ISSUES IN GLOBALIZATION

Edited by
Stuart Bruchey
Alan Nevins Professor Emeritus
Columbia University

A ROUTLEDGE SERIES

ISSUES IN GLOBALIZATION

STUART BRUCHEY, *General Editor*

ARMS DIFFUSION
The Spread of Military Innovations in the International System

Thomas W. Zarzecki

Routledge
New York & London

Published in 2002 by
Routledge
29 West 35th Street
New York, NY 10001
www.Routledge-NY.com

Published in Great Britain by
Routledge
11 New Fetter Lane
London EC4P 4EE

Routledge is an imprint of the Taylor & Francis Group
Printed in the United States of America on acid-free paper.

10 9 8 7 6 5 4 3 2 1

Library of Congress Cataloging-in-Publication Data

Zarzecki, Thomas W., 1969–
    Arms diffusion : the spread of military innovation in the international system / Thomas W. Zarzecki.
        p. cm. — (Issues in globalization)
    Includes bibliographical references.
    ISBN 0-415-93514-8 (HB) ✓
    1. Military weapons. 2. Arms transfers. 3. World politics—1989- I. Title. II. Series.

U815 .Z37 2002
327.1'743—dc21

                                                        2002020841

This book is to be returned on
or before the date stamped below

1 8 JUN 2004

Contents

List of Tables

List of Figures

Acknowledgments

M ANY THANKS GO OUT TO ROBERT E. HARKAVY, D. SCOTT BENNETT, Lee Ann Banszak, Christine White, Eric Plutzer, Suzanna DeBoef, and David Sacko of the Pennsylvania State University for their numerous helpful suggestions, comments, and various other forms of assistance rendered along the way; Professor Edward Keynes, Ulrike Schumacher, Jan Techau, Bettina Holtz, and the rest of the faculty and staff of the *Institut für Sicherheitspolitik* at the Christian-Albrechts University in Kiel, Germany, for their hospitality and access to invaluable research resources from March-August 1998; William J. Parente, for encouraging me to pursue the study of politics; Thomas Beech, in appreciation for endless hours of commiseration during the writing of the dissertation which became this book; and, finally and most importantly, to Brian Zarzecki for sparking my interest in all this business in the first place.

The views herein are those of the author, and not necessarily the U.S. government or U.S. Department of State.

ARMS DIFFUSION

Chapter 1
The Global Diffusion of Arms

INTRODUCTION

THE GLOBAL SPREAD OF ADVANCED MILITARY ARMAMENTS CAN BE USEFULLY characterized as a diffusion process, defined as the communication of innovations among the units of a social system over time. But what causes innovations in military technology to diffuse across the international system? The answer to this seemingly basic question is critically important to any understanding of the spread of arms. Despite this, it is rarely posed or addressed in so general and direct a manner. Scholars and policy analysts have written volumes of specific case studies on arms exporters, arms importers, and categories of military technologies. These studies usually contain numerous implicit and explicit explanations of why nations acquire armaments. Many descriptive and prescriptive overviews of the arms trade also attempt to explain the rationale behind arms transfers. However, there have been few if any empirical studies which attempt to systematically measure the rate of the spread of specific arms technologies across the international system as a whole. Fewer still then use this data to test theoretical causal hypotheses. This project attempts to fill this gap in our understanding of the arms proliferation phenomenon.

This chapter is divided into three parts. The first part centers on the significance of the global spread of arms in the post-Cold War era. The changed global strategic environment has clearly placed arms proliferation at the center of current security concerns. I discuss the key factors which have lent it this newfound prominence. The second part details the views of arms spread throughout the Cold War period. I explain how these perspectives evolved over time to accommodate changing global circum-

3

stances. The third part outlines how the idea of arms diffusion provides a new framework for analyzing the spread of arms in the post-Cold War era. Arms diffusion is conceived of as a singular global process. This allows it to be tracked, measured, and analyzed in a systematic fashion. A concluding segment outlines the chapters that follow.

THE IMPORTANCE OF THE SPREAD OF ARMS

Many policy-makers now publically rank the global spread of armaments as one of, if not the most, critical global security issues of the post-Cold War era. U.S. Representative Lee Hamilton (1992, 40) has argued that "the greatest security danger of the 1990s is weapons proliferation." Shortly after taking office, the Clinton Administration promised an "enormous priority placed on the issue of counter-proliferation" (Starr 1993a). And in the view of the Pentagon, "the spread of nuclear, chemical, and biological weapons represents a threat nearly as big as the specter of global conflict between Moscow and Washington during the cold war" (Weiner 1996).

These views are not restricted to U.S., or even Western, decision-makers. Sergei Kortunov, a Russian Ministry of Foreign Affairs official, has described weapons proliferation as "the major challenge of the 1990s" (Kortunov 1994a). In 1993, then-Russian Foreign Minister Yevgeny Primakov claimed that "tracking international proliferation" was a "priority task" of the Russia Foreign Intelligence Service (Starr 1993b). According to Masahiko Hosokawa, a senior official in Japan's Ministry of International Trade and Industry, Japan considers it "especially important" to restrict arms proliferation in the East Asian region. As a result, Japan planned for the first time to undertake a major regional security initiative to put an export control regime in place in the 1990s (Ebata 1993). Finally, no less multinational a body than the United Nations Security Council issued a congruent statement at the end of its January 1992 summit. It read that proliferation of weapons of mass destruction (WMD) was "a threat to international peace and security (codewords for justifying the use of force), and committed [member states] to concerted follow-up actions to strengthen non-proliferation approaches" (Roberts 1993, 139).

Contemporary scholarly assessments echo these sentiments. Many further claim that such attention is warranted by the increasingly rapid spread of arms. Keller and Nolan (1998,120) exemplify this argument in writing that:

> Military industry and technology is spreading around the globe at an accelerating rate . . . the scale, sophistication, and destructive capability of military technology entering the international marketplace are also increasing dramatically.

Undoubtedly, warnings of ever more rapidly spreading weapons have always characterized scholarly work on the arms trade and proliferation. However, they are particularly common in the current wave of literature. Molander and Wilson (1995, 3), while outlining a number of possible nuclear proliferation scenarios, chose to emphasize "the prospect of nuclear chaos" in the title of a recent work. Shukman (1996, 235) claims that a new wave of advanced conventional weapons is "joining the arsenals of a growing number of countries." Roberts (1993, 145) claims that newly-developed weapons are being exported much sooner than ever before, thus leading to more rapid proliferation. Klare (1994, 145) predicts that the arms trade is "on the verge of a new expansionary cycle." Finally, a number of authors (Keller 1995, Moodie 1995, Bitzinger 1994) have emphasized the increasing internationalization of arms production technologies. They argue that the growth of international arms projects and the spread of production technologies are making proliferation essentially uncontrollable by national governments.

Clearly, such concern over global weapons proliferation is not new. But from its earliest days, when attention was focused almost exclusively on the spread of nuclear arms, the field of proliferation studies always existed in the shadow of more pressing security concerns. The new centrality of proliferation to both scholars and policy-makers thus marks something of a watershed in the development of the issue area. How can this newfound significance be explained?

Three critical, interrelated changes in the global strategic environment of the 1990s have led to this heightened status. First, the immediate threat of war between the superpowers has been eliminated. Second, the Soviet collapse has spawned new proliferation fears. Finally, Operation *Desert Storm* and its aftermath have led to renewed appreciation of the possible consequences of the global spread of arms. When combined, these three factors served to raise proliferation to the central position it now occupies in the minds of many observers. The impact of each is detailed below.

The End of Superpower Rivalry. The end of the Cold War enhanced the awareness of arms proliferation as a security issue in two important ways. First, in the minds of scholars and policy-makers alike, the Cold War's conclusion removed the ongoing threat of a superpower conflict as the preeminent concern. After World War II, the possibility of a war involving nuclear weapons between the U.S. and USSR tended to drown out most other security fears. Representing as it did both an immediate and overwhelming threat to all of human life, the superpower nuclear balance was also the crux of strategic planning and arms control efforts. With the likelihood of that event largely eliminated, other, previously less encompassing and immediate threats had a chance to move to the forefront of concern (Roberts 1995, 247; Lockwood 1993, 23). Weapons proliferation thus ranked much higher on the scale of global threats after the end of the Cold War than before, even though wide acknowledgment of the phenomenon predated the Soviet collapse.[1]

A second, related issue involved the scope of conflict in the new global geostrategic landscape. Immediately after the Cold War's end, some observers predicted that the "end of history" had been reached. They expected that the failure of communism as a socio-political and economic system would lead to a more tranquil international environment dominated by the norms of liberal, capitalist democracy (Fukuyama 1989). But others feared that the world would witness a renewed scramble for power (Mearsheimer 1990, Gati 1992). To these thinkers, the Cold War period appeared in retrospect to be a time of relative global stability. Freed from the constraints of their respective blocs by the Cold War's end, the divergent goals and interests of various states and other international actors could now breed a "new world disorder."[2] Historical ethnic, national, and religious differences seemed ready to explode in many regions. The resultant conflicts, it was hypothesized, could spark an increased demand for arms and encourage the proliferation of destabilizing types and amounts of military hardware. From this viewpoint, even if arms proliferation had long been a feature of the international system, systemic changes during the late 1980s and early 1990s were only going to make the problem worse.

The Impact of the Soviet Collapse. A second factor which enhanced proliferation's status as a security threat was the expected direct effect of the Soviet collapse itself. From the early 1990s, many observers expressed fears that ex-Soviet arms would flood the international system, fueling the conflicts mentioned above. Two sources of such proliferation were envisioned. Analysts warned of the immediate diffusion of existing weapons held in the arsenals of the rapidly disintegrating Soviet armed forces throughout the FSU. Over the longer term, they feared a threat from unrestricted Russian exports of newly-constructed arms incorporating cutting-edge technologies.[3]

The earliest worries about proliferation after the Soviet collapse focused on the fate of the existing Soviet arsenal under emerging conditions of lawlessness. The Soviet Union had been perhaps the most heavily armed state on earth. Conventional arms were forward deployed and stockpiled throughout the former republics. Research and production facilities for nuclear, biological, and chemical (NBC) weapons and ballistic missiles were similarly widespread. Weapons designers at these facilities often went unpaid for months and were vulnerable to recruitment by foreign governments (Goldanskii 1993). In such a chaotic situation, it took little imagination to envision scenarios under which this technology could fall into the "wrong hands" and proliferate "among local warlords, criminals, and terrorists" (Galeotti 1992, Fulghum 1992; Allsion et al. 1996). Rumors of the availability of advanced weapons at "fire sale" prices only fueled these concerns (Friedman 1992b, Nelson 1993).

As the Soviet break-up appeared to be progressing in a less chaotic fashion than initially feared, a second strain of thinking began to emerge. The Russian Republic, inheritor of the most complete portion of the Soviet-era military-industrial complex, was expected to become a dangerously uninhibited arms exporter (Friedman 1992a, Zaloga 1992, Smart 1992, Covault and Rybak 1993). Russian government and arms industry officials predicted an economic windfall from arms sales under the new laissez-faire export policy (Kortunov 1994b). U.S. intelligence agencies agreed, saying that economic hardship conditions in arms factories would force Russia to:

> . . . offer more advanced systems...at lower prices or in barter deals . . . [and while] Russian officials have repeatedly said they would carefully control such sales and exercise discretion in choosing clients, dire conditions could encourage individual plants to attempt unauthorized sales (Greenhouse 1992).

This sparked predictions that "dangerous new technologies will spread as Russian factories win more freedom to seek customers" throughout the world (Erlanger 1993, "Russia's Swords" 1993). Stories abounded of Russia using arms sales profits to help convert into a free market economy. Many analysts were "convinced arms sales [were] being made in a reckless manner...[and that] Russia could be subject to heavy economic pressure in the form of curtailed transactions with the West and lost investments" ("Iran Eyes" 1992). Reports of massive arms orders by various buyers, particularly Iran and China, seemed to substantiate these claims.[4]

Operation Desert Storm. Finally, the impression that the waning of the Cold War had dramatically altered the global strategic environment was unmistakably driven home by the Iraqi invasion of Kuwait and the subsequent international response. Operation *Desert Storm* and its aftermath placed the significance of arms proliferation on the center stage of world attention in a manner that the Soviet collapse by itself would never have been able to accomplish. Several aspects of the Gulf War lent it this importance.

First, Saddam Hussein's attempt to gain control over Middle Eastern oil supplies forced the realization that, rhetoric of a "new world order" governed by international legal norms aside, the utility of military force in the international system had not ended along with the Cold War. Both Iraq's invasion of Kuwait and the U.S.-led Coalition's subsequent response boldly underlined this fact. The Gulf War served to mute much prior speculation about the replacement of traditional military threats by new security problems like environmental degradation, refugee movements, and other non-military phenomenon.[5] And if military force was still relevant after the Cold War, then the weapons possessed by states engaged in armed conflicts would also obviously continue to matter. By conducting an openly military invasion of Kuwait that generated a clearly military response from the Coalition allies, Iraq thus demonstrated that the impact of the global spread of weapons was an issue of continuing importance.

Second, the arsenal that Iraq had amassed was large and in some ways quite sophisticated. Undoubtedly, Iraq's military did perform poorly in the war. *Desert Storm* was indeed a showcase for the U.S. high-technology approach to conventional warfare. On the other hand, pre-war assessments stressed the scope of Iraq's conventional capabilities. These included its vast armor and infantry forces, its dense national air defense system, and its stocks of Silkworm and Exocet anti-ship missiles (Timmerman 1991).[6] And it did take six weeks of intensive, uninterrupted Coalition bombing to destroy just half of this fielded military equipment. The war also shed light on Iraq's NBC weapons projects and force of modified Scud ballistic missiles. Postwar United Nations inspections provided detailed descriptions of the extent of Iraqi success in creating and weaponizing chemical and biological agents like VX and anthrax (Hewish and Lok 1998). Iraq's ballistic missile attacks on Israel also raised the specter of an Israeli nuclear response. As Keller and Nolan (1998, 117) point out, "the idea that a small, semi-industrialized country like Iraq could acquire such a destructive arsenal was a wake-up call for some policy-makers." This aspect of *Desert Storm* also dramatically underscored the fact that weapons proliferation, conventional and non-conventional, was both a reality and a potential threat to global security.

Finally, the war clearly demonstrated how quickly threats to regional and global stability could emerge from unpredictable directions. As a result of this, at least from the U.S. perspective, the defense and foreign policy apparatus that had focused on the Soviet Union would thus need to shift its attention to other potential opponents. These new threats were more "fragmented and varied" (Clark 1998), and, individually, would not pose the same grand strategic challenge as had the USSR. But the analytical challenge of determining their exact nature and scope would thus require a new set of planning tools and assumptions (Davis 1994).

Unfortunately, the war revealed many U.S. weaknesses in identifying, assessing, and countering these non-Soviet military threats. U.S. pre-crisis intelligence on Iraq's military infrastructure was limited. After the war, it was revealed that strategic bombing had destroyed little of Iraq's NBC weapons complex because the existence and location of much of it was unknown to Coalition targeters.[7] Postwar assessments of the campaign against Iraq's ballistic missile force were similarly critical. Offensive strike missions had a very difficult time locating and attacking mobile ballistic missile launchers.[8] The Patriot missile's success at intercepting incoming ballistic missiles became the subject of contentious debate (Postol 1991). Much was also made of the fact that Iraq's defeat might not have been so certain had it seized Saudi ports and airfields early on, before the U.S. had time to mobilize heavy forces and transport them to the region (Bennett, et al. 1994, 497). Concerns arose that the U.S. was ill-prepared to deal with opponents demonstrating more strategic sense than had Saddam Hussein. The end result was the realization that the global proliferation of weapons and threats had imposed operational and intelligence requirements on existing military structures that the former emphasis on the singular Soviet threat did not.[9]

VIEWS OF PROLIFERATION: THE COLD WAR AND AFTER

Each of the three factors detailed above helped to raise public and elite awareness of the dangers associated with the global spread of armaments. But heightened awareness was not the only effect of the Cold War's conclusion. The end of bipolarity also marked the beginnings of a shift in the manner in which arms proliferation was perceived and understood. In order to understand the significance of this shift, it is best to explore how views of proliferation changed over the course of the post-World War II period. In the interest of clarity, I divide the period into three phases reflecting evolving perspectives on the spread of arms. I simply term these the early Cold War, late Cold War, and post-Cold War periods.

Early Cold War Period. From the late 1940s into the early 1960s, the spread of arms as an independent phenomenon was largely paid little attention by scholars or policy-makers. Instead, changes in the composition and distribution of global military forces were viewed as part of a two-party *arms race dynamic* which had emerged between the East and West Blocs. Driven by realist conceptions of systemic determinism (Waltz 1979) and Richardsonian arms race models (Etcheson 1989), scholars often interpreted the global spread of arms as a subset of problems linked to the larger U.S.-Soviet conflict.

The Cold War encouraged the evaluation of global conflicts by their significance to the arms race between the superpowers. This bipolar conceptual lens fostered three critical assumptions regarding the worldwide spread of arms. First, the transfer of new weapons by one superpower to its allies and clients was seldom primarily viewed as an "arms proliferation problem" by the other. It was first assessed in terms of its impact on strategic planning for regional political and military conflict with the opposing bloc.[10] Second, this mindset fostered the view on both sides that each superpower had a major influence over the military activities of its client states. Proliferation was thus a reflection of the degree to which both sides wished to engage in arms competition in a given area (Sanjian 1998: 98). The manner in which the U.S. and USSR regulated the arms flow to key clients in Europe, Asia, and the Middle East reinforced the perception of ultimate superpower control over the extent of proliferation.[11] A third assumption was that each superpower had the ability to maintain tight controls over its most critical technologies. The only real threat to its technological position could come from the other superpower. The likelihood of a similar threat coming from a developing country, for example, was considered low.

The initial atomic tests conducted by the Soviet Union (1949), Great Britain (1954), France (1962), and China (1964) did draw considerable attention to the increasing number of nuclear-armed states. These fears "reached their height in the early 1960s when President John F. Kennedy said that more than 20 nations might have the bomb by the 1970s" (Albright and O'Neill 1995). The term "proliferation" was originally coined during this period to refer exclusively to nuclear weapons, reflecting the concerns of the times. But the British nuclear program was integrated with that of the U.S. to a high degree, and bolstered overall Western defenses. The French program, despite public proclamations to the contrary, was also arguably an asset to the Western Bloc. And even though China's independent nuclear force was aimed at both blocs, China's pro-Soviet stance on issues like the Vietnam War placed it in the Soviet camp in Washington's eyes until the late 1960s (Dunn 1982, 11). Nuclear proliferation thus still largely unfolded within the perceived context of the two-bloc system during the early Cold War period.[12]

Late Cold War Period. The two-bloc perception of global politics began to weaken in the 1960s and 1970s. China, Japan, and Western Europe emerged as potential third forces in the global balance-of-power. The 1973 oil embargo and the Arab-Israeli War demonstrated Arab economic and military potential. And India's nuclear test explosion of 1974 showed the military potential of non-Western developing societies. These and other events signaled the spread of power and military capabilities from the superpower-led blocs to other states around the globe. Throughout this period, the central focus on the superpower balance and its arms race dynamic remained firm. But a second conceptual tool for understanding the spread of arms, a *proliferation dynamic*, also gained ground in the minds of policy-makers and scholars alike.

The proliferation and arms race dynamics existed side-by-side as explanations for how and why arms spread throughout the international system. The spread of arms among the superpowers and their key allies in Europe and Asia was seen as part of the bipolar arms race underway since the late 1940s. The spread of arms to some superpower clients in the developing world, such as Iraq, Taiwan, or South Korea, straddled both concepts. These states played key roles in the bipolar struggle, but could also have independent agendas, goals, and interests. The spread of arms to the rest of the world was seen as motivated by a variety of political and economic factors only occasionally or tangentially linked to Cold War concerns. The latter two categories were increasingly referred to as "arms proliferation," as the term began to outgrow its nuclear origins.

The development of the proliferation concept underscored how changed global conditions had undermined superpower control over the spread of arms. The number of states engaged in weapons production grew throughout this period. The superpowers also began to rely more heavily on the proceeds from arms sales to defray the escalating costs of new weapons developments. These and other factors increased purchaser leverage to request more sophisticated arms. The superpowers still retained an overwhelming military advantage in qualitative and quantitative terms. But by the late 1980s, Kolodziej and Kanet (1989, xiii) were ready to argue, for example, that:

> . . . the global and regional diffusion of economic and military power further reinforces barriers to easy extension of Soviet influence in the near term . . . [as a result], the constraints imposed by developing states . . . must be given greater weight then they have until now in explaining Soviet policy toward the Third World . . .

. . . a policy which included arms sales as a major component. The line between proliferation and the arms race was never a clear one. Nevertheless, the change in terminology reflected a definite change in thinking about the problem of spreading arms.

Post-Cold War Period. The end of the Cold War and the collapse of the USSR brought the two-bloc view of world politics to a close. It also ended the U.S.-Soviet arms race as a possible explanation for the continuing global spread of arms and related technologies. With the central arms race dynamic no longer a factor, the proliferation dynamic assumed center stage. The language and ideas of proliferation had already been developed in numerous works on the arms trade. It seemed only natural to use these as a starting point for grappling with the changed environment.

There are problems, however, with approaching the spread of arms simply through the language of proliferation. First, "proliferation" as such is only a descriptive term for the process of the spread of arms. Arms increase in number, and are acquired by larger numbers of states; proliferation thus occurs. Unlike an "arms race," the term conveys no specific, underlying theoretical explanation as to why arms spread.

Second, during later phases of the Cold War, the prevalence of the *idea* of the central arms race led many to look for the cause of proliferation itself in smaller, regional dyadic arms races outside the superpower context.

Arms races between India and Pakistan, or Israel and its Arab rivals were viewed as similar to those of their superpower counterpart (Sanijan, 1998). But much of the proliferation in the early post-Cold War era has taken place in areas like East and Southeast Asia. In these regions, the open, two-party conflicts, of either the cold or shooting varieties, that are central to the arms race motif are not universally apparent. As Ball (1994, 94–95) notes:

> The characterization of the regional military acquisition programs as "an Asian arms race" has a singular deficiency: it does not accord with any generally accepted definition of the term "arms race." Any arms race should have two principal features: first, a very rapid rate of acquisitions, with the participants stretching their resources in order to ensure that they remain at the head of the race; and second, some reciprocal dynamics in which developments in the defensive and offensive capabilities of one adversary are matched by attempts to counter the advantages thought to be gained by another. . . . There is little of this in the current acquisition programs in the region . . . more generally, imitative dynamics have entered the acquisition processes through concerns common to many defense establishments that their capabilities for surveillance of air and sea approaches and of activities in disputed maritime areas be as effective as those of their neighbors, and of particular countries to reap the prestige that is attendant on the acquisition of modern technology and to demonstrate that they are just as capable of operating and maintaining high-technology systems as their neighbors.

Gill and Kim (1995, 116) also note that "an 'arms race' does not properly or comprehensively define the current dynamic of military modernization in the [East Asian] region." The authors leave unstated what exactly does define this dynamic. In such cases, it is sometimes difficult to identify just exactly who a given state is "racing" against in its acquisitions of advanced arms. Under such circumstances, arms competition often takes on the character of "keeping up with the Joneses" technologically more than responding to specific military threats.[13] In cases like the Middle East, two-bloc behavior (the Arabs versus Israel) can more realistically be postulated. Still, bloc unity is very loose, and intense intra-bloc conflict undermines simple arms race models.

Third, despite the work of the 1970s and 1980s, the word "proliferation" still retained its original connotation. As Keller (1995, xiii) notes,

> If the word defense is too big and indiscriminate, another term, proliferation, must be expanded and enriched. Proliferation typically refers to the spread and multiplication of nuclear, biological, and chemical weapons. But this limited usage excludes the spread and multiplication of advanced conventional weapons, strike aircraft, for example, which are now routinely sold throughout the world. Many of these aircraft were specifically designed to deliver

nuclear, biological, and chemical ordnance. Their proliferation should be a matter of great concern.

Undoubtedly, attention paid to nuclear, chemical, and biological arms and their delivery systems is not misplaced. However, as Keller and Nolan (1998, 18–19) further observe,

> Mass destruction is an ancient phenomenon, and need not employ nuclear, chemical, or biological ordnance . . . as the Gulf War demonstrated, the destructive power of a coordinated conventional attack can achieve levels of devastation associated with weapons of mass destruction, even on the battle-field . . . the category of "weapons of mass destruction" is based more on historical usage than on logical grounds or on analysis of the characteristics of various weapons.

As we can see, the heightened awareness of threats from the spread of arms is paired with the inadequacy of existing concepts to handle them. The post-Cold War period has thus led decision-makers and planners to develop a new approach for dealing with the situation. The nature of this new approach is detailed in the next section.

EMERGENCE OF A DIFFUSION MINDSET

New Planning Challenges. The collapse of the bipolar system has been accompanied by the continuing global spread of arms. This has led to problems for the West in general and the U.S. in particular in planning for future military contingencies (Klare 1995, 4–5). Uncertain and contested assessments of the degree and rate at which new generations of arms can be expected to spread across the globe now figure prominently in the weapons procurement plans of major and minor powers alike. These have replaced assessments of a single superpower threat as the criteria by which defense projects are judged.[14] Consider the following six examples.

- The U.S. F-22 Raptor and the European EF-2000 fighter aircraft have very high price tags. Supporters defend their costs on the grounds that the advanced versions of the Soviet MiG-29 and Su-27 they were designed to combat continue to spread across the globe despite the Soviet Union's disintegration.[15] F-22 backers also contend that the EF-2000 itself, and other similar European fighters (i.e. the Swedish Gripen and French Rafale), will also diffuse globally. These will add to the "potential threat base" and justify procurement of the F-22 at a per unit cost of some $70–100 million for 438 fighters (Fulghum 1997, 42–3; Lorell, et al. 1996, 64–8; "Affordable Superiority" 1993, 100–2). The radar-evading B-2 stealth bomber was designed to carry out nuclear attacks on the USSR's mobile land-based ICBMs. Its massive cost has similarly been justified in the post-Cold War environment by noting the continuing diffusion of Russian fighters and surface-to-air missiles (Buchan 1994, 399). These systems will "progressively degrade the ability of existing long-range bombers to carry out missions without extensive suppression of enemy air defenses" ("The Case for the B-2" 1991).

- In 1996, a tremendous debate erupted over the release of the National Intelligence Estimate NIE 95–19. The NIE argued that the U.S. military's national missile defense (NMD) plans could be scaled back. It claimed that the technology to build intercontinental ballistic missiles (ICBM) was not diffusing rapidly enough to warrant early deployment of anti-missile defenses. The heart of the controversy centered on whether or not the analysis accurately predicted the rate at which long-range ballistic missiles would spread to so-called "outlaw" or "pariah" nations like Iran, Iraq, Libya, and North Korea (Karp 1996).

- In one of the most urgent Western military development programs of the post-Cold War period, the U.S. and its European allies have engaged in a crash effort to develop a short-range air-to-air missile that matches the capability of the Russian AA-11 Archer. The AA-11 entered service in 1985. When the USSR revealed the technical details of the AA-11 in 1991, it was at least a decade ahead of Western developmental missiles that had yet to enter service. The major concern stemmed from the fact that the missile had already diffused to several air forces around the world. These included a number considered potential threat countries by the U.S. (Cook 1991, 89). Israel had also begun exporting the equivalent Python-IV, which it had developed independently.

- The U.S. balked at a request from Thailand to include the AIM-120 AMRAAM air-to-air missile in an order for a batch of F/A-18 Hornet fighters. The U.S. argued that it did not want to be the first nation to introduce current generation beyond-visual-range missiles into the region at such an early stage of their global diffusion. Thailand threatened to cancel its purchase and buy Russian aircraft instead. The U.S. then relented and agreed to sell AIM-120s. The U.S. logic was that by the time the ARMAAMs were delivered, Russia would have already introduced comparable missiles into the region. An earlier order for AMRAAMs by Saudi Arabia was rejected on similar grounds ("USA Rejects" 1993, "USN Gets" 1995).

- China was aware that the U.S. Patriot surface-to-air missile of Gulf War fame was being sold to states across the globe. It thus reportedly attempted to acquire sample Patriots from Israel for examination (Fulghum 1993; Gates and Kim 1995, 83; Clarke 1995, 89–109). China did not necessarily intend to copy the Patriot itself. It already had the similar Russian SA-10 Grumble. Instead, it intended to use the knowledge it gained to develop methods for making its own ballistic missiles more difficult for the Patriot to shoot down. China then planned to market its ballistic missiles with the claim that they had been designed specifically to defeat both the Patriot and SA-10, missiles its customers would likely face in the future.

- Despite the Soviet collapse, Russia is continuing to build advanced submarines and sell them to states like China, India, and Iran. U.S. Navy planners have identified this diffusion as a major justification for production of its *Seawolf*-class submarine, as well as follow-on submarine classes of even higher performance and cost (Ryan 1995, 14–18).

A common thread runs through these examples. For many states, including the U.S., the identity of future enemies is unknown, or could realistically be any one of a number of possibilities. The nature of the global arms market is also such that one's enemy can be armed with weapon systems produced by friendly states. This is as true of advanced conventional weapons systems as it is of weapons of mass destruction. Long-term defense planning thus hinges at least as much on which technologies have spread across the system as a whole (among allies and enemies alike) than on the military developments within any single state. As the above examples show, defense and foreign policy planners are aware of this situation, and have begun to think in these terms.

The Diffusion Approach. The process of the spread of an innovation across a system with numerous individual members is called *diffusion*. The end of the Cold War has thus encouraged an *arms diffusion* mindset to replace earlier understandings of the spread of arms (Keller 1995, Krause 1992). Arms diffusion, *the generalized global spread of military technological innovations*, has become a greater concern to planners and decision-makers than the development of any specific state's military capabilities. This is more than just a semantic distinction. It represents a new way of looking at the global spread of arms.

Advantages accompany this adoption of a diffusion mindset. First and foremost, the fact that planners themselves are perhaps unknowingly developing the practice of looking at proliferation using the language of diffusion is important. It demonstrates that experienced professionals recognize the value of diffusion-related concepts in examining current global military problems. This provides an important clue that the subject is worthy of further study. Second, diffusion research is a well-defined field which has investigated diffusion patterns across a variety of different innovations. Conceiving of the spread of arms as a diffusion process thus allows one access to a broad array of new theoretical and methodological approaches. These may lead to a better understanding of the phenomenon. At the very least, they provide some new tools for examining proliferation, including hypothesis testing, that may yield new insights into the underlying process. Third, the internal logics of arms diffusion and previous frameworks are not necessarily coterminous. They approach the phenomenon of spreading arms from different angles. The differences between considering arms diffusion as a singular process in the international system rather than separate arms race and proliferation dynamics is a prime example. As a result, they may uncover new relationships between dependent and independent variables.

Finally, as the specific examples above show, envisioning the spread of arms as a diffusion process invites the development of a new set of questions. In the cases of NMD and AMRAAM, an understanding of the *rate* of the diffusion of a specific weapons was considered critical to making decisions about if or when a matching or countervailing system would or should be deployed. With the case of the Russian AA-11, failure to appreciate that rate has left planners scrambling for remedies. In other cases, understanding *which* technologies will spread and which are unlikely to might be important. Another set of questions could revolve around to *how many* states certain technologies will diffuse, or *how many* units of a given system the *average* operator is likely to acquire. Properly framing and satisfactorily answering questions like these will be a crucial part of developing a research program around the arms diffusion approach.

OVERVIEW OF THE STUDY

The chapters of this study can be divided into three parts. The first part lays the theoretical groundwork for studying arms diffusion. It examines the existing literature on diffusion processes and how these can be applied to arms proliferation. It then develops a number of theoretical explanations for arms diffusion which can be tested using empirical data. Finally, it outlines definitions and categorizations of military technological innovations (MTI) relevant to the study. The second part begins by explaining the data selection process for the MTIs to be examined. It subsequently presents an overview of this data by addressing some basic questions about arms diffusion. Then, it tests hypotheses derived from the theories of arms diffusion in the first part. The third part evaluates these theories explicated in the first part using results presented in the second. The study concludes with a final section on projected future developments in the arms diffusion process. The manner in which future changes in the development of military technology may affect arms diffusion, as well as our ability to understand it, are discussed.

NOTES

[1] A telling quote regarding this point is found in Mann (1998). Elisa Harris was the director of nonproliferation in the Clinton Administration's National Security Council. She says of the newfound interest in developing world chemical and biological warfare programs that, "The reality is that CBW programs existed outside of Europe [before the end of the Cold War]. We just didn't pay a great deal of attention to them because our direct national security issues were most affected by the Warsaw Pact threat...*it is hard to think of a single CBW program that has emerged since the end of the Cold War.*" [emphasis added]

[2] For a typology and analysis of possible post-Cold War international configurations and conflict scenarios, see Harkavy (1997).

[3] The validity of some of these arguments is examined in Zarzecki (1999a).

[4] See for example Ibrahim (1992), which details a "secret" $7 billion plan by Iran to acquire mostly Russian arms.

[5] These new security concerns have disappeared from neither the key literature on security studies nor the agendas of policy-makers. But the Gulf War served to stem the de-emphasis of future military threats prominent in much thinking of the late Cold War and early post-Cold War period. For an examples of the continued serious treatment of non-military security threats, see Levy (1995) and Homer-Dixon (1991).

[6] Towle (1991) highlights how the media incorrectly assessed Iraq's conventional military capabilities prior to the war's onset. For an even more detailed analysis, see Record (1993, 57–69).

[7] Venter (1998), for example, cites a CIA report that U.S. intelligence could not confirm destruction of a single biological weapons facility during the war. For a more recent example of concern over the accuracy of targeting information in "counterproliferation" strikes, see Bender's (1998) report on the U.S. cruise missile strike on Sudan.

[8] According to Buchan (1994, 407), "the U.S. performance in finding and destroying Scud mobile missiles in Desert Storm was abysmal."

[9] By way of example, two-thirds of U.S. intelligence expenditures during the Cold War focused on NATO/Warsaw Pact issues. Some 25% were directed at China, 7% at the Middle East, 2% in Latin America, and 1% on the rest of the world (Betts 1981).

[10] Earlier editions of *The Military Balance* demonstrate this tendency. Entitled *The Communist Bloc and the Free World: The Military Balance* (1960), they cluster all states not in formal alliances with the U.S. into a single "communist bloc" for the purposes of reporting military strengths and equipment holdings. See also Joshua and Gibert (1969, 6), which primarily views Soviet arms transfers from the perspective of the U.S.-Soviet rivalry.

[11] Heikal (1978, 13–14) is particularly vivid in depicting the asymmetrical arms relationship between Egypt and the USSR. He claims that eventually, the Soviet Union was viewed by Arab states *primarily* in terms of its "ability to supply or withhold arms."

[12] These perceptions sometimes lagged reality due to the hidden nature of some nuclear proliferation activities. The Israeli nuclear program, which reportedly reached weaponization by the 1960s, was not generally acknowledged until the 1970s (Day 1992). This program was geared more toward regional than super-power threats. Israel also had no formal security arrangement with the U.S., although it was, of course, aligned with the Western Bloc.

[13] Regarding arms races involving more than two states, Nicholson (1989, 159) notes that "while the *n*-party Richardson model is comparatively easy to specify, it is not very easy to analyze," and proceeds to attempt to do so using a 3–party arms race scenario. This does allow one to get at a number of very important conceptual issues. The problems of attempting to analyze the spread of arms across a 200+ actor international system using a Richardson-style arms-race model, however, are large, to say the least.

[14] For a discussion of some of the differences between "threat-specific" and "threat-ambiguous" planning, see Stephens (1997). See Davis (1994) for the differences with planning under conditions of uncertainty during and after the Cold War.

[15] The Eurofighter EF-2000 is a multi-national project under development by Germany, Great Britain, Italy, and Spain.

Chapter 2
The Arms Trade, Proliferation, and Diffusion: A Literature Review

THE PREVIOUS CHAPTER DISCUSSED THE SPREAD OF ARMS IN THE MODERN world in very broad terms, outlining the scope of the issue, as well as the various intellectual approaches that have been developed to grapple with it. The purpose of the current chapter is twofold. First, I will review the literature related to the question of what causes the spread of arms and analyze its strengths and weaknesses. Second, I will review the literature on diffusion processes, explaining how the terms and concepts central to it can be used to study of the spread of arms. My ultimate aim in mating these two research traditions is to develop a framework within which important but thus-far neglected questions related to the arms diffusion process can be asked and investigated in a systematic fashion.

This chapter reviews the three major existing types of literature on the spread of arms, divided according to their thematic and methodological approach to the topic. The first type consists of case studies of specific individual states that purchase, sell, or produce arms. Such works exhibit a high degree of detail, but usually make little or no attempt to generalize their findings to other cases.

The second type of literature consists of works that describe the arms proliferation problem from the perspective of more than one country. These studies often focus on a single category of arms (i.e. nuclear proliferation, ballistic missile proliferation), a single region (i.e the Middle East or Latin America), or a set of suppliers or recipients with some common feature (i.e. Third World producers or pariah states). These works provide much technical detail and policy prescription, often of a generalized nature. However, they rarely attempt to explicitly develop or test theories about the subject matter.

Works of the third type attempt to assess why and how arms spread from a macro perspective, and are the least-frequently encountered type of scholarship in this field. Usually embracing the entire international system, these macro level works can be divided into two varieties, descriptive/empirical and theoretical. Descriptive works attempt to catalogue the spread of arms by detailed data gathering and subsequent analysis to detect underlying, recurring patterns. Theoretical works seek the development of causal models to explain the empirical regularities observed during descriptive analysis. Some type three works use several of the concepts and approaches found in multidisciplinary diffusion-of-innovations research. By applying these concepts and approaches in a more systematic fashion, we can gain a better understanding of the factors motivating the diffusion of arms throughout the international system.

THE LITERATURE ON THE ARMS TRADE AND PROLIFERATION

Since the rise of the modern international system in the 17th Century, armaments and the technology of war have continuously spread from state to state. Military technological innovations, or MTIs, are ostensibly developed by individual states to increase their battlefield capabilities relative to those of their opponents.[1] It seems that it is never too long, however, before these innovations begin to be purchased, copied, or captured by allies, neutrals, and enemies alike. Before very long, what started out as an advantage for one's own forces inevitably becomes the newest emergent threat, and the menace against which one's next round of innovations is geared towards defending.

Despite the relative antiquity of this basic process, at least four major trends have forced the issue of the spread of new arms technologies on to the agenda of both the scholarly and policy-making communities alike since the 1960s. First and foremost, technological development has expanded the number and diversity of MTIs to such truly staggering proportions that the arcane intricacies of the modern world's "baroque arsenals" defy easy analysis (Kaldor 1981). Compared to prior eras, the unparalleled diversification and specialization of modern technology since World War II has produced a technological-industrial base capable of churning out tremendous numbers of the most sophisticated instruments of warfare the planet has ever seen on a steady, regular basis. As Dunnigan (1996, 3) has noted, "never before in history has there been a period where there were so many new weapons in such a short period of time." As a result, there has certainly been no shortage of MTIs to spread.

Second, the expansion of the number and type of MTIs capable of being spread has been matched by a dramatic increase in the number of states that might find such weapons desirable. After the numerous waves of European decolonization since the end of World War I, the number of independent states had risen to over 180 by the late 1980s. The fragmentation of a number of multinational political entities in the early 1990s, like Yugoslavia and the Soviet Union, has pushed this number to over 200. In the late 19th Century, the initial adopter of a newly-developed major military technology might have to worry about its innovation being spread to a dozen states at most, these usually being the major global powers. Today, modern weapons system can easily be acquired by forty or more states in the span of a mere decade or two.[2]

Third, the growing economic resources of many of these new states have meant that those who desire to purchase new military technologies often have the means to do so on a consistent, institutionalized basis. The states of the Middle East, Asia, Latin America, and, to a lesser extent, Africa have all been able to spend heavily on MTIs. They have become regular members of what in the previous century was largely a Europeans-only club. The increased resources made available for military products has also been matched by the stratospheric growth in the sophistication of global arms-producing firms. Usually in close alliance with their host governments, arms merchants have become savvy peddlers of their wares in the world marketplace. This combined maturation of both buyers and sellers has meant that the global structure for arms acquisitions has been institutionalized to such a degree that most buyers with the proper resources can acquire much of what they want most of the time.

The fourth and final reason for the increased interest in the study of the spread of arms has been the growth in the importance of weapons themselves as a deciding factor in the outcomes of war. As McKinlay (1989, 24) has noted, "technology has transformed the means of force such that, other things being equal, quality and quantity of firepower are more important that human power." As technological advances have made weapons more lethal, the status of their spread has become a more important topic of study than it would be if their importance to battlefield outcomes remained marginal. Of course, the human elements of military power–leadership, morale, political organization, and so on–remain critical. However, it is difficult to argue that gaps in the level of technological sophistication between the sides in a conventional armed conflict are not also of vital importance in determining its outcome.

The combination of these four factors has precipitated the creation within the larger discipline of international relations of an empirically rich and intellectually active subfield focusing on the arms trade and the proliferation of military technologies. This is turn has led to a veritable explosion of literature on the spread of armaments since the 1960s.

SINGLE-STATE CASE STUDIES OF MILITARY PRODUCERS, EXPORTERS, AND IMPORTERS

A common form of scholarship on the spread of military armament is the case study of the arms producer, importer, or exporter. This literature consists of detailed, focused examinations of single arms manufacturing, exporting, or importing countries which explore the dynamics of the subject state's participation in the global arms trade. Such works may address any of numerous facets of the state's arms-related conduct. These include, but are not limited to, detailed descriptions of the state's weapons inventories; examinations of the policies which govern its arms import and/or export activities; historical accounts of its military acquisition programs; explanations for the state's behavior in these areas; and normative prescriptions for altering the unfavorable aspects of that behavior.

The rest of this section is devoted to examining some of the key works in this research tradition. Because the number of published works on these topics is sizeable, I have tried to select for review pieces that are either of high quality or representative of overall trends in the literature. Although there is some overlap, I divide this examination of case studies for simplicity's sake into three sub-sections corresponding to the primary subject matter of the work at hand: arms producers, arms exporters, and arms importers.

Arms Producers. Case studies of arms producers have not usually been included under the heading of the "arms trade" or "proliferation" in scholarly analysis. Nonetheless, the decision of a major arms producing nation to develop and deploy military hardware is undoubtedly a decision leading to arms diffusion. This is true even if, as the previous chapter suggests, analysts tend to mentally cordon off the major superpower arms producers from other "proliferation threats."

Although truly vast, the case study literature on arms producing nations and production processes can be divided roughly into two broad categories of works. The first category emphasizes the detailed internal decisionmaking processes which lead to the development and deployment of new weapons systems. These policy-oriented case studies emphasize the technical and bureaucratic details of the weapons procurement process, either lauding incidences of its successful operation (Bugos 1996, Kelly 1989, Armacost 1969) or, conversely, citing the process' failures and calling for reform (Farrell 1997, Zakheim 1996, Stevenson 1993, Kotz 1988).[3] Obviously, studies on the superpower arms producers dominate this field of study, due to the size and importance of their weapons procurement programs. However, excellent works on smaller producers also exist (Kolodziej 1987).[4] A second group of works encompasses much of the "strategic studies" branch of the international relations literature. These works analyze force build-ups and/or build-downs (and thus, explicitly or implicitly, weapons acquisitions) from the perspective of their impact on the military balance between states (Cordesman 1999, Lambeth 1975). By analyzing the external, strategic dimension of procurement decisions, they flesh out our understanding of the specific, often idiosyncratic internal processes by which arms diffusion takes place that works in the first category of describe.

Some of the best scholarly efforts in these areas attempt to develop, or at least test, theory which explains arms procurement processes, thus lifting analysis beyond the level of the specific weapons systems to that of the general pattern of military innovation. Two excellent examples of this type of scholarship are Evangelista's *Innovation and the Arms Race: How the United States and the Soviet Union Develop New Military Technologies* (1988) and Johnson's (1998) *Heavy Bombers and Fast Tanks: Innovation in the U.S. Army, 1917–1945.*

The main purpose of Evangelista's *Innovation and the Arms Race* is, simply enough, to develop an understanding of why nations, particularly the superpowers, develop new military technologies. He addresses this question through a comparative case study of the process of military innovation in the U.S. and the USSR, particularly in the case of tactical nuclear weapons. The result of Evangelista's research is a richly-woven analysis which illuminates the strengths and weaknesses of existing arms race, balance-of-power, and bureaucratic politics models. In the end, the author argues for a more nuanced approach, claiming that his comparative case study demonstrates that:

> . . . the openness and decentralization of U.S. society encourage technological innovations in weaponry, whereas the Soviet Union inhibits innovation with its obsessive secrecy and centralization. These same characteristics do, however, allow the USSR to concentrate its resources and respond to U.S. initiatives in ways that ultimately redound to the disadvantage of both countries (Evangelista 1988, 269).

Evangelista's case study provides readers with a detailed and comprehensive look at the military technological innovation process in two very important arms producers. Furthermore, his rejection of numerous standing explanations of why states adopt arms–the aforementioned bureaucratic politics and arms race models, and so forth–does help to develop theory on arms innovation processes. However, Evangelista's explanations are tied to state/societal features intimately related to the cases under investigation. The nature of his case study methodology (as well as his selection of an innovation–tactical nuclear weapons–which, while obviously significant, has not widely spread throughout the international system) also limits his conclusions' applicability to a wider set of adopters. These factors can be considered "strengths" or "weaknesses" depending upon the use to which one wishes to put Evangelista's work. For the purposes of the current study, however, *Innovation and the Arms Race* is a classic example of an excellent study on the adoption of military innovations which suggests avenues of approach for the broader study of the spread of arms but which itself is necessarily limited in scope.

Less concrete in its conclusions but more detailed in its narrative is Johnson's *Heavy Bombers and Fast Tanks*. While the author describes as "elusive" causal links between specific institutional arrangements and policy outcomes, he uses the single case of American interwar innovation in the fields of armor and airpower to illustrate his conclusion that:

> . . . .in the final analysis, the U.S. Army that entered World War II was a reflection of the biases and institutional arrangements that existed in the War Department throughout the interwar era. Branch parochialism, a largely powerless War Department General Staff, tension between air and ground officers, a conservative culture, and disparate views about technology all conspired to inhibit innovation and intraservice cooperation. Although the War Department's focus on personnel enabled it to create and deploy a mass army in World War II, it constrained weapons research and development throughout the interwar period (1998, 229).

The bulk of Johnson's writing is a finely detailed analysis of the personalities and institutions involved in the process of military innovation in the U.S. during the 1917–1941 period which outlines the foundations and limitations of this conclusion. Unlike Evangelista, Johnson is less interested in trying to fit theory unambiguously to empirical data than he is to demonstrate why existing theories flounder in the face of such data's complexity and contradictions. Both case studies, however, provide no small amount of insight into why arms producing nations adopt the weapons that they do. Because of this, Evangelista, Johnson, and similar works are valuable contributions to the literature on why arms spread for the snapshots of innovation processes in critical cases which they provide.

Arms Exporters. More in the mainstream of arms trade and proliferation research are the wealth of case studies on arms exporting countries. Works on major weapons exporters naturally predominate this literature. However, the rise of smaller, developing world exporters since the 1970s has generated additional studies of the lower end of the supplier spectrum. In this section, I discuss key works on each of the five major arms exporters–the United States, Soviet Union/Russia, France, Britain, and China–as well as several of the smaller suppliers. Once again, the detailed case study style of analysis is evident across these works.

The United States, the world's most significant arms exporter in the post-World War II period, has unsurprisingly attracted the most scholarly attention of any of the arms supplying nations. In particular, case studies on the export activity of the U.S. have been a staple of arms trade literature since the 1960s. As one source (Hammond et al. 1983) notes, however,

> . . . the vast majority of these writings have decried what their authors perceived as the enormous growth of arms transfers, citing the dangers and charging that U.S. arms transfers have gotten out of hand. Various instruments for reestablishing "control" over arms transfers have been proposed. Often scholars have recommended that the United States attempt to become a "more reluctant supplier."

A classic example of this strongly normative case study approach to the analysis of U.S. arms export policy is Klare's *American Arms Supermarket* (1984). Written just after the Reagan reversal of U.S. President Carter's "policy of restraint" on arms transfers, Klare's book provides readers with a focused, in-depth case study of American arms exports throughout the post-World War II period with a strong normative (i.e. anti-arms sale) flavor. After beginning with an overview of U.S. arms export policy "from Kennedy to Reagan," Klare lays out in careful detail the U.S. arms sale decisionmaking process. He follows this up with regional analyses of U.S. policy in action in Latin America and the Middle East. Klare's later chapters examine the link between U.S. arms sales and human rights policies, and compare U.S. with Soviet and European arms sale behavior. The final chapter contains the obligatory call for arms sale restraint under an "alternative policy framework."

Klare's pattern of outlining U.S. arms sale policy, detailing actual U.S. export behavior, and then attempting to hammer home the negative consequences of such behavior (usually through in-depth description of the use of U.S.-supplied arms by recipient states or detailing of the arms' high economic costs) is also characteristic of a number of more recent major works on U.S. arms sale policy (Tirman 1997, Hartung 1994, Friedman 1993). This style of presentation, however, is not universal among researchers. Authors of shorter pieces on U.S. arms transfer policy, as well as those of narrower, more regionally-focused works, lack the space or the interest in addressing the large issues that Klare embraces (Pierre 1979).[5] These works often focus on less politically charged concerns, such as Lefebvre's (1991) analysis of the effect of U.S. arms sales to Somalia and Ethiopia on the course of conflict in the Horn of Africa, or Campany's (1986) study of those to Turkey. Nonetheless, given the importance of the U.S. as a global arms supplier and the political passions aroused by arms sales, the richly-detailed, strongly normative case study approach to the analysis of U.S. arms export policy has and will continue to exist in the post-Cold War period.

Published works on arms transfers by the Soviet Union are far fewer in number than those on U.S. sales, and tend to lack the latter's often sensationalistic and/or normative bent. This is partially a matter of their intended audience. Case studies of U.S. exports by American and other Western authors were often, at some level, ultimately aimed at criticizing U.S. policy in an effort to change it and restrict arms sales. As such, many such studies were aimed at influencing public opinion as well as at dispassionate analysis, and were thus intended for an audience somewhat broader than the usual academic and policy community readership. In contrast, Soviet arms export policy was not primarily influenced or determined by such activities. As a result, the case studies written on Soviet behavior tended to be more analytic than normative and aimed at reaching a narrower, specialist audience. The (often unstated) intention of such works was to help the West understand and *react to* Soviet arms export policy rather that to change the course of Soviet policies through written argument.[6]

A second result of this appeal to specialists is the relative dearth of book-length treatments of Soviet arms export policy. Research on Soviet arms transfers is instead more likely to be found in formats aimed at specialized audiences, such as professional or scholarly journals, or in edited volumes on broader arms trade topics. This bias toward shorter works is also a reflection of the comparative lack of detailed information on Soviet arms trade activity, particularly information allowing for the comprehensive analysis of bureaucratic procedures and decisionmaking. The knowledge gap on these issues results primarily from the closed nature of the Soviet system, which did not go out of its way to illuminate the dynamics of the internal functioning of national security decisionmaking apparatus for the benefit of Western scholars.

Typical of much scholarship on Soviet arms transfers is Uri Ra'anan's "Soviet Arms Transfers and the Problem of Political Leverage," published in the edited volume *Arms Transfers to the Third World: The Military Build-Up in Less Industrial Countries* (1978). Ra'anan's work is an assessment of the amount of political leverage which postwar arms transfers have given the Soviet leadership over their clients in the developing world. Drawing heavily on data on transfers to Egypt, Ra'anan draws the conclusion that the continuities in Soviet arms export policy (guided by consistent national strategic goals) outweigh the "temporary ups and downs" (p. 154) often attributed to supplier and client attempts to exert political leverage over one another over time. Ra'anan's work is typical in that its brief treatment of a narrow topic wrestles with the lack of knowledge about Soviet goals and intentions through the use of careful backward reasoning from Soviet actions to Soviet motives. The article also demonstrates the problems with the reliability of data on Soviet transfers, as it draws conclusions regarding at least one significant transfer that would later prove to be based upon erroneous information.[7]

Key exceptions to this pattern of shorter pieces include several works on the role of Soviet arms sales in regional conflicts in the Third World. Among the best of the early works (and still one of the few book-length treatments of the subject) is Joshua and Gibert's excellent *Arms for the Third World: Soviet Military Aid Diplomacy* (1969).[8] Here, the authors have crafted a region-by-region analysis of Soviet arms transfer policy to the developing states, explaining the political and economic motives for overall policies as well as specific transfer packages. More typical of the extant literature is Porter's *The USSR in Third World Conflicts: Soviet Arms and Diplomacy in Local Wars, 1945–1980* (1984). Porter's book, while of excellent quality, is seriously limited in scope, tending to focus on the diplomatic aspects of Soviet behavior and covering only arms transferred to combatants during military conflicts. Needless to say, neither book covers Soviet transfers to states in Eastern Europe, the primary recipients of Soviet military exports.

The literatures on the other three major arms suppliers–Britain, France, and China–follow paths similar to their Soviet rather than U.S. counterparts. Although book-length treatments are, as with the Soviets, not numerous for these states, those that exist are superior examples of comprehensive scholarship. The key English-language work on France's arms exports (which also includes an extensive analysis of France's role as an arms producer) is Kolodziej's *Making and Marketing Arms: The French Experience and Its Implications for the International System* (1987). Kolodziej provides an extremely detailed and exhaustive examination of France's motivations for producing and exporting arms, placing arms export policy within the broader perspective of French economic, security, and foreign policy's rich tapestry. No similarly extensive work exists for Britain, although narrower efforts like Miller's *Export or Die: Britain's Defence Trade with Iran and Iraq* cover some of the same conceptual territory.[9] The literature on Chinese transfer policy is exemplified by Gill's *Chinese Arms Transfers : Purposes, Patterns, and Prospects in the New World Order*. Although lacking Kolodziej's sophisticated conceptual framework, Gill's book provides a thorough grounding in Chinese security policy before launching into a detailed analysis of China's relationship with each of its arms clients.

In many respects, the more limited scope of French, British, and Chinese transfers make it easier to cover them comprehensively in a single volume than those from either the U.S. or the USSR. This trend is amplified in the case of the literature on the smaller arms exporters in the international system. These consist primarily of a handful of NATO states like Canada and Italy, Australia, and several states in the developing world like

Israel and Brazil. Israel is a favorite subject for writers on this topic, spawn-
ing no less than five books on its arms export policies. The best of these is
perhaps Klieman's *Israel's Global Reach: Arms Sales as Diplomacy* (1985),
which contains a comprehensive look at who Israel arms and why.[10] As
with Kolodziej's work on France, Klieman's book seeks to place the need
for exports within the larger context of Israeli security policy and the quest
for the development of as independent as possible a defense-industrial base.
Klieman details the bureaucratic structure of decisionmaking on arms
export policy within the Israeli state, and then provides a host of region-
by-region case studies of military assistance. A similar approach is taken in
Franko-Jones' (1992) study of Brazil's defense industry, which also rose
and fell on the back of its foreign sales.

Arms Importers. Since the vast majority of states in the international
system are arms importers, one might expect that the case study literature
examining the recipients of arms transfers would be far more extensive
than that on either arms producers or exporters. In fact, while arms
importers have also generated a considerable body of research since the
1960s, this has been far outstripped by the amount of attention garnered
by the other two categories of states. Furthermore, only a handful of
importers–particularly Israel and Arab states, Iran, and perhaps a few others–have received the lion's share of scholarly notice.

There are a number of reasons for these obvious disparities. First,
regarding the concentration of interest around a few major importers, it is
unsurprising that the largest importers attract the greatest attention from
observers. The larger importers often tend, in no small part due to their
arms imports, to be militarily significant states in the regional context, and
economically significant to their suppliers. This tends to draw attention to
their arms import activities, particularly as these relate to larger security
and economic issues. Second, the small size of the import orders of many
other states (as well as the size of the states themselves) lends itself toward
the making of more abstract generalizations about arms import activities
across a larger number of seemingly similar cases. Researchers often
assume that the arms import behavior of, for example, Somalia or Uruguay
is similar enough to that of other states in Africa or Latin America to warrant the use of a broad analytical brush. Finally, a lack of data on many of
these states also renders the writing of detailed case studies difficult or
impossible. Many of the shorter (article-length) case studies of smaller arms
recipients frequently rely upon inference and/or deduction to illuminate the
rationales and motivations for arms acquisitions rather than detailed
knowledge of the policy-making process within the states in question. Part
of the motive for this is political. Many smaller states with closed political
systems and unstable security situations simply have not historically
released military information of the kind and depth needed for detailed

case study analysis. Another motive, however, is more practical. The intensity of research necessary to probe the inner workings of, for example, the U.S. or French military-industrial complex might be justified by the size and global importance of those entities. Such efforts are presumably less justifiable in the case of smaller states, which, even of theoretically accessible, are by themselves of questionable interest and importance to a wider audience.

An example of a comprehensive book-length treatment of an arms importer is Gill and Kim's *China's Arms Acquisitions from Abroad: The Quest for 'Superb and Secret Weapons'* (1995). China's status as a significant arms exporter sometimes obscures the fact that it is also a major importer of arms (a condition true of Israel and a few other states as well). Gill and Kim do an excellent job of placing present-day Chinese arms acquisitions in all of their technical detail within the larger context of Chinese military and strategic history. The authors explain how the competing needs for military modernization, military independence, and technological progress in the defense-industrial base often collide with one another in Chinese foreign procurement policies. A second such work is Smith's *India's* Ad Hoc *Arsenal: Direction or Drift in Defence Policy* (1994). Like Gill and Kim, Smith provides a detailed look at how India, one of the world's major arms importers, makes procurement decisions on the basis of strategic military need, economic benefit, and internal bureaucratic alignments. Analyses of Saudi Arabia (Cordesman 1997, Safran 1985), Iraq (Timmerman 1991), Jordan (Cordesman 1983), and other countries follow similar patterns.

As the above paragraphs clearly show, the case study literature on arms producers, exporters, and importers provides researchers with a wealth of qualitative analysis (much of it historical) of why arms spread throughout the international system. Each of the case studies discussed above contains numerous explicit and implicit explanations for the spread of arms to the individual states examined in each work. When considered as a single body of scholarship, the detailed contextual understanding of arms acquisition processes which case studies yield provides fertile ground for extracting testable explanations for why arms spread at differing rates throughout the international system. Such studies are also invaluable for testing specific theoretical explanations in the context of single cases.

On the other hand, however, because of their single-state focus, these works run the risk of putting forward explanations for arms acquisitions (and thus, indirectly, for arms diffusion) valid for their primary subject but perhaps of less relevance to other states. One solution to this problem that stays within the research tradition–conducting more case studies of a more varied lot of states–is unlikely for reasons previously discussed. Furthermore, the premium placed on investigating "important" subjects, as well as those about which sufficiently detailed information exists for lengthy examination, also encourages case studies to focus on only a handful of "major" powers and/or importers/exporters. This bias aggravates the consequences of the single-state focus, weighting our understanding of arms diffusion dynamics in favor of a small sub-set of the overall adopter pool. Based on the case study literature, we have no way of judging, for example, to what degree the arms acquisition processes in Indonesia and Angola are similar to those in the U.S. and France. To those interested in the global spread of arms, case studies are an invaluable first step toward understanding the process, but must be supplemented by works featuring other methodologies and approaches.

MULTI-STATE CASE STUDIES

A second body of literature on the spread of military armament encompasses works geared toward analyzing issues and problems which involve more than one state. Whereas the previous group of case studies focuses in-depth on the arms procurement activities of a single state (or, in a few instances, like Evangelista's work, provide parallel in-depth studies of a pair of states), this broader form of scholarship interests itself in drawing conclusions about these processes from a larger number of state cases. The often strong policy orientation of this literature is a result of the importance of the issue of the spread of arms to government and other decision makers in the defense and foreign policy fields and their critical need for timely, policy-relevant advice and analytical support for their day-to-day activities. Clearly, both these works and the previously-discussed case studies on arms acquisition often contain a mix of narrative description and (frequently unstated) theoretical assumptions about why arms spread. However, the works reviewed in this section eschew the more historical/descriptive edge of many case studies to focus on aspects of arms proliferation issues of more immediate interest to their readership.

Given the scope of this branch of the literature, it is much more difficult to develop the same sort of typology of works which I devised for looking at case studies. Many works, for example, combine normative and analytical approaches or cover the same subject from several different conceptual angles. However, a rough breakdown, with much overlap between the categories, might include two broad classes of works: state class studies and technical studies. *State class studies* carry the logic of the state-level case study to the level of geographic regions or classes of states. *Technical studies* address the problems stemming from the spread of a specific type of weapons technology. Each of these is discussed separately in the paragraphs that follow.

State Class Studies. State class studies of the arms proliferation process attempt to extend the logic and methodology of the single-state case studies to the next geographical level. In these works, states are categorized according to geographic region or some other distinguishing factor (hence, considered as a "class" of states) and analyzed as a group. Common grouping factors for works in this genre include "Third World" or developing world status (Parker 1999, Ohlson 1988, Brzoska and Ohlson 1987, Mullins 1987, Kearns 1980, Ra'anan, Pfaltzgraff, and Kemp 1978); developing world producer states (Brzoska and Ohlson 1986, Katz 1984); "pariah" or rogue state status (Klare 1995); and various regional groupings, including the Middle East (Karsh, Navias, and Sabin 1993), Latin America (Vargas 1985), and East Asia (McIntosh 1987).

This approach, by virtue of its inclusion of a larger number of states in the analysis, takes the first steps toward exchanging the high levels of detail found in single-state case studies for the broader explanatory power of more global studies: instead of looking at the problems of Iraq's acquisition of new military technologies, for example, we examine the larger problem of the spread of arms in the Middle East, or among rogue nations. However, the approach's focus on only a sub-set of the states of the international system obviously still limits the generalizability of its conclusions. From the perspective of policy formulation, centering one's attention on a small group of states with similar problems is an extremely useful way of coming to grips with political or military problems which are not unique to a single state or region. However, from the theoretical perspective, the result of this approach is the segmenting of the globe into many smaller blocs of states, each with its own self-proclaimed proliferation dynamic which may or may not be linked to other groups of states.

Technical Studies. Technical studies of the spread of arms use a weapons system or category of arms as their "case" for analysis.[11] It is not unreasonable to argue that different types of weapons systems have different dynamics of spread. It therefore often makes sense to analyze the different weapons separately across some or all of the states in the international system. Unsurprisingly, such studies typically focus first on the technological aspects of the weapons in question, followed by an analysis of the weapons' patterns of spread, and finally the incipient risks which accompany those patterns. The most popular subject of such works is undoubtedly nuclear weapons (Bee 1995, Spector 1987, Myer 1984, Weissman 1981). However, ballistic missiles (Navias 1993, Nolan 1991), chemical and biological weapons (Karsh, Navias, and Sabin 1993) and various categories of advanced conventional weapons, including combat aircraft (Zarzecki 1999a, Lorell, et al. 1995, Forsberg 1994), tanks (Albrecht 1998), and precision guided munitions (Blair 1996) have also been extensively researched. Technical studies can also overlap studies of particular classes of states by examining the spread of a particular weapons system among a particular group of states (i.e. the spread of ballistic missiles in the Middle East (Navias 1993)).

To the extent that technical studies broaden the scope of investigations into the spread of military armaments, they are useful in deepening our understanding of the process. However, they share many of the same limitations of the previous categories of studies. These include a great emphasis upon technical and/or bureaucratic detail and the coverage of only a subset of states in the international system.[12] To these is now also added the new problem of focusing upon the spread of only a single type of weapon, which may or may not be representative of other weapons categories. Once again, these limitations may be irrelevant if the intended audience for these works is the policy community. In such cases, in-depth knowledge and a narrow focus is essential for crafting specific policy solutions to individual arms proliferation problems. However, if the goal is a better understanding of the spread of arms from a theoretical perspective which permits hypothesis testing over a broad range of cases, technical studies, like state class studies, are not the best approach.

MACRO APPROACHES TO THE ARMS TRADE

A final category of literature on the spread of arms deals with macro or global-level approaches to the topic. Unlike the first two categories of scholarship, this category emphasizes the functioning of the arms production and transfer system at the level of the international system rather than at the level of individual nations or smaller groups of states. Literature in this category can be clustered into two groups of works: descriptive/empirical and theoretical. Each of these is examined separately in the following sections.

Descriptive/Empirical Works. Descriptive/empirical studies of the arms trade and arms proliferation processes form the first group of macro approaches to the subject of the spread of arms. Scholarship in this category involves descriptive or empirical studies of the arms trade as a whole, encompassing numerous states and regions across the globe, and multiple weapons technologies.

More qualitative works in this genre often read like the single-country case studies of the U.S. or one of the other major arms producers writ large. A classic example of this is Anthony Sampson's *The Arms Bazaar: From Lebanon to Lockheed* (1977). Sampson's work is a comprehensive, if often anecdotal, look at the inside workings of the global arms trade in the 1970s. Jumping across numerous suppliers and recipients from chapter to chapter, the author attempts to expose the corrupt underside of the defense trade. Along the way, Sampson explores numerous aspects of the arms trade, including supplier competition, the motivations of buyers and sellers in the marketplace, and the role of domestic politics in the carrying out of arms sale policies.

While Sampson's book features American arms merchants strongly (due to his extensive coverage of the Lockheed and Northrop scandals of the period), the authors of other works spread their attention around more evenly. Pierre's (1997) edited volume and Howe (1980) span multiple producers, suppliers, and transfer modes, providing comprehensive looks at many facets of the arms trade. Still other works examine the global arms trade from a specific "angle," several recent works on the globalization of military industry being prime examples (Keller 1995, Bitzinger 1994).

Such qualitative macro-level studies of the arms trade are few in number for two main reasons. First, when covering such broad territory, authors must undoubtedly find it difficult to decide what to include and what to omit in their works. These decisions are presumably heavily influenced by the slant (political or subject-wise) which the author chooses to take in approaching the topic. Nevertheless, keeping a tighter focus by writing on a single country, region, or weapons system is clearly an easier task. Second, it is unclear that such broad works serve the interests of policy analysis which drive so much of the arms trade and proliferation literature. As previously noted, policy makers need specific, detailed advice about narrow issues of policy formulation and implementation. Studies like Sampson's, while undoubtedly illuminating of the processes by which arms spread, must be translated into specific policy recommendations by other authors in order to have value to decision makers. The result of these factors is that single-country case studies and smaller multi-state and technical works predominate the literature on the spread of arms, with all of the implications for the scholarship that this implies.

Much more common in the literature on the spread of arms are descriptive quantitative analyses of the arms trade. As one scholar has noted:

> In fact, most of the arms trade literature is rather descriptive. Patterns of global arms flows—in short, who sells what to whom—are a common focus, as are the transfer policies of specific arms-producing nations. Ironically, such an emphasis has generated a good deal of quantitative data on arms transfers but, at the same time, has generally failed to make use of it in any rigorous way to explore relevant causal relationships (Kinsella 1994, 557–8).

The shelves of arms trade literature are filled with works that list, classify, and catalog "who sells what to whom" in the way of weapons, summarize this data in various manners, and/or provide descriptive analysis of the tabulated results. In this sense, much of the arms trade literature reads like analyses of the stock market, with the questions of who's up, who's down, what is the volume of trade, and what are the past and future trends dominating the discussion. Examples of this research trend include Brzoska and Ohlson (1987), who exhaustively tabulate the arms trade to the Third World from 1971–85, Lesser and Tellis (1996), who catalog proliferation of weapons of mass destruction in the Mediterranean basin, and Catrina (1988), who analyzes the dependence of arms recipients on their suppliers through an extensive cataloging of supplier-recipient patterns. In addition to these works, organizations such as the Stockholm International Peace Research Institute (SIPRI) and the International Institute for Strategic Studies (IISS) have compiled and published extensive lists of arms holdings and transfers for all nations around the globe since at least the 1960s.[13] The result is a tremendous amount of data on the arms trade that has served as grist for the mill of descriptive/empirical scholarship on the topic.

Clearly, such works often lack the strong policy orientation or tight analytical focus of many of the works in the preceding two categories. Needless to say, however, the wealth of data on arms holdings and transfers and the handful of more qualitative works on the arms trade are welcome for their broad scope and attempts at comprehensive treatment of the subject. If nothing else, such works provide researchers with the raw material necessary to perform more directed analysis of the global arms production and transfer system. Even more importantly, the mining for patterns within the arms production and transfer data conducted in many of these works hopefully provides a foundation for researchers to take their analysis to the next step, to the level of theoretical explanation.

Theoretical Explanation. The final category of works on the spread of arms indeed encompasses that scholarship which attempts to find theoretical explanations for the structure and functioning of the global arms production and transfer system. The above quote by Kinsella (1994) is very instructive in framing an examination of the theoretical literature on the spread of arms: simply put, the level of descriptive data about the arms trade has thus far not been matched by an equally sophisticated level of theoretical analysis. By way of further example, Gleditsch (1990, 2–3) noted in analyzing the spread of arms among the hostile Cold War alliances:

> The descriptive literature about the East-West arms build-up has increased enormously, but has not been matched by theoretical innovation. Even in the field of Soviet studies–where lack of openness has impeded data collection–Meyer (1985, 45) argues that the main deficiency is not lack of data, but failure to 'exploit such data beyond simple descriptive analysis.'

As explained in Chapter 1 of this study, the literature on arms races lends us somewhat of a "default" understanding of how arms spread. According to arms race hypothesis advocates, the spread of arms across the globe is fueled by the existence of numerous arms races between competing states. The problems with and criticisms of this approach, again noted in Chapter 1, need not be repeated here. It is sufficient to note that the arms race literature ignores (at least in practice, if not necessarily in theory) the interactivity *between* various arms races, and ignores the larger systemic factors which influence arms flows across the international system.

These larger factors have been analyzed in a handful of theoretically-oriented works that seek to examine the spread of arms comprehensively at the level of the international system. This does not necessarily mean that these works seek *explanations* for why arms spread only at the systemic level (although many of those they investigate are to be found at that level). In fact, domestic, state or sub-state level factors may also be important motives. However, these works view the spread of arms as a global phenomenon which, *conceptually speaking*, is best viewed from the systemic level, rather than from the level of individual or small groups of states, as in the previously described bodies of literature.

The primary work in this vein is Harkavy's *The Arms Trade and International Systems* (1975), which was written with the above shortcomings in the then-existing literature in mind. As noted in the opening pages of his book:

> The lack of emphasis in the scholarly literature of international relations [on the arms trade] is particularly striking with respect to general, theoretical, or macrolevel analyses which might serve to relate the patterns of arms flows to some of the other traditional staple concerns of the discipline: alliance patterns, the extent and rigidity of bloc polarization, the ideological content of international rivalries, the distribution of power among leading nations of a period and the mood or zeitgeist of an epoch as reflective of varying emphasis on totality of conflict (1975, p. 1)

Harkavy casts four aspects of the arms trade (supplier market structure and behavior, donor-recipient patterns, distribution of transfer modes, and the extent of dependency and/or autarky in weapons acquisitions) as the dependent variables in his study, and correlates these with various aspects of the international system's structure to uncover causal linkages. His finding that the power relationships in the international system (bipolarity vs. multipolarity) are key determining factors of the patterns of arms flows in that system still stands as one of the major theoretical findings in the arms trade literature.

Harkavy's work has been followed up by a number of scholars, although the literature they have generated is far from voluminous.

Neuman (1984) and Buzan (1987) detailed further the "stratification" of the global arms system. Krause (1992) has taken this avenue of investigation a step further, examining in greater detail the structure and evolution of what he terms the arms transfer and production sub-system (ATPS) of the larger international system. According to Krause, the ATPS has a fixed structure, consisting of "tiers" of states categorized according to their relationship to the means of producing military armaments; however, the identity of the states in each tier can and does change in succeeding historical eras. Laurance (1992) has also followed in the tradition of the systems approach to the arms trade, casting his work as an "update" of the earlier scholarship for the post Cold War period.

The works in this body of theoretical literature on what causes the spread of arms share two key assumptions which will form the basis of my study. The first of these is that it is important to consider the spread of arms from the global, systemic perspective. There already exists a vast amount of literature on specific fragments of global arms trade and production processes, as exemplified by the various case studies and other works detailed in the preceding pages. These works have made a critical contribution to our understanding of the process of arms spread, and will undoubtedly continue to be a main feature of future scholarship in this field. However, it is also important to look at larger patterns of activity across larger cross-sections of the globe. This study will thus consider the entire international system as a whole in examining arms spread, even if some of the variables that are believed to be motivating that spread stem from state or sub-state level activities.

A second critical assumption of my study derived from these works is that the spread of arms should be examined as a dependent rather than an independent variable. A segment of the published theoretical research on the arms trade seeks to link arms flows with various systemic outcomes, especially conflict initiation and/or duration (Kinsella 1994, Baugh and Squires 1983, Schrodt 1983). Answering the question of what the spread of arms causes, as opposed to what causes the spread of arms, does allow us to test the normative claims of many critics of the arms trade (Sampson (1977) and Hartung (1994), for example). However, as Isaacson, Layne, and Arquilla (1999, 1) note, "the current international security environment puts a premium on predicting military innovation," for all of the reasons discussed in Chapter 1. As a result, the importance of determining how quickly military innovations will spread–i.e. using the spread of arms as a dependent variable–is also growing, and thus worthy of additional investigation.

THE SPREAD OF ARMS AND THE LITERATURE ON DIFFUSION PROCESSES

As noted in Chapter 1, one of the most useful and increasingly suggested ways of looking at the spread of military technologies across the international system is to characterize that spread as a diffusion process. In this section, I will define "diffusion" and its key ancillary concepts more precisely, review the extant diffusion of innovations literature, and begin the process of casting the spread of arms in the diffusion mold.

Definition and Literature. The standard social science definition of "diffusion" is "the process by which an innovation is communicated through certain channels over time among the members of a social system" (Rogers 1995, 5). For a process to be considered diffusion, therefore, it requires an innovation, plus a population (social system) *among which*, channels of communication or commerce *by which*, and a time period *during which* the innovation can spread. Individual units of the social system or population which "take on" the innovation are known as *adopters*. Those that fail to do so are *non-adopters*. The specific operational definition of adoption (i.e. deciding when an adoption actually takes place) can vary from innovation to innovation. However, it is always assumed to be constant across all adopters of a single innovation.

The innovation diffusion process begins when a member of the population creates or invents something *new*, i.e. an idea, opinion, or product which has never before been seen or experienced (Valente 1995, 2).[14] If this *innovation* is found to be useful and the first innovator *adopts* it for personal use, he/she/it becomes the *first adopter* or the *initial innovator* in the diffusion process.

In order for diffusion of that innovation to proceed further, knowledge of the existence of the innovation and of its initial adoption must somehow be communicated through channels to other members (called at this point *potential adopters*) of the population. In a population of individuals, these channels can include word of mouth, organized marketing (of a new commercial product, for example), or simple observance of the innovation's existence firsthand. Once word begins to spread of the innovation, the diffusion process truly begins to unfold, as additional population members must decide whether or not to adopt the innovation for themselves.

Key to an understanding of the diffusion process is the role of the interaction between adopters and non-adopters in shaping the course of the process. According to much of the theoretical and empirical literature on the diffusion of innovations, we should not assume beforehand that the spread of an innovation will take place at a constant rate. In the initial stages of spread (shortly after the first adopter's adoption), an innovation may seem costly, risky, or alien to existing practices and technological forms. Only those members of the population willing or able to take risks will choose to adopt at so early at point in time.

As the innovation spreads further, it in essence becomes "easier" or "safer" for other potential adopters to step forward and become adopters. At this point, the rate of diffusion increases beyond that of the initial stages. Once the innovation is largely considered of low or little risk by the population, the pressure to adopt shifts, in a sense, in the opposite direction. Now, instead of considering the risks of *adoption*, holdouts (those who have put off adoption) must face the potential costs of *non-adoption*. The classic example here is the adoption of new production technologies by business firms, which would optimally like to avoid the risks inherent in adopting untried technologies and practices but which must also not fail to adopt before they lose their market advantage to other firms that have already done so (Nasbeth and Ray 1974). As time passes, there are fewer and fewer holdouts, but those that exist are presumably holding out for very strong reasons (lack of financial resources, a high degree of isolation from the rest of the population, etc.). As a result, the rate of diffusion drops off dramatically as the innovation reaches its saturation point in the population.

The interactive nature of diffusion means that if we graph this process by plotting the cumulative percentage of the population which has adopted an innovation in a given time t, we should expect an S-shaped curve, as shown in Figure 2.1 (from Mahajan and Peterson (1985, 9)).

The above outlines the essence of a diffusion process. Among both social and natural scientists, diffusion is seen as a generalized process which takes place in a many of settings involving a variety of innovations. In the social science realm, diffusion research has examined a bewildering array of sociological phenomena, amounting to hundreds, if not thousands of studies (as cataloged, for example, in Rogers and Shoemaker (1971, 346–85) and Crano, Ludwig, and Selnow (1981)). Most of these studies have investigated either the diffusion of an innovation through a human population (for example, the diffusion of new farming technologies in rural areas) (Valente 1995, 6) or the diffusion of business/manufacturing innovations among a group of firms (Mansfield 1961). A smaller number of authors have applied the model to political phenomena, including Walker (1969), Gray (1973), and Eyestone (1977), all of whom examined the diffusion of policy innovations among U.S. states. Despite this relatively limited use in political literature, it is clear that the terms and concepts of the diffusion framework have been applied to a wide assortment of phenomena at a number of levels of analysis. Applying them to an analysis of the spread of arms in the international system is thus an eminently reasonable proposition.

Arms Diffusion. In Chapter 1, I described what is clearly a conceptual shift in the perceptions of many observers of the global spread of armaments away from the existing "arms race" and "proliferation" schools of thought and towards what might be termed a "diffusion mindset." I argued that this has been brought about primarily by the collapse of the Soviet Union and the end of the Cold War. The uncertainty of future opponents' identities and the continuing global spread of military technology has spurred a growing realization that the U.S. and its allies must pay more attention to the general spread of military capabilities across the international system rather than focus on the armament of any single state. In the present chapter, I have already noted and described the large extant literature on the arms trade and weapons proliferation issues, detailing the many divisions of that body of work, as well as their strengths and weaknesses. This has provided us an understanding of the various main methodological and conceptual approaches authors have already taken when addressing the subject, as well as the roads less taken. The remaining step in making the conceptual leap away from arms race/proliferation and toward arms diffusion modes of thought is to specify exactly the nature of the substantive differences are between the two. In this final section, I will first explain the differences between these two mentalities. Then, I will finally show how the arms diffusion concept allows us to better address many (but not all) questions about the spread of arms than its predecessors. Possible answers to these queries, in the form of hypotheses derived from various theoretical models, are reserved for Chapter 3.

If we look at military technologies or weapons systems as "innovations," (that is, weapons systems that states adopts which they have not previously employed), we can immediately make the leap from the study of arms proliferation to the study of arms diffusion. As in Chapter 1, I define *arms diffusion* here simply as the *spread of military technological innovations among the states of the international system over time.*[15] A weapons system is said to diffuse globally when it is adopted by more than one state over a given time period.

What is the distinction between looking at the spread of arms in the traditional sense (as part of an arms race or less-defined "proliferation" process) and looking at it as a diffusion process? At least two major differences are apparent.

First, *use of the term "diffusion" implies the existence of a specific interactive process between the members of the population through which the innovation diffuses. This is a very useful way to conceive of arms spread processes.* As explained in the previous section, a diffusion process takes place because of the communication of information about innovations between existing adopters and non-adopters. Population members are assumed to be aware of and affected by one another's activities, rather than simply being autonomous actors when it comes time to make adoption decisions. Clearly, in most diffusion processes, not *all* members of the system will have access to or be influenced by *all* other members (the so-called "completely intermixed population"). Communications nets (or webs of influence) will be denser among some sub-populations than others, leading to the existence of regional "leaders" and "followers" (Walker 1969) in the overall population. Nevertheless, the image created by the diffusion model suggests a system whereby population members make adoption decisions based upon general diffusion trends in the overall population, as well as calculated judgements about when it is safe and/or necessary to "jump in" on the process by becoming an adopter.

In many ways, this is a far more compelling and realistic view of much of the spread of military hardware that takes place in today's world than the one provided, for example, by existing arms race models. In Chapter 1, I defined the term "arms race" to mean a competitive armament process between states that is marked by:

> . . . a very rapid rate of acquisitions...and...some reciprocal dynamics in which developments in the offensive capabilities of one adversary are matched by attempts to counter the advantages thought to be gained by another (Ball 1994, 94–95).

This is simply an inadequate description of much of the arms acquisition which is taking place in the world today. As Ball further notes, arms acquisitions in East Asia in the 1990s, for example, are being driven by the perceived need of states to develop modern capabilities which are not necessarily directed at neighboring states (with whom relations are generally non-hostile), for purposes of national prestige or honor, or to remain militarily prepared against future contingencies. I would also add to this list of causal factors the perceived need of states to remain "players" in the international military game by remaining competitive with at least some of the latest technologies. Unfortunately, few of these motives is captured well by the arms race motif, and its emphasis on direct, sustained military competition between hostile, threatening opponents.

The arms diffusion perspective on the global spread of arms resonates deeply in the post-Cold War period. In this view, individual states are to varying degrees constantly looking over their shoulders at the military preparations of their neighbors and at the latest military developments taking place in other regions of the globe. When a new weapons system is first devised and adopted (usually by one of the major arms producing nations, like the U.S., France, or Russia), other states pay attention to this development. These states make very calculated decisions about when they should "jump in" on the bandwagon and adopt the innovation themselves, decisions that are influenced by a variety of motivating factors. If we can't produce it ourselves or make something similar, is the weapons system being offered for sale? How expensive is it? Does it work? Do we need it now (i.e. are we, for example, at war, or in immediate danger of being attacked by another state with a matching system?) Do we have the finances to afford it now, or must we wait until better economic times?

Obviously, for some states, events in their regional neighborhood and the arms activities of potential enemies will bear greatly on these decisions. In such cases, the global arms diffusion rate might be sped up by the activation of an arms race between two states in a particular location. An arms race could thus be considered a special case of the overall diffusion dynamic, or even a spur to global arms diffusion. But even so-called "arms races" of a regional kind often assume such a complex, multi-sided nature that the traditional two-party arms race model is less effective at understanding the process of arms spread than the arms diffusion approach. As one source (Blanche and Lennox 1999), for example, recently noted about the spread of advanced military technology in the Middle East:

> "It is all too clear that proliferation is taking place throughout a region where a long series of localized conflicts and arms races has developed the characteristics of an interactive system" . . . each new advance in technology transfer and weapons acquisition influences the entire region and acts to increase the overall pace of proliferation.

Clearly, Anthony Cordesman, the long-time observer of the Middle Eastern military scene responsible for the quote in the above passage, has noticed both the "interactive" nature of armament processes in the region, as well as the subsuming of numerous localized "arms races" within a larger arms diffusion dynamic. As Cordesman confirms, analyzing the spread of arms through an arms diffusion perspective less invalidates the arms race school of thought than it does help to explain phenomena which it has largely ignored.

This is an important point. The use of arms diffusion as an analytical tool for understanding the spread of arms goes beyond a simply apt descriptive metaphor for the post-Cold War period. If that were so, it would be inappropriate to use the diffusion concept to examine the spread of arms prior to the early 1990s. In fact, the interactive processes described above have *always* been features of the international arms production and transfer system. I would argue (as detailed in the previous chapter) that the diffusion nature of arms spread simply became more *visible* to scholars after the end of the Cold War. The weakening of the hegemony of arms race discourse in strategic studies scholarship that had been generated by the Cold War, as well as the real shift in concern over non-Soviet threats after the late 1980s, helped to spur the use of diffusion-style language in the proliferation literature. The purpose of this study is to further that trend by specifically using diffusion concepts to analyze the vast amount of data on arms production and transfers which exists for sizeable spans of the Cold War period, as well as that which exists for the brief post-Cold War era.

A second major distinction between the arms diffusion perspective and its predecessors is *the nature of the questions it allows us to ask about the arms spread phenomenon.* Arms diffusion is not simply a spurious linguistic convention lacking in theoretical import. When we look at the spread of arms through the arms race dynamic, the definitional rules of that model serve as limits on the kinds of questions we ask about the phenomenon. How many arms does one side or the other in a specific arms race have? How quickly are they arming, either qualitatively or quantitatively? What is the balance of forces between them? These are the types of questions which the arms race model suggests, and which have been the subject of much of the research which that model has generated.

On the other hand, we cannot ask how quickly arms will spread generally across the globe, both to states involved in arms races and to those not involved in competitive armaments processes. We cannot ask how quickly arms are spreading to countries outside the hostile dyad of states because of the arms race itself. Nor can we ask to how many states a given category of arms is likely to spread in the absence of an unambiguous arms race. These questions require that the dynamics of the diffusion process, as described above, be taken into account. Because, as outlined in Chapter 1, these are both interesting and important questions, there is a need for an analysis of arms diffusion which has thus far been lacking.

CONCLUSIONS

This chapter has detailed the scholarly background and conceptual foundation for my examination of arms diffusion in the following pages. My review of the literature on the arms trade and the global spread of arms has shown that, while vast, this body of work is lacking in theoretical content and sophistication. Existing arms race models and the policy-oriented proliferation literature are inadequate for answering many of the questions about the global spread of arms which both scholars and decision makers are finding increasingly important. My solution to this shortcoming is to adopt the comprehensive systems-level approach of the arms trade scholars who have been driven by theoretical concerns and apply to it the concepts derived from research on the diffusion of innovations. The resulting perspective–which I simply term arms diffusion–allows us to ask new and important questions about the spread of arms, and, as shown in the following chapters, to answer them in a rigorous and systematic fashion.

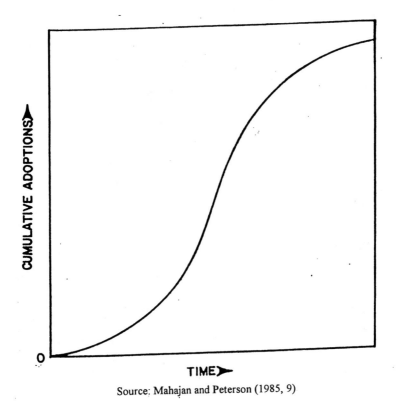

Source: Mahajan and Peterson (1985, 9)

Fig. 2.1: The Standard S-shaped Curve from the Diffusion of Innovations Literature

NOTES

[1] A thorough definition and exploration of the term "military technological innovation" is left for Chapter 4. For the purposes of this chapter, it can simply be understood as a piece of military hardware, i.e. a weapons system.

[2] Quantitative data on the rates of modern arms diffusion can be found in Chapter 5 of this study.

[3] MacKenzie's (1990) "historical sociology" of the development of nuclear missile guidance systems stands out as one of the few exceptions to this dichotomous division of scholarship.

[4] These tend to overlap with the works on arms exporters, q.v., below.

[5] One of the few book-length case studies on the subject which is *not* largely critical of U.S. arms sale policy is Hammond et al. (1983).

[6] This pattern has shifted since the Soviet collapse, with works on Russian arms transfers now sharing many of the hallmarks of those on U.S. policies. See, for example, Anthony (1998) and Cooper (1997). For a more detailed look at the treatment of Russian arms transfer policy in Western publications, see Zarzecki (1999a).

[7] Ra'anan notes that the continuation of strong Soviet-Egyptian ties are reflected by the Soviet transfer of at least 50 MiG-23 fighters and "the very latest Warsaw Pact model" MiG-27 Flogger-D attack aircraft from 1974 to 1977 (p. 151). In fact, Ra'anan (and all analysts of the period) were unaware of the distinction between downgraded export MiG-23BN which the Soviets supplied to Egypt and numerous other states beginning in the mid-1970s and the externally similar MiG-27 (which the Soviets did not export until the late 1980s, and then only to India). They were also unaware that the MiG-23s transferred to Egypt in 1974–75 were very early models with a radar set identical to that of older MiG-21s, which the Egyptians considered of approximately equal performance. See Nordeen and Nicole (1996).

[8] For a similar, contemporary treatment of the subject, see also Ra'anan (1969).

[9] In light of the recent progress on European integration, an emergent literature on the export policies of the European Union has also produced several works. These include Navias and Willet (1996) and Cornish (1995).

[10] Like those on the U.S., works on Israel have tended to be more polemical than those on other suppliers. See Ben-Menashe (1992), Beit-Hallahmi (1987), Bahbah (1986). For a more analytical view, see also Reiser (1989).

[11] Formal definitions of these terms for use in the analytical section of this study can be found in Chapter 4.

[12] Two notable exceptions to this pattern are Myer (1984) and Davis and Frankel (1993), both of which focus on uncovering theoretical explanations for the spread of nuclear weapons.

[13] See Chapter 4 for details of these data bases.

[14] The specific definition and parameters of the military innovations investigated in this study is found in Chapter 4.

[15] This is a broad theoretical definition. A more detailed, operational definition is provided in Chapter 4.

Chapter 3
Developing Theoretical Models of Arms Diffusion: Why Do Arms Diffuse?

HAVING DEFINED THE CONCEPT OF ARMS DIFFUSION AND EXPLAINED HOW IT fills gaps in the existing literature, it is now appropriate to return to the original question: why do arms diffuse and what determines the rate of their diffusion? Below, I suggest five broad explanatory frameworks for answering this question. I term these models realpolitik, exporting militarism, domestic political factors, economic factors, and the technological imperative.

The *realpolitik model* argues that security-seeking rational states populate an anarchic international system which heavily influences or determines their behavior. The rate of arms diffusion is thus likely affected by the level and intensity of security threats and conflict within the system as a whole. Within this approach, I explore hypotheses related to the degree of hegemony or power concentration and the frequency and intensity of wars and militarized interstate disputes. The *exporting militarism* argument links the needs of military-industrial complexes in core industrial states and the overall global economic situation to patterns of global arms flows. Here, arms diffusion is viewed in light of economic incentives to export weapons in core countries, particularly downturns in military spending or overall economic growth. The *domestic political factors* approach seeks explanations for foreign policy behavior at the level of domestic politics. Hypotheses derived from this approach posit links between the propensity to acquire modern arms and democracy and civil conflict. The *domestic economic factors* approach views arms diffusion as a function of the resources available for military spending. Thus, hypotheses linking diffusion to the levels of global economic wealth, growth, and defense spending are derived and tested. Finally, the *technological impera-*

45

tive approach suggests that features of various categories of weapons themselves have important impacts on the rate of arms diffusion. In this model, variables such as weapon category, type, cost, manufacturer(s), and design generation are all posited to exert influence on the rate at which arms spread.

Each of these five models is drawn from the literatures discussed in the previous chapter, and represents less a formal theory than a major research tradition. From these, explanations for arms diffusion can be postulated by either formalizing existing explanations (as taken, for example, from the policy literature on proliferation) or by extrapolating from their core assumptions. The ultimate intention is to identify a series of independent variables that explain the dependent variable "rate of arms diffusion," and to state these explanatory relationships in hypothesis form. I will then gather data on various military technological innovations (MTIs, as defined in Chapter 4) and test these hypotheses (in Chapter 5).

MODEL 1: REALPOLITIK

The *realpolitik model* is derived from the dominant realist and neorealist paradigms of international relations theory (Waltz, 1979). These paradigms emphasize:

> . . . the anarchic nature of the international system, in which there is no effective legislature, judiciary, or police force. In such a system, according to the realpolitik model, nation-states pursue their own national interests and conceive these national interests primarily in terms of power. Nation-states are fearful of conquest by other nations, and therefore build up national capabilities (including armaments) and form coalitions (including military alliances) to protect themselves (Wayman and Diehl 1994, 5).

The model is based upon the neorealist concept of the systemic basis of state behavior, that is, that "it is not possible to understand world politics simply by looking inside of states" (Waltz 1986, 52). Rather, neorealists believe that state behavior is heavily influenced by the central properties of the international system itself, particularly the distribution of power. Realists conceive of states as the primary ensurers of their own security, sensitive to military threats from other states, and responsive mainly to stimuli from outside their own borders.[1]

Given this, the realpolitik model states that *arms diffusion is the result of the military competition between sovereign, security-seeking nation-states operating within the context of an anarchic international system. The rate of arms diffusion is primarily influenced by the degree to which states feel their security threatened by other states, or by military conditions within the international system as a whole, rather than by domestic political or economic conditions.* This model seeks explanations for the rate of innovation diffusion in the central features of the international system, the three most important of these being (1) the level of interstate war in the system; (2) the number of militarized interstate disputes; and (3) the global power distribution. The rationale behind each of these explanations is detailed below.

Interstate War. There are four reasons to expect that the level of interstate military conflict in the system is positively related to the rate of arms diffusion. First and most importantly, states at war should be more likely to acquire new MTIs than states not at war. During military conflicts, combatant states have an immediate incentive to innovate, to introduce new weapons systems that they hope will aid in winning the war (Clark 1979). The pressures of wartime encourage or necessitate that state-level decision-makers take greater risks or bear greater cost burdens associated with new technologies than they probably would in non-war periods. This is particularly the case for longer wars, when states have the necessary time to evaluate, acquire, and deploy new major weapons systems. During the eight-year Iran-Iraq War, for example, Iraq purchased new generation warplanes, precision-guided munitions, and tanker aircraft. Iraq attempted to increase its air attack capability with these procurements in order to force Iran's surrender through a campaign of strategic bombing (Bergquist 1988). Even though under partial international embargo, Iran acted similarly, acquiring new ballistic and cruise missiles to bombard Iraq into submission (Cordesman and Wagner 1991). Short wars are postulated to have a similar impact on states' decisions to adopt new MTIs. But because MTI procurement cycles and lag times tend to outlast the duration of these wars, the new weapons systems tend to be adopted after short conflicts are over. This sometimes takes place in preparation for another round of fighting.[2]

Second, interstate wars should tend to enhance the rate of MTI acquisition among non-combatants as well. A military conflict in a region tends to breed an overall regional sense of insecurity, even among states not directly involved in the fighting. States are well aware that conflicts can quickly spread, and that victorious aggressors (now armed with newer generations of weapons systems) can rapidly shift their attention to other opponents. This knowledge is often incentive enough for non-combatant states to seek new levels of military technology. Examples of this phenomenon are numerous. In the 1950s, fighting on the Korean Peninsula sparked a Japanese rearmament drive that led to Japan's acquisition of numerous new weapons systems (McIntosh 1986: 51). It also spurred a massive infusion of Soviet arms technology into the arsenals of mainland China, which soon became involved in the fighting (Segal 1985: 102). Similarly, the escalation of the Vietnam War during the 1960s led to the introduction of new generations of weapons throughout Indochina.[3] And most recently, the

Iran-Iraq War of the 1980s spurred major arms purchases by Saudi Arabia, Kuwait, and numerous other regional states. These arms included fourth-generation combat jets, third-generation main battle tanks, airborne early warning aircraft, and modern anti-ship missiles (Cordesman 1984). This pattern was repeated after the Gulf War of 1991, which saw a "dramatic increase in the demand for technologically advanced arms" (Pedatzur 1998, 63).

A third reason to expect interstate war to lead to more rapid arms diffusion might be termed the "baptism of fire" or "free publicity" effect. In short, wars often serve as publically-observable proving grounds for new military technologies. This free publicity lessens the risk of their adoption by additional states. As Spence (1994, 28) argues, "an innovation is likely to be adopted more readily and more widely if it is open to inspection and, above all, if it can be seen to work." Due to the classified nature of the details of their operation, however, many military innovations are *not* open to such inspection, at least not to all potential adopters, and especially not to hostile nations. Even with MTIs that are openly advertised for sale or other transfer, peacetime testing and evaluation are rarely seen as convincing substitutes for combat success in determining a system's true value on the battlefield.

There are a variety of reasons for this. Potential adopters know that arms producers have economic incentives to exaggerate the performance characteristics of their wares. They are also aware that the producers themselves may not have accurate and reliable data about how their systems will perform under combat conditions difficult to simulate on a test range or computer (Hampson 1989; Farrell 1997; Holland 1997). And with such a plethora of weapons systems for every conceivable battlefield niche available, it is often difficult for both producers and non-producing adopters to determine which systems will be most important in combat. Finally, although relevant to only a small number of adoption cases, wars also provide the opportunity for states to capture the MTIs of their opponents and subject them to examination. If captured intact, these MTIs can be pressed into service with one's own forces. If not, they can perhaps be examined, imitated, or even directly copied.[4] Peacetime rarely affords such opportunities to reduce the risk and uncertainty inherent in the adoption of new MTIs. Furthermore, even the *unsuccessful* combat debut of an MTI might still foster arms diffusion. Such an event clues potential adopters in to which MTIs *not* to adopt, or exposes gaps in existing operational concepts that need to be plugged with new MTIs. By increasing the total amount of available information of the relative value of different MTIs, it may clarify alternatives and enhance the chances that more useful or valuable MTIs *will* be adopted.

Jervis (1976, 242) provides an opposing view. He writes that:

> . . . in choosing weapons systems, nations are also more heavily influenced by their own experiences than by others...the amount one learns from another's experience is slight even when the incentives for learning are high and the two actors have much in common and face the same situation.

To support this contention, Jervis cites several examples from the 1870–1945 period in which states failed to learn from the military successes or failures of other states. This provides an interesting countervailing hypotheses to the one stated above. However, Jervis' examples are drawn from a time period outside the time frame of this study and from a very select set of cases, the major powers. The strongly institutionalized military structures of the major powers may act as a drag on ready adoption of MTIs, and contribute to these states' relative unwillingness to learn from the lessons of others. In addition, non-major powers, whose military establishments may be smaller with fewer vested interests who find it to their advantage to resist innovation, are not discussed in Jervis' work. Power status aside, the wealth of information about global military affairs in the modern world (due both to the information revolution of the second half of the Twentieth Century and to the increased sophistication of national intelligence agencies) may also have changed the relationships noted by Jervis. As shown by several of the examples above, states are now much more aware of military developments around the globe Arms producing firms are also much more sophisticated about using combat success as a marketing tool for their wares. As a result of these factors, there is reason to believe that Jervis' contentions are inapplicable for the period and cases in this study.

Examples of the impact of war on arms diffusion which counter Jervis' claims are numerous. The Spanish Civil War of the 1930s was widely viewed as a testing ground for various new military technologies, including the German *Luftwaffe's Stuka* dive bombers and Messerschmitt Me 109 fighters. These later saw wide service in all theaters of World War II with numerous users. In 1967, the sinking of the Israeli destroyer *Eilat* by Soviet-supplied Egyptian Styx anti-ship missiles shocked naval establishments around the world and "revolutionize[d] contemporary naval strategic thought...on the formation and procurement programs" of small navies (El-Shazly 1998, 193). The Styx, which had been in Soviet service for almost a decade by 1967, subsequently became the most widely-adopted anti-ship missile of its generation and the standard armament of East Bloc-supplied maritime forces. The demonstrated success of the next-generation Exocet anti-ship missile in the Falkland Islands conflict of 1982, in which Argentine Exocets sank two British ships, similarly increased its export sales (El-Shazly 1998, 196). More recently, as Pedatzur (1998, 65) notes,

. . . the impressive success of the advanced weapons systems operated by the American forces during [Operation Desert Storm] persuaded most Middle East decision-makers including high-ranking Arab officers who took part in the fighting and were exposed to the weapons used against Iraq, that they should themselves acquire these or similar weapons.

These successful weapons include the Patriot SAM, which has been sold to Israel, Saudi Arabia, and Kuwait after the war and is under examination by the United Arab Emirates. Patriot has also since been ordered outside the region, by Taiwan, Italy, and Greece.[5] In contrast, Israel's invasion of Lebanon in 1982 and the subsequent fighting between Israeli and Syrian forces demonstrated the inadequacy of existing Soviet-supplied armaments provided the Arab states. As a result, the late 1980s saw the spread throughout the Middle East region of a new generation of Soviet fighter aircraft, SAMs, and other systems designed to rebuild the Arabs' technological parity with U.S.-supplied arms.[6]

The fourth and last reason that global military conflict may accelerate arms diffusion is simply that combat usually results in equipment losses of existing systems on both sides. After conflict termination, these losses have often been replaced with more modern generations of technology. Again, this sometimes takes place in preparation for the next round of fighting. Particularly if the destroyed or worn-out equipment is very old, replacement with technologically innovative armaments may make more economic sense, in that spare parts and support equipment for the older weapons may be difficult to obtain. This is particularly true for non-arms producing states, which are dependent upon the status of the technological state of the art in supplier countries. If the suppliers' defense firms have already moved on to producing newer generations of systems, recipients may not have the option of simply replacing losses with older technologies already in the recipients' arsenals. From the perspective of internal bureaucratic politics, combat losses may also represent a strategic opportunity for bureaucratic actors to make a strong case for the acquisition of more technologically modern systems. Such actors can employ pragmatic arguments to justify such purchases ("If we have to buy *something*, why not buy something new?"). But, since combat losses by definition take place in the context of a war or other military crisis, bureaucratic actors can also appeal to the fear of the possibility of technological inferiority in the face of future threats to justify buying new MTIs ("If our old systems were lost to enemy action, they were ineffective, and should be replaced with newer ones.")

Again using the case of the Iran-Iraq War, Iran's postwar rearmament drive has largely centered on obtaining modern Russian arms to replace its older, U.S.-supplied ones. More recently, both Ethiopia and Eritrea have acquired advanced fourth-generation MiG-29 and Su-27 fighter jets to replace older third-generation MiG-21s and MiG-23s lost in previous rounds of combat between the two states. Conversely, states like Austria, which essentially never engage in interstate wars, continue to fly older generation aircraft until they are figuratively ready to fall out of the sky before replacing them. Finally, in the wake of the 1991 Gulf War, the U.S. replaced the handful of losses of older A-6E Intruder bombers by ordering production of a similar number of newer F/A-18 Hornet strike aircraft because the former were no longer in production.

The level of conflict in the international system can be understood in two ways. It can refer to the *scope* of conflict, meaning the extent of conflict in the system. In this sense, the greater the number of wars in the system, the more likely the overall systemic tendency toward faster arms diffusion. Conversely, "level" can also refer to the *intensity* of conflict in the international system. From this perspective, all wars do not have the same impact on arms diffusion. Wars that are more intense–for example, those which result in a greater number of casualties–are likely to be seen as more serious by combatants and non-combatant alike. These are thus likely to enhance arms diffusion, as compared to those marked by lower levels of intensity.

With this distinction in mind, I offer the following hypotheses derived from the "military conflict" strain of the realpolitik model of arms diffusion.

H_{R1}: *The greater the scope of military conflict in the system, the greater the rate of subsequent arms diffusion.*

H_{R2}: *The greater the intensity of military conflict in the system, the greater the rate of subsequent arms diffusion.*

Militarized Interstate Disputes. Interstate war, however, may not be the only, or even the most significant, security-related factor that spurs the diffusion of arms. Interstate wars are relatively infrequent events which are often precipitated or followed by a variety of other militarized interactions between states. These militarized interstate disputes, or MIDs, involve a variety of events that fall short of all-out war, including border clashes, armed raids, shows of force, and other low-level hostile actions. Because they do not carry the costs of full-scale war, and because they are an often effective tool of international affairs, MIDs are generally more frequent than interstate wars. MIDs may encompass inadvertent fighting that breaks out in the middle of a tense situation, or pre-meditated acts meant to demonstrate the seriousness of a nation's political stance over a given issue. In either case, MIDs have formed a significant element in the conduct of international affairs, and have been linked to a variety of other international phenomena.

I posit that the relationship between MIDs and arms diffusion is essentially similar to that between interstate war and the spread of arms. Increasing numbers of MIDs should thus lead to an increase in the diffusion of armaments for many of the same reasons cited for interstate war. These include states' need to confront the deterioration and/or uncertainty in their general security situation which the MIDs represent; the imminent need to solve pressing military problems; and the role of MIDs as proving grounds for new technologies. It is even possible that MIDs might have a greater influence on arms diffusion than interstate wars, particularly full-scale wars of high intensity. During high intensity wars, states may direct more of their resources toward increasing their inventories of proven, existing armaments rather than engaging in risky deployment of new, untried technologies. In contrast, the short and sporadic nature of MIDs gives states time to evaluate military requirements more freely, develop new arms technologies, and consider the relative value of different arms innovations in light of combat experience.

Example of this phenomenon are numerous. In the case of the major powers, the many military clashes fought by the United States throughout the post Cold War period have served as proving grounds for new weapons technologies. In the post-1991 policing actions of the no-fly zones over Iraq, the U.S. has deployed and field tested a variety of a new weapons, including the AIM-120 AMRAAM air-to-air missile and the AGM-130 and AGM-154 (JSOW) air-to-surface missiles. The constant sparring between the U.S. and Iraq has also served to heighten regional tension and keep foreign arms imports flowing to other regional states. Likewise, the military confrontation between China and the U.S. over Taiwan in 1996 has sparked a Chinese drive to improve its naval forces with new generation warships, submarines, and anti-ship missiles. Examples involving lesser powers are almost too numerous to mention. The continuing tension on the Korean peninsula, which occasionally involves shooting incidents and cross-DMZ territorial violations, has kept new arms technologies flowing to the Northeast Asian region despite the absence of full-scale war for better than half a century. A similar situation holds in South Asia between India and Pakistan, where a simmering low-level conflict has fueling arms acquisitions. In a final negative example, post-Cold War Latin America has seen relatively light arms diffusion. One U.S. diplomat attributed this phenomenon to two factors:

> One, there's peace in the region, and, two, these [Latin American] militaries are looking at this [weapons purchases] in the long term, as part of their modernization plans.

The absence of MIDs throughout the region has stifled fears of larger conflicts, and led states to scale back their arms acquisitions.

These observations lead us to the following hypothesis.

H_{R3}: *The greater the number of militarized interstate disputes, the greater the rate of subsequent arms diffusion*

Global Power Distribution. The third element of the realpolitik model posited to explain variation in the rate of arms diffusion over time is the global distribution of power. Neorealists look to the distribution of power in the international system to understand the behavior of both the system as a whole and its constituent units (Waltz 1979). Traditional realists also use power as a central theoretical construct in their models, but find the international system playing a somewhat less deterministic role in influencing state behavior (Wayman and Diehl 1994). The theoretical distinctions between these schools of thought are often quite abstract. Both schools, however, assume that states are sensitive to the changes in the power status of other actors in the system, and to the manner in which power is distributed across the entire system. My analysis proceeds on the basis of these two assumptions.

The realpolitik model seeks explanations for the link between power distribution and the rate of arms diffusion in the theory of hegemonic stability. Hegemonic stability theory is an elaboration of the basic neorealist approach which argues that:

> . . . the presence of a single, strongly dominant actor in international politics leads to collectively desirable outcomes for all states in the international system, [while] the absence of a hegemon is associated with disorder in the world system (Snidal 1985, 579).

This "single, strongly dominant actor," is labeled a global hegemon. Because of its size and power, the hegemon can solve the dilemmas of collective action by absorbing the costs of other nations' free ridership while still generating both collective and individual benefits through concerted action (Olson 1965). This means that hegemons can impose order upon an often unruly and chaotic international system. Conversely, when the dominance of the hegemon declines, the system is characterized by a propensity toward "violence and disorder," as the political power landscape is reconfigured and states scramble for position in the newly emergent world (Huntington 1993, 83). A frequent, although not uncontested, theme in the hegemonic stability literature is that of American decline (Higgott 1994, 161). According to the "declinists," the power of the United States, the reigning global hegemon since 1945, has been on the wane since the early 1970s. Declinists argue that the ebb of U.S. power has had and will continue to have a significant impact on the course of world politics, the parameters of which they seek to identify and understand (Keohane 1984, Russett 1985).[7]

Pierre (1979, 1) notes that "arms transfers are an important element of the diffusion of power which is in process around the globe." If this is true, then the global spread of arms may also be related in some fashion to the larger phenomenon of the waxing or waning of hegemonic power. I posit that the linkage stems from the hegemon's role as a "first tier" arms producer and supplier.

Krause (1992, 26–27) argues that the international system of any historical era is marked by the co-existence of an arms transfer and production sub-system (ATAPS) with certain structural features. The most important of these features is the division of the ATAPS into numerous tiers, with the states belonging to each tier having a certain set of relationships with the overall ATAPS in common. First tier states are marked by an ability "to innovate and advance the technological frontier...and to produce weapons systems for all military applications" (p. 27). Second tier states may produce a wide variety of advanced arms, but find it difficult to innovate across most arms categories. Third tier producer states lack even the technological resources of the second tier. They are reduced to attempts to build enclave arms production industries with technology acquired from first and second tier states, and can only hope to produce a limited selection of arms. Finally, fourth tier states lack the means for indigenous arms production, and can only purchase arms from states in tiers one through three. Although these categories remain constant over time, states can and do move from one tier to another as time passes. The U.S. and USSR were undoubtedly first tier arms producers throughout the post-1945 global system. However, after 1991 in particular, the Soviet regime and its Russian successor state have exhibited a steady downward slide through the tiers as their ability to innovate at the cutting edge of technology across many arms categories increasingly falters.

Because of the hegemon's status as a key military technological innovator, other major arms producing and supplying nations must react to the hegemon's activities, in terms of developing competing or countervailing weapons systems. Hegemonic first tier states are also likely major arms exporters, upon which numerous other recipients are dependent for innovative technologies (Catrina, 1988). As a result of these factors, global hegemons that are first tier arms producers–like the United States–are likely to play a major role in the global diffusion of arms. I postulate two possible specific theoretical links between arms diffusion and declining hegemony (i.e. the deconcentration of global power) which depend upon the fact that the hegemon is a first tier state in the global ATAPS.

First, the declining hegemon, witnessing the ebb of its global influence, may be more likely than a non-declining hegemon to export its latest military technologies, and thus increase the rate of innovation diffusion. Declining hegemons, fearing an increasing scarcity of resources available for defense purposes, are less likely to conduct military operations abroad and less likely to undertake forward basing and other peacetime foreign commitments (Gilpin 1994, 97). This leads to an increased demand for new-generation weapons on the part of allies seeking to compensate for the loss of the former hegemon's security guarantees. The hegemon may also see it in its interest to attempt to distribute their common defense responsibilities among its allies and clients more broadly. When the hegemon's power was more secure, it may have been willing to assume a greater share of this common defense burden without complaint. As financial strictures become more of a problem, however, the hegemon may insist that its allies pick up a larger portion of the defense burden. This can lead to an acceleration of the arms diffusion process, as arms and technologies the hegemon once reserved for its own use are now exported.

The so-called Nixon Doctrine of the early 1970s was a classic example of this approach to hegemonic management. By 1970, the war in Vietnam was consuming a large portion of the U.S. military's attention and resources. The frustrations of that war were similarly eroding U.S. domestic support for further overseas military involvements. The subsequent U.S. policy of downsizing many overseas U.S. force commitments and arming regional allies to assume a greater share of their own defense, termed the Nixon Doctrine, reflected all of the concerns outlined above. One result of this doctrine was the arming of states like Iran, Saudi Arabia, South Korea, and South Vietnam with new generations of U.S. weapons systems in an attempt to balance the perceived growing Soviet influence in the Middle East and Asia (Hartung, 1994: 22). This basic policy has been extended into the 1990s with Israel, Saudi Arabia, Egypt, and other U.S. allies. Ball (1994), in fact, describes "uncertainty about the future U.S. presence" in East Asia and the downsizing of U.S. forces in the region as key elements fueling advanced weapons acquisitions by East Asian states in the post-Cold War period.

A second and perhaps more important impact of declining hegemony on arms diffusion is the growing inability of the hegemon to control the global arms trade. At the height of its power, the hegemon is both a dominant arms producer and supplier and has a tremendous amount of influence over the military decision making activities of its allies and clients. The hegemon can refuse altogether to transfer a given set of arms technologies of which it may control a dominant market share. The hegemon can also make liberal use of other political and economic carrots and sticks to prevent other states from obtaining weapons systems from other sources that it does not want them to have. These powers are far from absolute, particularly if there exists a hegemonic challenger that is willing to offer a similar set of technologies. But on the whole, these aspects of its position in the ATAPS yield it considerable ability to influence outcomes in the arms diffusion process.

The declining hegemon faces two problems regarding these matters. First, the diffusion of power which marks declining hegemony presumably leads to, or has already led to, the rise of non-hegemonic arms suppliers. As other states grow in strength economically, politically, and technologically, their ability to produce and sell arms independent of the hegemon increases. Ironically, it is arms and technology transfers to allies and client states that often plant the seeds for these capabilities (Krause 1992, 48). In any event, as alternate suppliers proliferate, the hegemon's ability to control arms transfers of which it disapproves can dissipate rapidly. Second, as stated before, the declining hegemon faces a growing scarcity of resources and a concomitant risk-aversion when it comes to overseas affairs. This leads to fewer available carrots and sticks for the hegemon to employ in reigning in the behavior of its allies and non-allies alike in transferring the latest technologies abroad. In fact, many states may see opportunities in the waning of the hegemon's power to enhance their own power status through the acquisition or development of new military technologies. The increasing number of players in the arms market also generates more intense competition, demanding higher rates of innovation diffusion for individual players to remain competitive.

This pattern of an increasing number of arms producers and a shrinking ability of the U.S. to control the global arms market has been noted by a number of authors as characteristic of the post-1960s global arms trade. Summing up these arguments, Bajusz and Louscher (1988, 9–10) write:

> . . . in the 1960s, the U.S. and the Soviet Union accounted for 80 percent of the value of all deliveries of military equipment and services of other countries. Presently, their combined share has declined to 55 percent. The greatest decline has occurred for the U.S. where the market share was 60 percent in 1969 but has continued to decline to less than 20 percent by 1985. The Soviet portion of the market, however, has remained relatively constant at about 33 percent over the past twenty years . . . as the U.S. share of arms deliveries has declined the greatest increase in deliveries has been among a diverse group of suppliers. This diversification of suppliers is a major phenomenon...[encompassing] Great Britain, France, Italy, Brazil, Israel, Yugoslavia, the People's Republic of China, and South Korea.

This has resulted in the spread of advanced weapons to countries which the U.S. would most likely not have armed itself. French arms transfers to states like Libya, Syria, and Iraq during the 1970s and 1980s were opposed by the U.S. with little success. French, British, and Italian firms, among others, also freely sold advanced arms to Latin America, despite a decade's long U.S. ban on sales to the region (Myers 1998). Finally, despite its Operation *Staunch* and other efforts, the U.S. was unable to cut Iran off from external sources of arms resupply during the Iran-Iraq War. In contrast, dozens of states provided Iran with a variety of major weapons systems over the course of the eight-year conflict, including missiles, tanks, and combat aircraft. Even today, the U.S. would like to curtail the spread of beyond-visual range air-to-air missiles like its own AIM-120 AMRAAM to the developing world. However, the U.S. finds itself frustrated in these efforts by Russian and French offers to sell the comparable AA-12 Adder and Matra Mica, respectively, to interested parties.

The probable result of the interaction of all these factors is an increase in the rate of arms diffusion, as stated in hypothesis #3, below.

H_{R4}: *The less the level of hegemonic dominance, the greater the rate of subsequent arms diffusion.*

MODEL 2: EXPORTING MILITARISM

Although stemming from different conceptualizations of the core paradigm, the hypotheses H_{R1-R4} are all derived from the basic realist/neorealist school of thought. The second model draws its inspiration from a less dominant, but no less extensive body of work on peace research, economic determinants of the arms trade, and the world systems approach to international relations theory (Wallerstein 1979). I term this model *exporting militarism.*

Considering as it does the global economy as a single division of labor, the world systems approach finds the traditional class distinctions noted by Marx replicated at the level of the states system. A group of core industrialized states controls the bulk of productive resources, while the vast hinterlands of the periphery and semi-periphery serve as a pool of cheap labor and natural resources to fuel the core economies. Core states are seen as "economically, politically, and militarily dominant" over those in the periphery and semi-periphery. It is within the context of these underlying economic relationships that all political phenomena (including, presumably, arms diffusion) must be understood (Viotti and Kauppi, 1987: 412).

Building upon this approach, Model 2 depicts *arms diffusion as a process largely motivated by the need of the core world economies– the economies of the major arms producing states–to compete with one another in the production and export of the end-products of their military-industrial complexes.* It is more than mere coincidence that the world's primary economies belong to the states in Krause's (1992) first and second tiers of dominant players in the global arms transfer and production sys-

tem. The military-industrial complexes of these key states, even if originally developed in response to genuine security needs, have become a central
component of the world capitalist system. Employing millions of skilled
workers and benefitting from an intimate relationship with national governments, these complexes ensure their own prosperity through the maintenance of a war economy and a state of perpetual military confrontation.
In addition to encouraging the adoption of unneeded new weapons systems
at home (and thus promoting a generalized global military build-up), they
promote the export of new weapons abroad under the guise of "security
assistance," or "protecting the defense-industrial base." These actions fuel
the process of arms diffusion through a supply-push dynamic.

Core Military Spending. Model 2 suggests two causal agents for the
diffusion of military innovations in the international system. First, I posit a
link between core state military spending and subsequent arms diffusion.
During periods of relatively high domestic military spending in core states,
the market pressures upon first and second tier arms suppliers are expected to be lower than during times of defense spending contraction or
restraint. The logic of economies of scale and the need to recover sunk costs
over larger production runs means that exports are required to make up for
lost domestic orders. Similarly, money is less likely to be channeled into
costly research and development on essentially "unexportable" systems
(aircraft carriers or ICBMs, for example) and more likely to fund systems
for which international buyers can readily be found. During such times, the
logic of security (holding back export of new and sophisticated weapon
systems in order to curb possible security threats) surrenders to the
demands of the capitalist need for markets.

Support for the second model's argument can been seen in many writ-
ings which emphasize the purported increase in the role that economic factors have played in influencing the arms sale policies of the core exporting
countries since the 1970s, and especially after the end of the Cold War.
Hartung sees the economic incentives for arms exports as the deciding
factor in the Bush administration's decision to export advanced combat
aircraft and other systems to Israel, Saudi Arabia, and Taiwan in the midst
of the post-Cold War US contraction in defense spending. That these sales
were announced during a presidential election campaign in which the state
of the U.S. economy was a major issue is also not coincidental (Hartung
1994, 146, 274).[8] For the second tier major suppliers, like Britain and
France, the economic importance of defense exports is even more acute.
A recent work on Britain's defense trade with Iraq prior to Operation
Desert Storm (with the telling title *Export or Die*) emphasizes that the
primary motive of Britain's "disposition to sell" the products of its arms
industries "is economic rather than strategic," as "arms sales buck the
trends of Britain's economic decline" (Miller 1996, 5). Finally, the bulk of

the analysis of Russian arms exports after the Cold War has focused on the parlous state of Russia's economy as the primary influence on Russian export behavior (Zarzecki 1999b, Anthony 1998). The virtual collapse of Russian domestic defense orders have made defense exports vital to the very survival of Russia's defense industrial base. As a result, both individual defense firms and the central government itself are said to have abandoned the Soviet emphasis on grand strategy and ideological orientation in determining which states will have access to the latest Russian weapons technologies.

From these arguments, I derive Model 2's first hypothesis:

H_{E1}: *The greater the aggregate growth level of military spending in core (first and second tier arms producing) states, the less the subsequent rate of arms diffusion.*[9]

Economic Conditions. A second possibility derivable from Model 2 is the existence of a broader relationship between the rate of diffusion and general economic conditions within the core economies. The first hypothesis assumes that the defense sector is somehow isolated from larger economic trends. It suggests that the military industrial complex reacts primarily to economic stimuli within its direct sphere of interest. Because of this, arms diffusion is largely a result of pressure to maintain high profit levels in the defense sector of the economy, whether through direct foreign sales or state-subsidized military sales or aid. The second version of Model 2, however, views the production and export of military innovations as a means of raising revenue when general economic growth is stagnant or declining. In these situations, indigenous military purchases are used as a Keynesian-style economic stimulus to spark domestic growth. In addition to this, arms exports correct balance-of-payments problems, reduce trade deficits, and keep defense workers on the job instead of at the unemployment office. The actual effectiveness of this strategy for enhancing economic growth has indeed been debated (Looney 1988). Regardless of the soundness of the policy, however, I assume that appeals to government to be more aggressive in purchasing and marketing arms are more likely to find a receptive political audience in periods of economic distress than in periods of economic plenty.[10] This results in the second hypothesis from Model 2:

H_{E2}: *The lower the aggregate level of economic growth in the core (first and second tier arms producing) states, the greater the subsequent rate of arms diffusion.*

Both hypotheses H_{E1} and H_{E2} essentially assume the perpetual economic and military dependency of the peripheral and semi-peripheral states. Although smaller arms producers may emerge from time to time, their impact on the arms market, particularly for cutting edge technologies, is very limited at best, and their small size means that their continued survival depends highly upon fluctuating market conditions.[11] Even during a period of "globalization" in the international arms trade (Bitzinger 1994) in the 1990s, the core arms producing states continued to account for the lion's share of arms exports, particularly to the developing states (Schmitt 1995, Starr 1994, Pear 1992). One author even argues that, from a purely market perspective, the U.S. had become a monopoly supplier of arms to the world (Kapstein 1994).[12] All of these trends reinforce the image of global arms diffusion as a process best explained by the demands placed by the capitalist system upon a few super-sized national economies operating within a single global division-of-labor, an image suggested by the second model.

MODEL 3: DOMESTIC POLITICAL FACTORS

Models 1 and 2 emphasize systemic or global causal factors related to arms diffusion. In contrast, Models 3 and 4 shift emphasis to those factors which work at the level of the state and below (Singer 1961). Model 3 posits that *the global spread of arms is primarily motivated by political variables found at the level of individual states*. Political characteristics particular to the state itself, rather than external power or economic relations, determine whether and when a state will feel it necessary to acquire sophisticated new arms. As a result, global diffusion patterns are best understood as the aggregate result of these largely autonomous state-level political processes.

The domestic factors approach to explaining defense and foreign policy behavior has been widely employed, and has generated a vast literature (Allison 1971, Kissinger 1971, Rosenau 1967, Rosenau 1969, Kotz 1988, Hartung 1994, Vanhanen 1981, McKinlay 1989, Sorenson 1995, Leitner 1995). The great industriousness of scholars working in this research tradition has lead to an incredible proliferation of theories about the linkages between military affairs, the latter including weapons procurement decisions, and domestic politics. The possibilities of analyzing many of these theories, however, are limited by the nature of the explanatory variables they employ. Detailed bureaucratic or organizational politics models, for example, usually demand a wealth of qualitative detail for the case study analyses which scholars typically use for their examination.[13] This type of information is simply not available for the vast majority of countries around the world. Even if it were, such analyses often tend to ascribe specific acquisition decisions to the influence of unique constellations of actors and events at a given point in time (Meyer 1984, 17). This makes it difficult to test such theories across a large number of cases. In devising a model incorporating domestic politics variables into a study such as this one, the main task is thus to select variables which are potentially central to the process of arms diffusion and for which data across all of the states in our universe of cases is readily available. These issues led me to focus the analysis in particular upon two significant domestic politics factors: civil conflict and democratic polity.

Civil Conflict. The first causal factor included in the domestic politics model is civil conflict. As opposed to the interstate conflict included in Model 1, civil conflict, or intrastate conflict, is simply defined as armed conflict between various factions within a society. This conflict can include asymmetrical warfare between a state regime and one or more anti-regime groups (i.e. Nicaragua during the 1980s). It can also include symmetrical conflict between more evenly matched factions within a more broadly fragmented society (i.e. Afghanistan during the 1990s). A typology of civil conflict could include numerous descriptive labels applied to wars of varying characters, with guerilla war, insurgency, counterinsurgency, civil war, terrorism, revolutionary war, and low-intensity conflict commonly encountered.

There are two major reasons to presuppose that a higher level of civil conflict around the globe is negatively related to the global rate of arms diffusion. First, the character of intrastate civil conflicts is commonly assumed not to require the use of high-technology major weapons systems on an extensive basis. The conventional wisdom holds that civil conflicts are primarily infantry struggles by government forces against low-tech opponents. Guerilla wars generally consist mostly of small unit combat, intensive patrolling in often remote areas, police-type actions, or long-term, low-intensity fighting. Guerillas, by virtue of their non-state nature, do not have access to the financial resources or the operational environment (i.e. large fixed bases and logistics infrastructures) to operate large numbers of tanks, artillery, combat aircraft, and other major weapons systems. Similarly, government forces find such exotic and expensive weapons of relatively limited use in fighting lightly-armed, highly-mobile bands of partisan fighters across rugged terrain. In contrast, anti-guerilla campaigns require large expenditures on personnel and low-technology arms–small arms, mines, trucks, and simple fortifications–rather than high-technology, cutting-edge weapons systems. The greater the frequency of such conflicts, the more likely that states are forego purchasing "conventional" military systems and instead shift their expenditure toward less prestigious, less expensive items of military equipment. Finally, it may be true, as David (1999) writes, that "conflicts fought within the borders of a single state send shock waves far beyond their frontiers." But while states witnessing the civil strife of a neighbor may feel threatened by the conflict, they are unlikely to see further conventional armament as the solution to their insecurity. As a result, intrastate conflicts are not likely to spark the diffusion of major conventional arms among other regional states in the same fashion as their inter-state counterparts.

A second rationale for a negative link between civil conflict and arms diffusion involves the impact of civil conflict on the political and economic condition of the countries experiencing it. Major weapons systems are complex items which increasingly require extensive ongoing maintenance and high-cost logistical support to remain combat-effective. They also generally require a well-developed and well-funded defense-industrial base to design, produce, and procure. The complex social and industrial-economic systems necessary for the conduct of these activities are easily disrupted by high levels of civil conflict within a nation. Extended lower-intensity guerilla wars can sap the economic vitality of a nation and leave few of the resources required for advanced arms procurement. Over time, even the remaining resources are shifted away from either foreign arms purchases or indigenous military development and toward the meeting on ongoing needs for low technology consumables (i.e. ammunition, small arms, etc.).

Similarly, it is the mission of insurgents to bring about disruption of the existing political order to achieve their political aims. The unrest their activities causes can unhinge delicate social systems and the production processes they support. It would be difficult, for example, to manufacture arms in a province of a country which is under frequent guerilla attack, or which had been "liberated" from government control. If the conflict escalates to a higher level and brings about the overall fragmentation of society, even imports of major new systems may be rendered impossible by the ensuing chaos. To whom would an outside supplier sell arms, and how would these arms be maintained and based? In practice, civil conflict has not been a hallmark of the industrialized major arms producers for most of the post-World War II period. As a result, the long-term economic burden of civil conflict upon arms importers, particularly in the developing world, is likely to be of more salience for the rate of global arms diffusion than that conflict's interruption of arms production processes.

Examples of the relationship between civil conflict and arms diffusion are more apparent in broad regional trends than in any specific instances. One analyst explains the lack of major U.S. arms exports to Latin America in the 1990s despite the lifting of a twenty-year ban on sales, by noting that:

> . . . militaries in Latin America often face internal threats not easily attacked with supersonic fighters and air-to-air missiles. . . these countries are more likely to want more mundane equipment, like trucks and transport helicopters (Myers 1998).

Indeed, states with long-running insurgencies like Myanmar, Guatemala, and El Salvador have acquired few major weapons to wage these conflicts. In regions like the Middle East and Northeast Asia, where interstate conflict clearly outranks intrastate conflict among the concerns of most state decision-makers, conventional arms diffusion is much more pronounced. In some states, like Afghanistan, Somalia, and Lebanon, the complete collapse of civil order has restricted arms purchases by competing factions to the lower end of the technological spectrum. Prior to its disintegration, each of these states had important significant quantities of sophisticated arms. Afterwards, warring factions were reduced to employing the arms that were on hand at the time of the collapse. As these supplies dwindled, imports were generally restricted to small arms and ammunition, with only handfuls of obsolete armor and artillery perhaps reaching the combatants from outside sources. In the case of Afghanistan, some factions have in fact succeeded in maintaining small numbers of combat aircraft and helicopters. But even here, the groups have been restricted to obtaining only small numbers of additional examples of systems on hand at the time of the government collapse. Clearly, given their current conditions, the spread of new generations of weapons systems to these states is highly problematic.

If these observations are accurate, both the incentives and the resources states might have for early acquisition of new weapons systems are reduced by civil conflict. I thus posit the following hypothesis:

H_{P1}: *The greater the level of civil conflict within a state, the longer it is likely to wait before adopting a military innovation.*

Democratic Pacifism. A second domestic political factor plausibly related to the rate of arms diffusion stems from the basic tenets of the "democratic peace" school of international relations. The *democratic pacifism* approach posits that, for a number of reasons, democracies are more peaceful than states with other, non-democratic forms of government. Greater numbers of democracies in the international system should thus logically be linked to a decreased need for weapons and thus a reduction in the global rate of arms diffusion. The democratic peace argument is grounded in an increasingly sophisticated and well-researched empirical and theoretical literature (Crescenzi and Enterline 1999, Gleditsch and Hegre 1997, Gates, Knutsen, and Moses 1996, Russett 1993). This does not mean that a consensus has developed on the exact nature of the relationship between democracy and peace. In fact, there are a variety of competing explanations for the phenomenon. Nonetheless, because the subject has been so thoroughly explored, I will be able to present only its barest outlines before proceeding to tie its basic assumptions to arms diffusion.

Explanations for the link between democracy and a more pacific international system are numerous and varied. However, they can be divided into at least two major schools of thought. The first school characterizes the economic features of liberal democracy as inimical to the ready use of military force. Democratic states are usually free market capitalist states, in which the primary societal emphasis upon "commercial activity and material prosperity" dampens the enthusiasm for costly wars and military adventures (Onuf and Johnson 1995). In this formulation, commerce and combat are incompatible goals for individual states to pursue, and commerce is more likely to win over the hearts and minds of democratic decision-makers as they consider participation in a war.

A second school of thought stresses the pacific nature of domestic democratic polities and their impact on their structures of governance. One author (Cashman 1993, 125) summarizes this argument as follows:

> Democratic governments, being democratic, represent the wishes of their peaceful citizens (or at least they represent the will of the peaceful majority). By giving prospective soldiers and their families the chance to share in the decision to go to war, the probability of war is reduced. Few people will vote for an unnecessary war that might mean the destruction of their property, the reduction of their standard of living, and the death of themselves or their loved ones.

Thus, democracies are irenic because democratic citizens are both peaceful and able to exert influence on the political decision making process. This implies that democracies are both unlikely to initiate aggressive wars against other states, and that relationships between democracies are likely to be the most irenic of all (Doyle 1986). Another branch of this school argues, however, that democracies may not necessarily be less warprone than other states, because they often come into conflict with nondemocratic states. In this formulation, the "democratic peace" is a peace *between* democracies, and does not necessarily include their authoritarian or totalitarian counterparts (Cashman 1993, 129). However, clearly, as the number of democratic states around the globe rises and the number of potentially hostile dyads decreases, overall level of conflict should decline.

The linkage between the number of democracies around the globe and the rate of arms diffusion is fairly straightforward. If democracies are more pacific and less militaristic than other states, an increase in their number in the international system should decrease the overall rate of arms diffusion. Democracies should be less likely to foresee themselves getting involved in conflicts which require the use of armed force than their authoritarian neighbors, and less willing to expend budgetary resources on military purchases.[14]

As with the civil conflict argument, examples of the relationship between democracy and arms diffusion are more apparent as broad trends than as specific instances. The post Cold War period has seen a noticeable drop in the overall level of military spending, much of which is accounted for by the disarming of the now-democratic former Warsaw Pact nations in Europe. A 70% drop in military spending in the developed world between 1988 and 1993 is "mainly due to the severe budget cuts which followed the economic collapse in the former Soviet Union . . . [and the] six other countries of the former Warsaw Pact" (Schméder 1998, 12). The replacement of the totalitarian governments in these countries with democratic ones heralded the beginning of new relationships with the other world democracies based upon trade and dialogue rather than military confrontation. The results for numerous weapons programs of this cut in defense spending have been delays and/or outright cancellations.

This leads us to the following hypothesis.

H_{P_2}: *The greater the number of democracies in the international system, the lower the rate of global arms diffusion.*

MODEL 4: DOMESTIC ECONOMIC FACTORS

The *domestic economic factors* approach views arms diffusion as *a function of the state-level resources available for military spending. States with the economic resources to acquire new weapons do so. Those lacking such resources tend to delay adopting arms innovations as long as possible.* As a result, general upturns in the economic fortunes of the global economy are likely to herald broader diffusion of new military technologies.

Economic Prosperity. The arguments behind the domestic economic factors approach are straightforward and uncomplicated. First, the spread of military technological innovations is a game that only rich states, not poor ones, can play with systematic regularity. The more aggregate resources a state has at its disposal, the more it can afford to spend on developing its military capabilities. The very wealthy states tend to be first tier arms producers and will adopt new systems rapidly, before they begin to export them. If these states are economically prosperous, they will be able to acquire these systems more rapidly, and thus begin the export process earlier than would otherwise be the case.[15] Among middle- wealth states, the high (and increasing) cost of major weapons systems and their support infrastructures renders their acquisition even more hostage to the level of resources available in state coffers. Among less wealthy states, weapons acquisitions may be difficult or impossible without some form of outside military assistance to reduce their cost. As a result, poorer states do not necessarily adopt new weapons rapidly after their initial availability, as such assistance may only come in times of crisis, war, or other unusual, "random" circumstances.

Second, wealthier states, having more developed industrial economies, are more likely to rely on technological solutions to military requirements rather than upon quantitative increases in troop strength. This proclivity is linked, among other things, to the lower birthrate found in industrialized states and the increased amount of costly training necessary to prepare modern soldiers for combat (Luttwak 1993). From a broader perspective, military institutions tend to reflect the societies from which they spring. As a result, high-technology industrial societies are likely to support militaries that reflect their overall level of technological development. As the overall wealth of the world grows, this propensity for the adoption of high-technology arms can be expected to grow as well, fueling arms diffusion across the globe.

Examples of the link between economic resources and arms diffusion are legion. However, as with the links between democracy and arms diffusion, they are found in broad trends rather than specific instances. As Klare (1993, 138) notes of recent events in East Asia,

> . . . the steady rise in GNP in these countries has provided their governments with access to increased economic resources, which many have chosen to invest in the expansion and modernization of military infrastructures.

In contrast, the economic crisis which struck Asian states beginning in 1997 forced the curtailment or delay of many advanced weapons purchases, slowing the rate of regional arms diffusion considerably.

In even broader terms, Singer and Wildavsky (1993, xiv) note that "a society that cannot operate the highest quality economy cannot operate the highest quality fighting force." In their view, only the wealthy industrialized states possess such economies. Undoubtedly, the rich capitalist states of Western Europe, North America, and East Asia do have advanced military forces built on high-technology weapons systems that most poorer states lack. This heavy reliance upon technology has encountered critics over the years (see for example Gabriel (1985)). However, it clearly stems from the ability of the West, and the U.S. in particular, to purchase advanced weapons on a regular basis. Contrast this behavior with Russia's post-Cold War military situation, where domestic economic collapse has essentially placed almost all major military projects on the back burner (Butowski, 1996; Cook, 1995).

H_{E1}: *The greater the global level of economic prosperity, the greater the subsequent rate of arms diffusion.*

Defense Spending. A third argument for the importance of domestic economic factors focuses upon the level of global military spending. The amount of resources a state decides to allocate to the military sector (as opposed to its overall wealth) is expected to be the key determinant of the pacing of its adoption decisions on new arms take place independently of the size of its overall economy. Military budgets represent the "upper bound" of actual available funds for arms procurement. States with larger military budgets (the U.S., USSR, Britain, France, etc.) also tend to be military innovators, and thus acquire new arms earlier than their non-producing counterparts. The link between larger defense budgets and arms procurement may seem a logical one. However, the literature has shown that, to the extent that states spend military resources on funding large troop inventories or building military infrastructure, the connection is far from necessary (Sherwin and Laurance 1979, Goertz and Diehl 1990). It is thus in need of empirical investigation.

H_{E2}: *The more a state spends on defense, the sooner it is likely to adopt new military innovations.*

MODEL 5: TECHNOLOGICAL IMPERATIVE

Drawing from numerous other diffusion studies, the *technological imperative* model argues that *features of various categories of innovations themselves have significant impacts on the rates of their diffusion.* Studies on industrial and business innovations have focused on the influence that the productivity, cost, and other similar factors of new innovations have on the rate of diffusion (Mansfield 1961, Mahajan and Muller 1996, Mahajan and Peterson 1979). Weapons systems share some of these characteristics, but are unique in many other ways. The following hypotheses are thus derived from both the existing scholarly literature on technical innovations and an analysis of the technical literature on weapons systems for categorical features that might be expected to affect their spread.

Combat Effectiveness. Spence (1994, 30) notes that "if something new can be seen to be a major improvement on what currently exists, then it could well be adopted fairly quickly." Most studies of the diffusion of business innovations further argue that innovations which increase firm productivity the greatest are those that spread the fastest, because they provide firms with the greatest economic incentives to acquire them (Mansfield 1961). If we assume for a moment that what new weapons systems "produce" are increases in "combat effectiveness," then we should similarly expect that military innovations which provide greater leaps in combat effectiveness over their predecessors should spread more quickly than those which produce less dramatic jumps.

Combat effectiveness is a notoriously difficult concept to operationalize quantitatively (Sherwin and Laurance 1979, Laurance and Sherwin
1978). However, it is possible to make some distinctions between more and
less effective systems. In particular, we should expect that the first generation of any new category of arms represents a more significant jump over
existing military capabilities than subsequent generations, which typically
represent more modest leaps in performance. First generations of weapons
are thus likely to spread more quickly than subsequent generations.[16] New
categories of arms represent new dimensions of warfare that tend to tran-
scend existing capabilities dramatically. As such, the incentive to buy
matching or countering systems is usually overwhelming. New weapons
categories also demand the creation of new military institutions to develop
and employ them. Since this organizational infrastructure is presumably
easier to improve upon than to create in the first place, states may choose
to purchase first generation weapons to lay the institutional foundation for
further improvements that may be taken at a more leisurely pace, if at all.

H_{T1}: *First generation military innovations are likely to diffuse more
rapidly than those in later generations.*

Cost. A second factor is cost. As Spence (1994: 27) succinctly explains:

> Any new product or practice which is high in financial cost is likely to be
> adopted more slowly than one which involves lower expenditure, even if the
> eventual return for outlay is likely to be proportionately higher.

In the case of armaments, cheap military innovations are thus likely to
spread more rapidly than expensive ones. Not only will the decision to
adopt cheaper weapons be less monumental in terms of the potential
resource expenditures and risks involved, but these weapons will also be
affordable to a wider array of states, particularly those with fewer economic resources. By way of example, we can compare the relatively rapid
spread in the 1970s of inexpensive shoulder-fired surface-to-air missiles,
versus the relatively snail-like spread of second generation attack helicopters. The latter, although extremely effective, have barely diffused to a
dozen states in the ten years since their initial appearance in the mid-1980s.

A sub-hypotheses related to cost is system complexity. Again citing
Spence (1994: 28):

> Ideas and practices which are relatively simple to understand and operate by
> the end-users tend to be adopted more readily and quickly than those of
> greater complexity.

Since there is no easy way to quantify the complexity of a system, we will use cost as a surrogate, arguing that less costly weapons are by their nature usually smaller and less complex than more expensive ones. While this may not be true in all cases, it is correct enough to use in our analysis.

H_{T2}: *The less expensive a weapons system, the more rapid its spread.*

Weapon Production Features. A third critical argument centers not specifically on technical features of weapons categories, but rather upon the nature of the relational system of their design and supply. A "generation" of weapons systems in a given category of arms can include a variety of specific systems from different manufacturers in different producing states which become available for operational service at varying points in time, and these features can be posited to affect the nature of diffusion patterns.[17] First, the rate of diffusion will be influenced by the length of time between the adoption of the innovation between the two major arms producing states (the U.S. and Soviet Union/Russia). Specifically, if an innovation spreads quickly between these two states, its rate of overall spread will be much greater. Both of these states served as "nodes" of diffusion, each having a list of client states for which, for political reasons, it was the sole or dominant arms supplier. If the U.S. and Soviet Union developed a given innovation within a short interval, they could both begin exporting it to their allies at roughly the same time. However, if one delayed adoption of a new innovation for whatever reason, its closest allies were essentially forced to wait until it became available from their supplier, as they were usually incapable of producing such a weapon indigenously and could not simply purchase it from the opposing state. This resulted, for example, in most of the Warsaw Pact states not receiving current-generation fighter/attack planes equivalent to Western model until the late 1980s, almost eight years after they began appearing in the air forces of the states of Western Europe.

H_{T3}: *The shorter the interval between the adoption decisions of the two major global arms suppliers, the greater the subsequent rate of diffusion.*

Second, the rate of diffusion for arms in a given generation and category is expected to be influenced by the selection of weapons systems available in that category. Generations which feature a variety of systems under production by number of supplier states can be expected to diffuse more rapidly than those in which fewer systems from fewer suppliers are available. An increased number of producers making arms of a given generation stimulates the so-called "dilemma of alternatives." This is the oft-cited argument that "if we don't sell this weapon to country *x*, then another producer will" (Pearson 1994). The sale of British Tornado strike aircraft to Saudi Arabia after the U.S. refused to supply F-15E Strike Eagles in the mid-1980s is an example of this phenomenon, as is a more recent threat from Thailand to purchase Russian-built Su-35s or French Mirage 2000s if the U.S. failed to supply F/A-18 Hornets. A larger number of individual systems in a given generation also usually means that at least some of them, although embodying the same basic technologies as their generational counterparts, have been designed to be cheaper or easier to operate. This makes the systems more accessible to a wider variety of potential adopters. Thus the Russian MiG-29 fighter has been supplied to 17 states by 1996, whereas only two had received the more costly and sophisticated Su-27.

H_{T4}: *The greater the number of individual systems in a given generation of arms, the greater the rate of subsequent diffusion.*

The five models outlined above capture most of the major explanations for why arms diffuse that many of the works described in Chapter 2 so thoroughly detail. The purpose of this project is to test these models using empirical data gathered over a significant period of time. Before testing can begin, however, I must operationalize the concept of arms diffusion in a systemic fashion, and explain how the data used for that testing will be gathered and coded. All of these issues are discussed in the following chapter.

NOTES

[1] Clearly, not all schools of thought within the realist and neorealist paradigms embrace identical conceptions of these relationships (Waltz 1997; Vasquez 1997). For this project, I draw liberally from both paradigms to develop and test causal hypotheses about arms diffusion. Since I am not primarily interested in using these hypotheses as critical tests of realism or neorealism, I omit consideration of whether (or which of) these variables represent the theoretical core of the two approaches.

[2] Examples of this abound. See, for example, Smith (1994, 79–85), who details India's burst of MTI adoption after its 1962 war with China. See also Glassman (1975), who describes the process as it occurred between Israel and the Arab states through the mid-1970s.

[3] Because the Vietnam conflict is often characterized as a low-intensity or guerrilla conflict, the amount of arms diffusion in the region to combatant and non-combat states is frequently overlooked. In fact, the Soviet Union and China sent massive quantities of modern arms to North Vietnam, including SAMs, radars, fighter aircraft, tanks, and naval vessels. South Vietnam, Thailand, Laos, and (after 1965) Indonesia received similar U.S. weapons systems. Cambodia received such arms from both the U.S. and China. See Brzoska and Ohlson (1987) for specific transfer lists.

[4] A recent example of this is the shooting down of a U.S. F-117A fighter during NATO's conflict with Yugoslavia in 1999. Some sources indicated that Yugoslavia planned to send the wreckage of the jet, and thus clues to its stealth technology, to Russia for examination and possible duplication (Schmitt 1999).

[5] Interestingly, these effects may also be system-specific, i.e. combat use is transferred not only to a generation of MTIs in a given arms category, but also to a specific system within that generation made by a specific producer. An example of this is the Russian S-300 SAM system. While similar to the U.S. Patriot in many respects, the S-300 has never been tested in combat. Possibly as a result of this, the S-300 has earned very few export orders after the Gulf War relative to its U.S. counterpart.

[6] Doctrinal innovation in combat may also be critical in identifying the strengths and weaknesses of existing clusters of military technologies. This also fuels subsequent arms diffusion. For a recent example of this phenomenon, see Andrews (1998).

[7] Since the end of the Cold War, the declinist school has largely been eclipsed by a "triumphalist" school which cites America's newfound status as the world's sole economic and military superpower as the basis for an unprecedented global hegemony (Valladão 1996, Nye 1990). Since (as the next chapter explains) my analysis focuses on the period from 1960 to the early 1990s, however, I will test the theories which predominated over the course of that period.

[8] For a dated but thorough statistical cost-benefit analysis of U.S. arms exports, see Bajusz and Louscher (1988).

[9] The term "lower" here is meant to indicate either lower rates of actual growth and/or negative growth or contraction.

[10] Possible support for this position is yielded by statistics supplied by Krause (1988, 11) suggesting that the 1973–1982 period saw a dramatic increase in the global arms trade, one which tapered off in 1982. Interestingly enough, this period began with economic stress on the core state economies due to the Arab oil embargo of 1973, and closed with the economic recoveries of 1982 and onward.

[11] The virtual collapse of Brazil's arms industry in the wake of the arms embargo on Iraq beginning in 1990 high-lights the problem of single-recipient dependence of many smaller suppliers. About 90% of Brazil's arms production was exported, most of it to Iraq (Catrina 1988, 258).

[12] Interestingly, this observation directly clashes with the theories of American hegemonic decline and its relationship to arms diffusion outlined in the global power concentration hypotheses of Model 1.

[13] The classic in this research tradition is Allison (1971). For an excellent recent example, see Tirman (1997).

[14] A possible confounding influence on this thesis is the purported propensity of democracies to substitute firepower for manpower in conflict situations. Democracies require popular consent to wage their military campaigns, and are thus highly sensitive to casualties among their own forces. Because many of the world's democracies are highly-industrialized, prosperous states, they have the ability to obviate the need for suffering high casualties by employing expensive, high-technology weapons systems in combat. I merely state this here as a possible alternate linkage between democracy and arms diffusion, and reserve final judgement on the validity of these arguments for the data analysis chapter of this project.

[15] Domestic adoption of a new weapons system is often a prerequisite for that system achieving success in foreign markets. Small foreign users often cannot absorb the risk of working the "bugs" out of new technologies. As a result, these users demand producer adoption as a sign of confidence in the design and as an assurance that production lines for spare parts and upgrades will remain available over the expected service life of the system (Zarzecki 1999a).

[16] I leave the operational definition of "categories" and "generations" of arms technology for the methodology section of this proposal.

[17] "Generation," "weapons category," and related terms will be defined and explored in Chapter 4. For breakdowns of specific generations and weapons categories and the individual weapons systems they contain, refer to the data appendices.

Chapter 4
Arms Diffusion and the Nature of Military Innovation

THERE ARE TWO PREREQUISITES CRITICAL TO EMPIRICAL RESEARCH ON THE diffusion of innovations. The first is a clear understanding of the concept of an "innovation." The second is a meaningful scheme for classifying innovations and tracking their spread throughout the diffusion medium. In this chapter, I address the first of these issues by defining exactly what I mean by military technological innovation (MTI). I address the second by generating a scheme for categorizing individual MTIs that is both theoretically and logically sound and can be employed operationally to conduct empirical research. Once these definitional issues have been settled, I use this scheme to operationalize dependent variables that capture some measure of the spread of military technological innovation throughout the international system. Finally, I explain how theoretical, empirical, and data constraints define the time frame and adopter population of this study and how specific MTIs were selected for analysis. This chapter thus draws a clear conceptual picture of arms diffusion and the angle from which I will examine it, as well as laying the definitional and operational basis for the two data analysis chapters that follow.

WHAT IS A MILITARY TECHNOLOGICAL INNOVATION?

In previous chapters, I discussed the importance of investigating the subject of the spread of arms in a systematic fashion. Critical to this task is crafting an unambiguous definition of military technological innovations that clearly identifies the objects whose spread we are investigating. The purpose of this section is to provide such an explicit definition. This is necessary not only for conceptual clarity, but also for facilitating operationalization of

73

our key dependent variable (i.e. the spread of new weapons technologies) with as much precision as possible.

Borrowing terminology from Tornatzky and Fleischer (1990, 11), I define a *military technological innovation (or MTI) as the situationally new development and deployment of any knowledge-derived tool, artifact, or device used by the military forces of a state in the conduct of or preparation for armed conflict.* Four components of this definition require further explanation. First, why are states the only adopters of military hardware included in the definition? Second, how does the definition interpret the relationship between the development of new military technologies and their "situationally new" deployment as a part of operational weapons systems by state military forces? Third, what do we mean by a "technological?" Finally, what is meant by a "military," as opposed to a non-military, innovation? The details of each of these elements of the definition require elaboration before we proceed further.

States as Actors. The definition of a military technological innovation considers only states as possible adopters of MTIs. It does not include the military hardware adopted by guerilla movements, paramilitary forces, terrorist groups, organized crime syndicates, and other sub-state actors. There are two reasons for this omission. First, the level of military technology operated by most of these groups for most of the post-war period has been relatively primitive, consisting mostly of small arms, mines, and various forms of explosives. This does not mean that these actors are insignificant to the study of security affairs or even of the arms trade. It does reflect the fact, however, that the threats they pose do not primarily hinge on the sophistication of the military technology they employ. Any study of military technology diffusion can thus safely leave such groups for others to investigate. Second, during the post-World War II period, states have been identifiable by certain common features (i.e. a territory, a population, and a government) that allow us to compare them with some degree of validity. Sub-state groups lack functional similarity, and are tremendously varied according to their structure, objectives, resources, and other features. This makes it extremely difficult to incorporate such actors into a systematic analysis of the type undertaken by this study. Can we meaningfully compare arms acquisitions by the PLO with those of the Cali drug cartel or the Baader-Meinhof Gang in a systemic fashion? Can their MTI adoption behavior be usefully compared to that of Israel, Colombia, or West Germany? Since their level of technological innovation is extremely limited anyway, it is best to omit such groups from consideration.

Innovation, not Invention. As described above, an innovation is defined as a device which is "situationally new," or *new to the entity which is adopting it.* This simply means that a state is said to "innovate" when it accepts for use a piece of military technology which it itself has never before adopted. This is true regardless of if or when the innovation was adopted by any other states. Using an example from the data for this study, consider the Soviet Union, which first deployed the MiG-21 fighter, its first third generation combat aircraft design, in 1960. In contrast, the African nation of Burkina Faso adopted the same aircraft type for service in 1988. Even though the MiG-21 was a 38-year old design *to the Soviet Union* by the time it was adopted by Burkina Faso, it is still considered an innovation for Burkina Faso, because that country had never before adopted that particular piece of military hardware. For the purposes of arms diffusion research, innovation is defined not in global terms, but in terms of the specific country or "situation" in which the technology is found.

This element of the definition of an MTI links together the concepts of innovation and adoption, demanding some common standard for the latter which is meaningful across all cases. In short, operationally speaking, we need to develop a clear definition of what exactly it means to "adopt" an innovation.

Here, the distinction between innovation and invention is critical. *Invention* is defined as the initial discovery or development of new basic scientific or technological principles (Rosenberg 1976, 67). Given the uneven global distribution of military industrial production capabilities, the invention phase of new product development is not necessarily shared by all eventual adopters of the product (Krause 1992). Further, particularly in the case of military technology, the path from initial conceptualization, to invention or test or prototype examples, to eventual use by military forces is far from straightforward. Most designs never make it off the drawing board. Only a portion of those that do ever see active service. It is thus best to consider the adoption of an MTI as taking place *at the time which it enters operational service with the armed forces of the adopting state* rather than at invention or some other point in time.

This makes sense for a number of reasons. Entry into operational service is clearly an event shared by all adopters of an MTI, whether or not they produce arms. The use of a deployment decision as the criterion for adoption also provides a clear conceptual break between true adopters and those who merely explore a technology's possibilities without integrating it into their force planning or military structure. While research and development programs can be costly, they pale in comparison to the financial, personnel, and training resources consumed by placing a weapons system into active service. Lastly, undeployed weapons are militarily useless weapons. Since, as discussed in the following section, military planners usually assess opponents on the basis of inherent capabilities, weapons which have yet to leave the proving grounds or the warehouse are seen as having little military value. They do not gain such value until they are placed in service and integrated into operational planning.

Military Uses. The definition of military technological innovation concerns itself solely with MTIs "used by military forces in the conduct of or preparation for armed conflict." For the purposes of this study, I consider this not to include civilian or dual-use (joint military/civilian) technologies that have not yet seen a military application. In the modern technological environment, the links between military and civilian or commercial categories of technological innovation are undoubtedly strong and growing (Anthony, 1997: 37–8). However, it is conceptually useful to maintain a distinction between deployed weapons systems and the component technologies they may share with non-military products. This project is interested in examining the spread of military technological *capabilities* as embodied in operational military hardware. In contrast, the spread of dual-use and component technologies represents a diffusion of military *potential* which may or may not eventually be converted into militarily-usable equipment.[1] While also important, the diffusion of dual-use technologies is beyond the scope of the present study.

Technology as Hardware. Finally, I limit the definition of technology to the "real, usually tangible tools by which we transform parts of our environment" (Tornatzky and Fleischer 1990, 11). The project centers attention upon military armaments, the visible, measurable tools of conflict that occupy so much of the attention of military establishments, arms controllers, and scholars alike. Some researchers have defined "technology" to include new, more efficient processes for accomplishing tasks. By way of example, Spence (1994, 26) notes that "an innovation might not be a material product, but a fundamental change of practice which is new because it puts an entirely different emphasis on well-established procedures." Fresh knowledge that allows existing devices to be used in new ways undoubtedly represents innovation in the broadest sense of the word (Rogers and Shoemaker 1971, 21). Under Spence's definition, for example, the German practice of using tanks in independent striking formations during World War II as opposed to mere infantry support vehicles can be considered as much a technological innovation as the adoption of the tank in the first place. But while obviously significant, this *doctrinal innovation* is not considered 'technology' within the bounds of this project, and is not the focus of the study's attention.

There are a number of reasons for excluding doctrinal innovation and instead focusing on military hardware. First, militaries themselves tend to plan around worst-case scenarios. They focus on the raw capabilities of an opponent rather than on more intangible assessments of that opponent's plans, intentions, or strategies. As a result, more attention is usually paid to weapons inventories and technological potential than to the specifics of stated policy or doctrine, which may or may not reflect the actual capabilities of the enemy's forces.[2] Second, most significant doctrinal changes must also be accompanied by concrete technological changes. New technologies are sometimes developed to better meet the needs of the changed operational requirements.[3] Concentrating on the spread of the technologies themselves can thus, to an extent, substitute for examining the spread of doctrines. Finally, doctrines may also be more difficult to identify and equate across a large number of cases. From a practical research standpoint, identifying and classifying hardware is a relatively straightforward process compared to evaluating written doctrine and/or training procedures. In the vast majority of cases, the latter information is either held secret by security-conscious military establishments, unavailable, too general to provide a useful measure of anything, or of questionable significance. Analyses of changing military doctrines are usually conducted using focused case studies and tend to center only on the doctrines of the major military powers (Posen 1984, Murray and Millet 1996). These studies provide in-depth information on the subjects that they choose to cover. However, they provide little insight into the defense planning of smaller powers, which may or may not be comparable in scope and detail.

DEVELOPING A SCHEME FOR CLASSIFYING MTIs

With an unambiguous definition of an MTI in hand, we must next develop some scheme for classifying MTIs that is logically sound, theoretically clear, and operationally useful. This step, however, is far more complex than simply defining an MTI. If we examine the spread of MTIs across the international system in the Twentieth Century, we immediately recognize, as Dunnigan (1996, 3) writes, that "never before in history has there been a period where there were so many new weapons in such a short period of time." The pages of defense trade magazines are brimming with advertisements and articles displaying the dozens of new weapons systems that vie each year for military dollars in the global arms marketplace. Military planners interested in adding a new fighter or tank to their arsenals have multiple options from which to choose, each offering a slightly different combination of sub-systems and capabilities. And this is just for current systems. If one were to add up all of the weapons developed and deployed in just the last fifty years alone, it is easy to agree with Van Crevald (1989, 217) that nations

> . . . from the earliest times have applied their genius to the design and production of better weapons, so that military technology has rarely stood still for very long but has been in a state of almost continuous turbulence with currents, tides, whirlpools, and eddies almost too numerous to analyze and understand.

Any scheme meant to make sense of the potentially confusing phenomenon of military technological innovation should be *inclusive, complex,* and *relevant.* First, it should allow, at least theoretically, for the inclusion of the broad spectrum of military technologies, ranging from the simplest to the most complex. This will render the conclusions we derive from our analysis applicable to the largest number of MTI diffusion cases possible. Second, the scheme should be complex enough to reflect meaningfully different levels of change in military technology over time, in clear recognition of the fact that military technological innovation is not a monolithic phenomenon. It should be able to track the development of Van Crevald's "currents, tides, whirlpools, and eddies" as they emerge from the undifferentiated stream of innovative activity. Finally, we are concerned with investigating the impact of various political, economic, and technological forces on the spread of arms. The scheme should therefore create categories that we might expect to reflect the influence of these forces. This is not to say that we want to stack the deck by generating categories we know will prove our hypotheses, a task that would be difficult–at best–to undertake *a priori.* It simply means that the scheme should be relevant to and allow for the construction of dependent variables that we might reasonably expect to be linked to the exogenous variables discussed in the previous chapter.[4]

Table 1 presents a simple scheme for understanding and classifying MTIs that meets all of these requirements. The scheme conceives of military technological innovation as a generalized process involving a progression of technological development that can be examined at any one of several *innovation levels of detail* described in Column 3.[5] Any specific MTI can be classified as one of these six *innovation types,* referred to either by the number in Column 1 or the name in Column 2. For purposes of illustration, Column 4 offers examples of the type of difference or change described by a given level of technological innovation. (Thus, the difference between tanks and aircraft is a variation at the weapons meta-categorical level, between the F-4 and F-15 at the generational level, and so on. For more details, see the relevant appendices.) The following paragraphs describe in detail each of these six innovation types, both explaining the nature of innovation at each level and providing real-world examples for illustration.

Meta-categorical (I). Meta-categorical MTIs are those which represent the most dramatic level of technological change. They lead to fundamental alterations in the way in which warfare is conducted and military institutions are organized. At their most dramatic, they create pressures for the generation of entirely new bureaucracies and service branches to administer their development and use. By way of example, the development of fixed-wing aircraft for military purposes completely changed the face of Twentieth Century warfare and spawned the worldwide growth of independent air forces equal in stature to traditional armies and navies. It also forced all military planners to consider the impact which enemy air power will have on their operations, and necessitated the development of counter-systems and plans in virtually every situation. This is the type of "significant" innovation analyzed in Evangelista (1988, 51–2), and is the most commonly analyzed in the scholarly case study literature on military innovation.[6]

Categorical (II). Categorical MTIs result from the usually rapid splitting of most meta-categorical innovations into a series of more specialized MTIs designed to accomplish specific operational tasks. This splitting results from the recognition that not every weapons system can be optimized for every mission. Specialized, often complementary, categories of designs make operational sense when the logic of a new technology's employment is played out. In the case of military aircraft, designers realized that aircraft designed to carry bombs had to be larger, heavier, and slower than those optimized for shooting down other aircraft. Both differed from those built to carry out reconnaissance over enemy territory. Soon, the development of separate fighter/attack, bomber, and reconnaissance aircraft weapons categories had split the larger meta-category into a number of clearly recognizable parts.

Generational/Initial and *Generational/Diversifying (IIIA & IIIB).* As new categories of arms are developed and fielded, initial systems provide a baseline for subsequent weapons, which incorporate clusters of major technological advances. A *technological generation* of weapons is consequently defined as a grouping of individual weapons systems which possesses technical features that represent a roughly comparable overall level of technological sophistication and marks a clear technological advance over the preceding grouping. Depending upon the overall complexity of the weapons system, generational advance can come about as the result of one fundamental technological change or multiple smaller changes. In this fashion, post-World War II fighter/attack aircraft have passed through four technological generations of development. These are represented by (1) swept-wing subsonics of the early 1950s; (2) the high-altitude supersonics of the late 1950s; (3) the missile-equipped swing-wing or multi-role bisonics of the 1960s and early 1970s; and (4) the complex, highly-computerized, highly maneuverable multi-role fighters of the 1970s and 1980s.

There are two types of generational innovations, *initial* (IIIA) and *diversifying* (IIIB).[7] Initial innovations are those which represent the first ever adoption of a given generation of technology generation by a state adopter. Diversifying innovations are those which add a particular weapons system not currently in the force structure but which represent the same generational level of technology. By way of example, the U.S.' replacement of its naval F-4 Phantom by the F-14 Tomcat fighter in 1972 was an initial generation-level innovation. Its deployment two years later of the Air Force's F-15, also a fourth generation fighter, was a diversifying one.

Incremental (IV). Incremental innovation, more often referred to as upgrading or modernization, takes place in smaller steps or stages than generational advance. It represents the alteration or improvement of existing weapons without their replacement by significantly more advanced platforms. In comparison to generational advance, incremental innovation takes on the role of "tinkering" rather than making fundamental improvements in overall technological sophistication and performance. One reality that allows us to make the distinction between generational and incremental innovation is that a twofold law of diminishing returns is in effect regarding weapons upgrades. First, each weapon system has a practical limit beyond which it is more cost effective to purchase next generation systems than to upgrade older ones. Second, most upgraded systems will lack one or more key components of the next generation's technological make-up.[8]

Incremental innovation takes place at the level of a weapon's components parts, also called sub-systems. Many modern weapons are very complex devices composed of numerous sub-systems, each with a specialized purpose in the overall system's functioning.[9] Being modular in nature, these sub-systems can often be: (1) replaced with newer sub-systems that improve performance; (2) interchanged with other sub-systems to optimize a weapons system for a particular mission or role; (3) altered to expand one set of operational parameters in exchange for limiting another set. In the latter two cases, simple design alterations at the component level may not necessarily be innovations in the sense of developing fundamentally new technologies. In practice, the process of upgrading usually involves elements of all three of these categories, as shown by our continuing example of the F-15. The basic F-15A was optimized for the air-to-air combat role, while the F-15E upgrade developed the original aircraft's ground attack capabilities. To this end, the F-15E gained larger fuel tanks and extra ordnance pylons not possessed by the F-15A, as well as a new digitized flight control system and APG-70 ground mapping attack radar. The additional tanks and pylons involved no new technologies, while the avionics did represent fundamental advances over the F-15A's APG-63 radar and analog flight control system. Neither of these, however, make the F-15E qualify as a generational advance over the F-15A from which it was derived (Donald 1995, 44), since the basic aircraft are similar in most other respects.

Continuous Innovation (V). Continuous innovation is a category of technological advance in which innovation lacks the discrete quality which allows easy measurement, although change can undoubtedly be seen to be happening over longer periods of time. The principal example of this is computer software code, which can theoretically be altered line-by-line to improve the performance of weapons platforms. With improvements of this nature, a clear distinction between one level of innovation and the next is usually indiscernible. In the case of aircraft radars, programmable microprocessors make it possible to add operating modes or alter electronic threat-identification libraries on a regular basis. Over time these improvements yield detectable differences in the aircraft's performance. But individual innovations are potentially so small, and data on them so hard to obtain, that for all intents and purposes, change can be construed as a potentially continuous process.

ARMS DIFFUSION AND TECHNOLOGICAL GENERATIONS

Since our primary interest is examining the diffusion of military innovations, we must now turn to investigating how best to use this classificatory scheme toward that end. Our first task is to determine at which of the six levels at which military technological innovation takes place it is best to conduct our analysis. As explained below, this project focuses on the generational level of detail for a number of theoretical and practical reasons.

Theoretical Reasons. The first major theoretical reason to investigate the spread of MTIs at the generational level of detail is that a number of significant studies have already been conducted about categorical and meta-categorical level changes, mostly among the small core of initial innovators that are also major military powers (Murray and Millet 1996, Hartcup 1993, Rosen 1991, Evangelista 1988, Kolodziej 1987, Smith 1985, Armacost 1969). These studies have analyzed at least the initial phases of the MTI diffusion process by examining how the military establishments of the major powers reacted to the development of new technologies that threatened to revolutionize the conduct of war. On the other hand, they tell us little about the diffusion process which occurs after the handful of first tier arms producers (Krause 1992) acquire an MTI, a process usually occurring through indigenous development. It remains to be shown that the motivating forces addressed in these case studies have an impact on the larger process of global diffusion beyond the first few adopters. Significantly, the process of arms diffusion among these smaller states in the second tier and below is the place where much of the arms proliferation that currently attracts the attention of policy specialists and military planners is taking place.

A second theoretical reason involves the position of generations in the hierarchical scale of innovation. Generational changes fall in between the broad changes of the higher levels of detail, which are infrequent in the real world, and the lower levels, which are less relevant. Given the number and scope of incremental changes states regularly make in their weaponry, it is far from clear that analysis of any single set of innovations across an identifiable category could reveal a marked impact on the technological balance between a state and its potential opponents. On the other hand, the impact of categorical level changes can itself be captured at the generational level by conceptualizing categorical/meta-categorical innovation as simply the diffusion of the first generation of a given technology. Limiting analysis by tracking only categorical level change (i.e. the spread of only first generation weapons) provides only an incomplete picture of MTI diffusion, that need not be so restricted.[10]

A third and final theoretical justification for examining arms diffusion at the generational level is simply that generational change and generational differences matter. A state possessing weapons systems one or more generations older than those of an opponent places itself at a severe disadvantage on the battlefield. This is not to say that victory in warfare is ensured by technological superiority alone. But those militaries which lack sufficiently modern generations of weapons must overcome a major rather than minor problem in their plans and decision making. The fact that the bulk of Iraq's arms were one-to-two generations behind those of the bulk of the U.S.-led coalition's arms, for example, had a decided impact on the lopsided outcome of the 1991 Persian Gulf conflict. This was true even though other factors also played important roles in Iraq's defeat.[11]

Practical Reasons. Two practical reasons for examining arms diffusion at the generational level are even more compelling. Most important is the fact that military decision makers and planners often conceive of military technologies, particularly in comparative perspective, in generational terms. The term "generation" used almost ubiquitously in the defense trade press and in military analyses dealing with force structures, military balances, and technological comparisons. The word is often too loosely employed and needs to be formally defined and operationalized for a study of this nature. However, the assumption that weapons systems can be clustered together into groups of technologically similar systems and compared is part of the common parlance of the field (Leitner 1995, 63; Epstein 1984, 44). This stems partially from the fact that weapons systems are meant to face each other in the competitive environment of the battlefield, and it is thus natural to attempt to compare and contrast their major technical features (described at the generational level of detail) to identify similarities and differences. It also derives from the reality that common operational problems often result in common technical solutions, resulting in the parallel evolution of the technological features of even those weapons designed by different firms and states.[12]

A second reason deals with the reliability and availability of data on military innovations. Data on incremental and continuous technological innovation below the generational level is almost impossible to classify and gather. In terms of classification, moving our analysis to the incremental and continuous levels of detail would obviate the advantage of relying upon published expert opinion to determine which weapons systems are important to include in our data base, the equivalency of various weapons systems, and thus their grouping into generational categories. (These issues are discussed in greater detail in the following section). While it is clear that, for example, tanks, aircraft, and missiles are vital components of modern conventional military power, it is unclear—or at least highly debatable—which specific components of these systems represent the most important elements of their overall capability.[13] Through experience, experts possess the ability to assess the relative value of the various sub-system and/or component parts of a given weapons system, and also to render judgements as to the quality of the system as a whole relative to other systems in the same weapons category. If we were to undertake analysis beneath the generational level, we would either be required to locate expert opinions on the relative quality of a tremendous quantity of sub-systems, or make such assessments ourselves. Unfortunately, the far more complex and often secret nature of such technologies means that such comparisons do not abound in the existing literature. In the absence of expert opinion, it is difficult to imagine that an independent effort for this study could arrive at data that was valid and useful.

In terms of data-gathering, even if important and distinct categories of sub-system/incremental MTIs could be established, obtaining data on adopters and adoption dates for these MTIs would be fraught with problems. Reliable data on when various models and sub-variants of weapons systems were adopted by various states is simply not available for most countries of the world. Even if it was, incremental change in weapons systems is not always reflected in clear-cut designation changes, particularly those found in the standard reference works on military inventories and the arms trade.[14] Local modifications and other small changes are much more prevalent at the incremental level or lower than at the generational level or higher. They may even go undocumented, either for security reasons or through simple neglect. If gathering reliable data at the generational level is difficult, gathering it at finer levels of detail is all but impossible.

While these are all strong reasons for examining arms diffusion at the generational level, the use of the term "generation" must be clarified. Earlier, I defined a generation as *a grouping of individual weapons systems which possess technical features that represent a roughly comparable overall level of technological sophistication.* I further pointed out that the term is widely, if sometimes loosely, used in professional military and security literature to identify similar weapons systems. This section will outline the definitional boundaries and complexities of the generational concept and methods for the construction of generational categories and the operational decision rules for coding data.

Issues Related to the Generational Concept. Before operational research can begin, a number of qualifications and caveats to the above definition of a generation that must be understood. First, MTI generations are defined as groupings of weapons systems which possess technical features that represent a roughly comparable overall level of technological sophistication. *This, however, does not mean that every system in a given generation must have every technical sub-system in common with every other system in that generation.* Most major modern weapons systems are very complex, and thus it is unreasonable to expect that any group of contemporaneous systems, particularly those produced by different manufacturers and in different countries, will have identical technical components and sub-systems. (By "identical," I mean of identical function, and not necessarily produced by identical manufacturers.) Generations are conceptualized here as *rough* rather than *exact* equivalents, and *similar* rather than *identical* in overall level of sophistication. By way of example, the Soviet fourth generation MiG-29 fighter aircraft is equipped with an infra-red search-and-track (IRST) sensor which U.S. fourth generation aircraft lack. In contrast, U.S. jets feature radars better than those of the MiG-29, and which are capable of engaging multiple targets at longer ranges. Similarly, the main guns of U.S. third generation main battle tanks (MBTs) lack the missile-firing capability possessed by their Soviet third generation equivalents. In both of these cases, however, the weapons systems in question have an overall level of capability which is roughly equivalent. This equivalence stems either from common features not mentioned in the above comparisons or to offsetting technical features which make up for other deficiencies or differences. Thus, the MiG-29's IRST makes it an equivalent or superior fighter to the U.S. F-15 in the short-range arena, while better radars make the U.S. jets superior at medium ranges. Similarly, U.S. tanks make up for their lack of Soviet-style guided missiles with more accurate fire control systems. Normal U.S. armor-piercing shells are thus more likely to hit their targets on the first shot. Soviet tank designs lack the Western emphasis on exotic armor, necessary to defend against larger Soviet guns and missiles. On the other hand, Soviet tanks are smaller are thus make less likely targets (see the relevant data appendices for details in both cases).

Second, and perhaps even more importantly, *different weapons systems may be optimized for different roles, even within an arms category and generation. However, they may also carry out secondary missions for which they are equipped but not specialized.* In looking again at combat aircraft (Appendix B), we can see that about ten modern aircraft can arguably considered "fourth generation." These ten systems share many common technological features and are of roughly the same level of sophistication. However, within this group of systems, at least three clusters of what I shall term *most similar systems* are apparent: multi-role fighters (those equally capable of carrying out air-to-air fighter and ground attack missions), interceptors (optimized for high-altitude, high-speed interception of enemy bombers), and strike planes (optimized for long-range low-level bombing missions). Further confusing matters, there is a lot of cross-over between these categories, depending on the specific variant of each specific system in question. The European Tornado and the U.S. F-15, for example, come in both interceptor and strike variants, both of which have radars and other avionics systems optimized for the primary mission but share most other features in common. The F-14, which has served primarily as an interceptor since its initial adoption by the U.S. in 1972, has only since the mid-1990s added a ground attack capability. This was done by adding to the F-14 items of equipment that could have been procured a decade before, had funding for such a project been secured.

Third, *the technical features of generational categories are not static, and incremental change takes place intra-generationally.* Many states frequently improve their weapons systems after initial service introduction by adding or upgrading sub-systems and component parts. This change can take place both *vertically* through a process of modernization (the addition of "new" sub-systems that did not exist before) and *horizontally* through the process of modification (the incorporation into a given system of already-existing components or the making of operational performance-altering trade-offs). The retrofitting of Global Positioning System (GPS) navigation systems to Russia's existing MiG-29 Fulcrums is an example of modernization, since that particular sub-system did not exist at the time of the Fulcrum's initial introduction. The adding of larger external fuel tanks to increase the MiG-29's range is an example of modification, as fuel tanks of all sizes existed in the Russian inventory prior to their mating with the MiG's airframe. It was only after the operational introduction of the Fulcrum that the aircraft's inherent range limitations became apparent, demanding a quick remedy from off-the-shelf (existing) technology. For the reasons stated above in Section II, these types of innovations rarely amount to generational- level change. When they do, the effect on the data (as will be demonstrated later) is usually minimal.[15] For our purposes, we assume an unchanging (at the generational level) innovation over the entire course of the diffusion process, although it is understood that incremental change may in reality take place.[16]

Last, *MTI generations are determined by technological features rather than calender time.* A generation of people is understood to be a grouping of individuals who were born in a given time frame and thus share some set of sociological characteristics rooted in their experience of a common context in whatever sphere is under examination (cultural, economic, political, etc.). For example, persons born in the 1945–50 period are often termed the "baby boomer generation." Such a generation's boundaries are marked by the period of the human lifespan and the normal physical stages of human development. In contrast, a technological generation is defined by the technical features of the MTI in question, and its member systems need not have been developed within a specific time frame to qualify for membership. In practice, most of the major arms-producing states need to deploy comparable weapons at about the same time in order to remain militarily competitive, and thus their production of chronologically new weapons systems that actually belong to generations prior to the current one is rare. However, in the case of smaller second-tier producers, MTIs may be developed and deployed which lag considered behind those of the major powers. In my framework, these MTIs are classified generationally by the level of technological sophistication they represent rather than by the year of their initial deployment. An example of this is the Chinese J-8 fighter aircraft. The J-8 it entered service in the early 1980s, over twenty years after the first Generation 3 combat aircraft and almost a decade after the first Generation 4 designs appeared. However, the J-8 is clearly a Generation 3 system by virtue of its technical characteristics, and is categorized as such in our data set.

Decision Rules for Identifying Generational Groupings. Now that the definition and boundaries of the term "generation" have been clarified, we can shift to the task of determining decision rules for identifying meaningful generational groupings. The question we must ask is this: operationally, how are systems in one generation to be distinguished from those in another?

Because the generational concept, though very common in the professional literature, is rarely formally defined, an inductive approach to divining generational breakdowns within various weapons categories is in most cases essential. Here, I use a four-step process to determine the number and content of MTI generations in any given arms category.

Step 1: Consult the defense, arms trade, and military-technical professional literatures to identify specific generational breakdowns or clearly-labeled, generationally-equivalent systems. Professional sources occasionally come right out an identify the successive generations of a given category of arms cross-nationally (Cordesman 1983, 70; Sapfir 1991, 199). More frequently, two or more systems from different manufacturers or different countries are compared, with terms like "almost identical," "similar," "equivalent," "comparable," and "derived from," being used in the comparison. By weighing these judgements and establishing the preponderance of professional opinion, one can begin to see the outlines of generational development across a number of individual weapons systems.

This is particularly true for the most widely discussed (i.e. usually the most important and widely-diffused) systems in a given arms category.

Step 2: Examine generational MTI replacement patterns within individual states and then structure cross-national categories. Establishing the successive generations of a given category of arms for a single country can be relatively easy: simply identify the earliest innovation in the arms category of interest for each major arms producer, and track its successive replacements over time. Generational breakdowns from single-nation analyses (Sweetman 1982) can then be cross-referenced with those from different nations to come up with coherent cross-national generations.

Step 3: Analyze technical features and search for commonalities. The most direct method of determining generational succession is to simply define a set of concrete technological criteria for each generation and search the military technical literature for systems which fit those criteria. Contemporary articles concerning new weapons systems, comparative analyses of systems in a given arms category, strategic assessments, and handbooks and manuals which describe the technological specifications of weapons all feature varying degrees of detail and are readily available.

Step4: Use the transitive method for comparing individual systems. As the number of individual systems in a generation increases, the number of individual comparisons of pairs of systems one would need to locate in the literature increases exponentially. With 4 systems (A, B, C, and D), one would only need 6 references (A = B, A = C, A = D, B = C, B = D, and C = D). With 6 systems, the number jumps to 15 references, with 8 systems 28 references, and so on. This situation rapidly becomes unmanageable, particularly when one realizes that, for less widely-dispersed or less significant systems, few if any direct comparisons are ever made. A solution to this problem is to apply the transitive property to individual weapons system comparisons, e.g., if an F-16 is cited as equivalent to a MiG-29 in one source, and a Mirage 2000 and an F-16 are equated in another, we must assume that the MiG-29 and Mirage 2000 are also equivalents. The latter is assumed even if no direct published reference to the latter effect can be found.

CRITICISMS OF THE GENERATIONAL APPROACH

Combining these methods, one can arrive at generational groupings which provide multiple, overlapping justifications for placing individual systems in a given generation that. Furthermore, these justifications do not rest on evidence from any single source. The combination of professional opinion, technical and operational substantiation, and logical deduction will produce enough evidence to create meaningful categories that unarguably cover the vast majority of adoption cases for a given innovation. But there are a number of potential problems and criticisms which might be leveled at this approach which are addressed in the following paragraphs. These involve (1) the cross-national comparability of different weapons systems, (2) the conceptual fit of individual systems to the broad generational categories, and (3) the reliance upon non-quantitative measures of technological equivalence. Descriptions of and counter arguments for these criticisms are discussed in the paragraphs that follow.

Cross-National Comparability of Weapons Systems. The vast majority of weapons systems in the world have been produced by either the U.S. and its NATO allies (particularly Britain and France) or the Soviet Union. While other nations may produce their own weapons, the bulk of the designs are either copied or derived from one of these two sources. Some analysts attempting to weigh the relative merits of East Bloc and West Bloc arms have claimed that the design philosophies of each producer are so different that any attempt at comparison is useless. In particularly, it has been asserted that Western militaries pursue a generational approach to weapons development while Eastern militaries have approached arms innovation as an incremental process. As Leitner (1995, 63) writes:

> The United States has long been noted for its generational improvements in major weapons systems. While minor upgrades to U.S. systems occur routinely, significant upgrades are usually embodied in follow-on generations of replacement weapons systems. U.S. weapons systems evolution has long been motivated by the evolving threat posed by the slower, but relentless, pace of military technology development in the former East Bloc. In contrast with the United States, the Soviets were the masters of incremental change, preferring to make a myriad of small improvements to an existing weapons system through rapid retrofits or modifications during the manufacturing cycle.

Slomovic (1987, 23) also discusses at length what she sees as the "evolutionary weapons development process" embodied by key Soviet weapons programs, using the MiG-21 fighter plane as a case study. Sherwin and Laurance (1979, 365–6) similarly claim that:

> . . . with Soviet weapons...proven solutions to recurring design problems are incorporated in subsequent weapons models, but . . . with U.S. weapons . . . the tendency is to build entirely new weapons systems, resulting in technical improvements and cost increases which rise in a step-wise fashion.

If these assessments are correct, the validity of comparing U.S. technological "generations" with Soviet ones is questionable at best. These arguments, however, contain a flawed view of the differences between the arms development processes of each bloc of producers. This flawed view stems from differences in designation systems and weapons system deployment patterns between Eastern and Western militaries. Regarding the first of these, Epstein (1984, 43–55) decisively points out that it is greatly differing Soviet and U.S. designation systems that create the impression of Soviet incrementalism rather than any inherently different approach to creating new weapons:

> . . . the extent to which a series of weapon systems, combat aircraft, for example, exhibits commonality or design inheritance depends upon naming. If the U.S. renamed the F-4B after every block number, or even airframe change, the resulting sequence of systems would exhibit remarkable commonality indeed . . . we would have exactly the same arsenal, but it would appear to exhibit far greater incrementalism in design.17

The manner in which designation systems variously describe innovations incorporated into an existing design is more fully developed in Appendix A.

A difference in deployment patterns has also led to a perception of Soviet incrementalism and Western generational advance. Soviet-era operational philosophy stressed the importance of mass and the quantity of arms on the battlefield, while Western deployment patterns focused on attaining qualitative superiority (Baxter 1986). As a result, Soviet forces were typically more reluctant to retire aging weapons systems than Western armies. The Soviets instead used these weapons to equip additional, non-frontline or reserve units and increase the total number of deployed systems on inventory.18 Modest modernization of this obsolete equipment was often undertaken to make it less vulnerable in a rapidly increasing threat environment, and this was often mistaken for an incrementalist approach to weapons innovation. In fact, the Soviets simultaneously pursued active development programs for new technologies, and fielded generation-level weapons advances, albeit at a somewhat slower rate than the U.S. But the confusion created by their accumulation of obsolete systems, frequently combined with a lack of open information about new weapons developments, fostered an incorrect incrementalist view.

The Conceptual Fit of Generational Categories. The differences between Soviet and Western design approaches are not a major impediment to developing cross-national generational categories, as can be fully seen in the manner in which the categorizations are developed in the data appendices. As the data appendices also show, a handful of systems (from both Soviet and Western suppliers) create conceptual problems due to their specialized nature. In operational terms, however, these problem cases have little impact on the study of arms diffusion because (1) they are almost always created by the major powers and are rarely exported; (2) if exported, they usually have only a few adopters due to their specialized nature;

and (3) they even less frequently represent the initial adoption decision for the generation in which they might be nominally placed. An excellent example here is the U.S.-built A-6 Intruder light bomber, which is not included in the combat aircraft section of the data. Some might label it a heavy attack aircraft and equate it with the U.S. F-111, which has even greater payload/range figures and some similar systems. But even if this was done, it would have absolutely no impact on arms diffusion data, since this nominally third generation aircraft was never exported and was preceded into U.S. service by the F-4 Phantom.

Reliance on Non-Quantitative Measures of Equivalence. A final potential criticism regarding the validity of the generational concept is its lack of a quantitative basis. The four step classification process outline above relies upon non-quantitative published assessments by defense experts and technical descriptions of operating characteristics for categorizing weapons systems into generational groupings. But should not a better, more precise, perhaps quantitative method for arriving at these groupings be used, one that could bring a higher degree of certainty to the accuracy of the classifications?

I answer this criticism by addressing separately its theoretical and practical implications. Sherwin and Laurance (1979) have discussed the possibility of rigorously quantifying the technological "value" of arms relative to one another for the purposes of arms trade research. After rejecting the validity of a number of existing approaches (in particular, factor analysis and multiplicative measures), they settled upon the use of the multiattribute utility technique (MAU) as a useful method for "[gauging] the military capability associated with conventional weapons (1979, 376). According to the authors, MAU:

> . . . capitalizes on the notion that, to date, human insight remains the most reliable means for synthesizing the interrelations among a complex set of international relations variables, and that one means of indexing an otherwise intangible concept is to tap the collective judgements of human experts. According to this notions, humans, by developing an intuitive expertise, determine what factors are salient; they interpret relevant information; and, by making weighted judgements, they differentially integrate several types of information to form subjective evaluations regarding key concepts (1979: 377).

The authors thus use human experts on a given category of weapons technology to rank the relative combat potential of systems within that category. They then derive quantitative measures of military capability from these rankings. Sherwin and Laurance argue that such scores, by relying upon the human qualities described above for their generation, bypass limitations imposed by strict numerical measures of various technical and/or performance features of weapons systems. Although eventually arriving at numerical measures for combat capability (at hence, in some sense, for technological sophistication), the authors make a sound theoretical case for the value of professional judgements in assessing such matters.

To the extent that the classifications in this study mirror the theoretical underpinnings and sources of authority used by Sherwin and Laurance, they are defensible means of establishing generational categories. But from a practical standpoint, conducting their sort of in-depth evaluative analysis for more than a select handful of weapons systems would require a large number of experts familiar with a broad array of technologies. Assembling such a mass of expertise would be impractical in a study of this magnitude. Furthermore, given the wealth of published information on the generational categorization of weapons systems, it is extremely unclear whether or not the additional precision of attaching numbers to the expert judgements that we do have at our disposal would be worth the added costs of collection. Such precision might be required for the technical analysis of the effectiveness of specific weapons systems or an assessment of military balances. But it is unnecessary for the simple categorization of systems into broad generational groupings.

SELECTING INNOVATIONS FOR ANALYSIS

The preceding sections have laid out the definitional and operational basis for this study. They have defined military technological innovation, provided a comprehensive scheme for classifying individual MTIs, explained why analysis should be conducted at the generational level of innovation, and dealt with some criticisms of the generational concept. The purpose of the rest of this chapter is to operationalize the dependent variable "arms diffusion" by determining upon which specific MTIs we should gather diffusion data, from what sources, and over which time frame.

Selecting Significant MTIs. The first task must be to specify which military technological innovations (MTIs) merit our attention. Logic dictates that we impose two criteria on the selection of cases for analysis. First, the MTIs must represent important elements of military power during the time from of the study. Second, reliable and reasonably complete data must be available for the MTIs selected. The finer points of these criteria and the manner in which they have shaped the data set for this study require further explanation.

Theoretically, we could examine the diffusion of any military innovation, from bullets to ballistas. Obviously, however, we are interested most in those MTIs which have the greatest effect on the global military balance. Ideally, we should restrict our attention to MTIs which have had a major impact on the shape, organization, and power potential of military establishments and their ability to influence battlefield outcomes. The MTIs must also be representative of major trends in the arms production and trade system. Numerous innovations, like aircraft carriers or anti-ballistic missiles, never leave the possession of the two superpowers or are adopted by perhaps a half dozen or so states. Since these systems have clearly not spread widely, methods of investigation other than statistical diffusion analysis, such as focused case studies, should be employed when examining them.

There are a number of possible approaches to the problem of identifying critical MTIs. The most straightforward of these is to simply consider the innovations which both policy makers and non-governmental analysts have found important during the time period of interest.[19] Fortunately, via both treaties and published analyses, these two groups of thinkers have provided us with their consensus views that are both easily available and complementary in their assessments. For this project, I have drawn upon numerous sources of such information. The most important of these are the Conventional Forces in Europe Treaty, the United Nations Register of Conventional Arms, and the SIPRI and IISS arms trade and holdings data bases. I examined each of these sources to see with which major categories of arms they were concerned, and how these categories classified various weapons systems. The categories common to all sources (as explained later in this section) were used as a base list of categories from which to select MTIs for analysis as part of this study.

The Conventional Forces in Europe (CFE) Treaty, agreed to in 1990 by all twenty-three member states of NATO and the Warsaw Pact, is an appropriate starting point for understanding the assessments of the policy making community. The CFE Treaty is the most wide-ranging attempt to limit conventional land forces in the 20th Century. Its extensive appendices list and classify major weapon systems deployed by the signatory nations in five strictly-defined categories: tanks, armored combat vehicles (ACVs), artillery, attack helicopters, and combat aircraft. The treaty then imposes exact national numerical limits for each category. It also encourages signatories to provide detailed information on systems in non-treaty-limited weapons categories, for the purposes of armaments transparency and confidence-building. With CFE, we thus have as part of the public record both an assessment of which MTIs are important enough to limit via treaty and an MTI classification system devised by policy makers from most of the major military powers.

The annual United Nations Register of Conventional Arms (UNRCA) is similarly informative. Founded in 1992, the UNRCA asks all U.N. members to submit comprehensive annual lists of their arms imports and exports. Collected data are then published in the hopes of building international trust through transparency in the arms trade. While there is no sanction for non-submission, which limits UNRCA's usefulness as a confidence-building measure, the classification system used therein provides additional clues to policy maker assessments.

UNRCA covers the five categories used by the CFE and adds two others, warships and missiles and their launchers. Since the UNRCA is not a limitation device and there are no verification procedures, these categories are less well-defined than those of CFE.[20] Nevertheless, both classification systems mesh to a considerable degree, with UNRCA containing all of the CFE categories.[21] We can comfortably say that combining the CFE and UNRCA systems provides us with a solid general idea of the conventional arms considered significant by the security policy making community during the period of this analysis.

Finally, I drew upon two major non-policy making, non-governmental analytical sources for additional information about military technology: annual editions of the Stockholm International Peace Research Institute's (SIPRI) *Yearbook* and the International Institute for Strategic Studies' (IISS) *The Military Balance*. Each SIPRI *Yearbook* contains an arms trade register which exhaustively list all known arms exports and imports for the previous year. Specific systems were identified as belonging to one of a number of categories, including tanks, ACVs, artillery, combat aircraft, warships, helicopters, and various types of missiles. Similarly, annual editions of *The Military Balance* list current country-by-country holdings of armaments in all of these categories, adding data on numbers of military personnel and combat units.

Other periodic sources, while less widely known, such as the *Defense and Foreign Affairs Handbook*, the Jaffe Center's *The Middle East Military Balance*, and editions of Keegan's *World Armies*, also provide lists of military equipment in corresponding categories. We can thus see that policymakers and non-governmental analysts are in broad agreement about the important categories and types of military hardware. As a result (as discussed in greater detail below), the analysis of arms diffusion in this study includes a representative sample of systems in these categories.

Ensuring Data Availability. Drawing cases from the major weapons categories listed above is also desirable because, as indicated, there are a number of available sources which list arms holdings and transfers using these classifications. Diffusion research requires adoption date data for all potential adopters within a given system, which in this case means the states of the international system. SIPRI's *Yearbooks*[22] and IISS' *The Military Balance* are thus invaluable for their annual state-by-state updates of military inventories across the globe. Because they largely cover the same empirical terrain, I also checked IISS and SIPRI against one another for accuracy.[23] I also supplemented their information with other periodic volumes that are released on a less frequent or regular basis, like the aforementioned *Defense and Foreign Affairs Handbook, The Middle East Military Balance,* and *World Armies* series.

Invaluable in working with the SIPRI material are Grenback's (1975) *Arms Trade Registers* and Brzoska and Ohlson's (1987) *Arms Transfers to the Third World, 1971–85.* The SIPRI *Yearbooks* list pending and unconfirmed as well as completed transfers, and succeeding yearbooks will frequently update canceled or misreported entries. This undoubtedly increases data reliability. The frequent information changes make it difficult, however, to track the progress of specific transfers across multiple yearbooks. Grenback and Brzoska and Ohlson compile in their two volumes all SIPRI data on completed transfers to the Third World from 1950 to 1971 and 1971 to 1985 respectively. They thus tremendously reduce the amount of time and effort necessary to generate adoption data from SIPRI sources.

Finally, specialist military technical publications, like the numerous and exhaustive volumes released by the Jane's Publishing Group, also provide adopter data on a weapons system-by-weapons system basis. While not as systematic as the TMB and SIPRI data bases, I was able to use data from Jane's for verification purposes, to double-check TMB and SIPRI accuracy. While using it for acquiring technical comparisons of systems, I also obtained a great deal of fragmentary, non-systematic adoption data from the defense trade and technical press as a whole. This was useful to flesh out TMB, SIPRI, and Jane's data, particularly for more recent events.

Time Frame of the Study. The criteria for the selection of significant MTIs and the need to ensure the existence of reliable data are critical first steps in outlining the dependent variable parameters of this analysis. Next, I focus on the interaction of these and other factors in determining the time frame covered by the study. As a general rule, researchers have an interest in maximizing the number of observations contained in their data sets. A large, robust data set tends to minimize the impact that random or transitory events have on the analysis and gives subsequent conclusions firmer evidential footing. From the time perspective of this analysis, the greater the number of years included in the data set, the better. Counterbalancing this, however, as outlined below, are both theoretical and data availability constraints which set certain limits on the time frame of the study.

As indicated in previous chapters, most approaches to diffusion research share the simplifying assumption that the nature of the diffusion medium (i.e. the number of potential adopters) remains constant throughout the entire period of diffusion. This is particularly important when examining the influence of motivating factors exogenous to the diffusion process itself on the rate or extent of spread. In such cases, we must assume a unchanging underlying structure of opportunity for adoption: *ceteris paribus,* an adopter must have an identical opportunity to adopt a given innovation at time t as at any time subsequent or prior to t. Only by assuming constancy in this underlying structure can we say that variance in the rate or extent of diffusion is due to our independent variables rather than to other changes in the adopter's opportunity to adopt.

Many studies deal with innovation diffusion over short periods of time through large, homogenous populations of individual human beings. In such cases, this constancy assumption is often trivial. Unquestionably, the total population may change by a few percentage points, and individual people are obviously born and die. However, these factors are usually posited to have little impact on the diffusion process relative to other variables and can safely be ignored. When the diffusion medium in question is the international system, however, such assumptions cannot be made, for two very important reasons.

First, the international system is very heterogeneous. States differ dramatically in size, population, wealth, and along other dimensions. Further, these quantities have changed dramatically over time as states have been formed and broken apart, grown powerful and collapsed. Determining which states should be considered "potential" adopters in any given case is thus not a straightforward task. Second, relative to most diffusion populations, the international system is very small, currently comprised of only about 200 states. Further, the quantity of member states in the system has fluctuated dramatically throughout history. This number has been growing since the Nineteenth Century, but has more than doubled since the end of World War II alone. The combination of large fluctuations in a population of small absolute size means that it we can only ensure a constant diffusion medium for relatively short periods of time. As a result of these factors, we cannot automatically assume a more-or-less constant and homogenous diffusion medium, as in other studies. We must either limit the study to a single period in which the diffusion medium was more-or-less constant, or segment the analysis into multiple constant periods and work with each separately.

In a second, more practical vein, data availability also places timeframe constraints on the data set. TMB and SIPRI were first released in 1959 and 1970, respectively. However, the level of detail and quality of inventory information in these early editions, particularly of TMB, were very poor compared to the high standards achieved later. Often, inventories are listed simply as "tanks" or "aircraft," with no indication as to what types are included. Data on smaller systems, like anti-tank missiles, is almost completely absent. Entire states are even omitted from one year to the next. Sometimes, a note informing the reader that the missing state's inventory had not "substantially" changed is all that assures one of the country's continued existence. As a result, information from this period is fragmentary and generally unreliable. A number of different sources must usually be cross-referenced to ensure accuracy.

The previously-mentioned *Arms Trade Registers* (Grenback, 1975) partially remedies this situation. Grenback's work extends back to 1950, long before the publication of the SIPRI *Yearbooks* themselves. It represents the only systematic record of arms diffusion during this early period, when IISS and others were at their most unreliable. On the other hand, it only contains data on arms trade to the Third World and completely neglects the holdings of the industrialized states of NATO and the Warsaw Pact. Data on these latter states are scattered and fragmentary and must be assembled from a variety of defense trade and technical press sources. In some cases, particularly with smaller weapons like anti-tank and anti-aircraft missiles, one is fortunate if one can find complete lists of users, much less specific adoption dates. Adoption data for the U.S. and U.S.S.R. are more available than data on the other NATO and Warsaw Pact states. But pre-1970 data on the Warsaw Pact is particularly difficult to obtain, due to both to the closed nature of those societies and the neglect of East European (as opposed to Soviet) forces by defense analysts in the West.[24] Even post-1970 Warsaw Pact data is far more suspect than similar data on Western MTI inventories, particularly for smaller systems.

THE RESULTANT CASE SELECTION AND TIME FRAME

The MTI diffusion data set collected for this project has been selected to bypass or mitigate most of the difficulties associated with these theoretical and data availability concerns. The data set consists of initial adoption year data on a selection of MTIs for the period 1960 to 1997 across 138 states of the international system. All states with a population of less than 500,000 in 1997 or which lack military establishments are excluded as potential adopters. A state enters the data base if it has existed for half or more of the years in the 1960–97 period.[25] These limits provide for a reasonably constant diffusion medium over a long-enough period of time to examine complete or near complete diffusion curves for multiple generations of a number of important MTIs. It also describes a meaningful potential adopter population base for which reasonably accurate and complete data is available, with some qualifications (as described in the following section).

Special cases are considered in as logical and systematic a manner as possible. Since they were independent entities for better than 50% of the diffusion period, North and South Yemen are counted as separate states, as are East and West Germany and North and South Vietnam. For the purposes of data continuity, post-unification MTI adoptions in these states are credited to the dominant country in the unification, i.e. North Yemen (post-1990), West Germany (post-1989), and North Vietnam (post-1975). Strictly speaking, the upper end of the data set (approximately 1960–1970) does not meet the equal-opportunity-of-adoption condition since a number of states gained their independence later than others during this period. However, most of these states are not likely to have been early adopters of the MTIs considered anyway. For those few states which became independent after 1970 (Angola, Mozambique, and a few others), I simply accept this as a limitation of the data, and include their MTI adoptions from the date of independence onward.

As explained previously, the year in which the MTI in question is made operational with any branch of the armed forces of the given country is considered the year of adoption. In terms of data coding, SIPRI and related publications (Brzoska and Ohlson 1987; Grenback 1975) were the primary sources used to determine adoption data for the developing world states after 1960, and for all states in the 1990s. SIPRI's arms trade registers list the *delivery year* of each major weapons system transfer. I derived the adoption year from this by simply adding a year; for example, a tank delivered to a state in 1977 is coded as adopted (i.e. put into active service) in 1978. This reflects the fact that it takes some time for states to absorb newly-delivered systems into their force structure. If deliveries are listed as taking place over a number of years (i.e. 1986–89), I coded the adoption date as the year after the *first* year of deliveries (in the case, 1987). For developing world states and all states in the 1990s, SIPRI sources were checked against adoption dates derived from annual editions of *The Military Balance*. In the vast majority of these cases, both sources were in agreement.[26] TMB lists active arms *inventories* and is valid for the Fall of the year in which the annual edition is published. As a result, I coded the first annual edition in which a given weapons system appears in TMB for a given state as the adoption year. For example, the first TMB edition in which Burkina Faso is reported as operating the MiG-21 fighter is *The Military Balance 1988–1989*. The adoption year for third generation combat aircraft for Burkina Faso is thus coded as 1988. For most developed nations, TMB is the also primary source of adoption data for MTIs prior to the 1990s. As mentioned previously, a variety of other defense trade and technical press reports were used to check and confirm adoption dates from SIPRI and TMB where possible. In a few instances, an MTI is reliably reported as being used in combat by a state's armed forces in the same year of delivery (according to SIPRI) or before the MTI appears for the first time in TMB. In these rare cases, I code it as having been adopted in the year it sees combat, since the system is obviously in operational use.

A total of fourteen MTIs were selected for analysis. These include innovations in three of the five CFE and four of the seven UNRCA categories, thus representing a majority of categories on both lists. The selections represent key components of land and air warfare in the post World War II period: aircraft, combat helicopters, main battle tanks, and the anti-aircraft and anti-tank missiles developed to counter them. Multiple generations from each arms category are also included, so that both inter-generational and inter-categorical variation can be examined. Summary data about each of these MTIs is listed in Table 4.2.

Naval weapons have been omitted for two reasons. First, naval weapons pose the theoretical problem of not being equally adoptable by all states. Some 24 of the 138 states (17.4%) in the data base lack access to the ocean and thus the opportunity or need to acquire significant naval arms.[27] This complicates our analysis by violating the equal-opportunity-of- adoption stipulation. Second, since naval vessels are very large, they are much easier to modernize at the sub-system level of technology. For our purposes, this poses the problem of identifying which sub-systems are of greater or lesser significance.

It also raises the question of whether sub-system level diffusion is theoretically comparable to categorical/sub-categorical level diffusion. These are important questions, and an analysis of naval arms would provide for very interesting comparisons with land and air systems. Because of the additional difficulties it would create, however, I leave this task for future research.

Two of the fourteen MTIs selected have adoption date ranges which partially fall beyond the parameters of the established time period. In the case of Generation 1 ATGMs, the initial adoption took place in 1956, four years outside the time frame. In the case of Generation 1 Long-Range SAMs, the initial adoption took place seven years too early, in 1953. Complete and reliable adoption data for all adopters of the ATGMs and SAMs is also not available until 1971 and 1963, respectively. Nevertheless, the existing data provides some diffusion information that can be usefully compared with that for the other MTIs in the data set. Further, adoptions in the years for which comprehensive and reliable data was available can be used in some segments of the analysis. As a result, both MTIs have been incorporated into the data set despite their limitations.

This chapter has established the definitional and operational basis for a systematic examination of arms diffusion. It has defined and created a scheme for classifying MTIs and then explained how data was selected and gathered to allow for empirical research on MTI spread. Chapter 5 will begin our analysis of arms diffusion by mapping out the empirical terrain over which we will be traveling, and providing some descriptive analysis of the arms diffusion phenomenon. Testing of the hypotheses derived from the theoretical models discussed in Chapter 3 will take place in Chapter 6.

No.	Innovation Type	Innovation Level	Examples
I	Meta-categorical	weapons meta-category	military aircraft vs. tanks
II	Categorical	weapons category	fighters vs. bombers
IIIA	Generational/initial	weapons system	F-15 Eagle vs. F-4 Phantom
IIIB	Generational/diversifying	weapons system	F-15 Eagle vs. F-14 Tomcat
IV	Incremental	weapons sub-system	APG-70 vs. APG-63 radar
V	Continuous	computer software	single vs. two-target tracking

Table 4.1: Types of Military Technological Innovation (Source: Thomas W. Zarzecki/Military Technological Data Set Version 1.0)

#	Innovation Name	G	IOC	Comp	# Yrs	# Adp
1	Combat Aircraft	3	1960	1992	32	90
2	Combat Aircraft	4	1972	nyc	25	54
3	Attack Helicopter	1	1967	nyc	30	39
4	Attack Helicopter	2	1986	nyc	11	8
5	Main Battle Tank	2	1960	nyc	37	60
6	Main Battle Tank	3	1980	nyc	17	20
7	Long-Range Surface-to-Air Missile	1	1953	1987	34	48
8	Long-Range Surface-to-Air Missile	2	1960	1989	29	55*
9	Long-Range Surface-to-Air Missile	3	1980	nyc	17	11
10	Point-Defense Surface-to-Air Missile	1	1969	nyc	28	54
11	Portable Air Defense System	1	1964	nyc	33	80
12	Portable Air Defense System	2	1977	nyc	20	56
13	Anti-Tank Guided Missile	1	1956	1988	32	70
14	Anti-Tank Guided Missile	2	1967	1997	30	71

G = generation
IOC = initial operational capability (initial innovation)
nyc = diffusion not yet complete
* = more innovations after complete diffusion (see text)
Comp = year diffusion was completed
#Yr = number of years to complete diffusion (Comp-IOC)
Adp = number of adopters at complete diffusion

Table 4.2: Military Technological Innovation Data Set Summary (Source: Thomas W. Zarzecki/Military Technological Innovation Data Set Version 1.0)

NOTES

[1] For an example of the gap between the military development of dual-use technology and its operational deployment by military forces, see Douglas (1985).

[2] The case of Iraq during the 1991 Gulf War is instructive. Throughout the 1980–1988 Iran-Iraq War, Iraq showed a persistent doctrinal unwillingness to sacrifice high-value assets like fighter aircraft in intense combat. True to this form, Iraq's aircraft played little active part in the 1991 fighting against Coalition forces. Despite this, the Coalition heavily targeted Iraqi air bases throughout the war. In fact, the most intense bombing took place after Iraq's air force had demonstrated its overwhelming desire to avoid combat. The underlying potential of Iraq's approximately 500 aircraft was seen as justifying the considerable effort being made to shut down their air bases, even though the planes were expected to remain largely inactive (Biddle and Zirkle 1997).

[3] By way of example, the organizational shift from the use of tanks as infantry support vehicles to an independent striking arm between World Wars I and II was also accompanied by the development of faster, more heavily armed tanks optimized for this new role (Murray 1996). Similarly, the shift to airmobile tactics spurred helicopter development during the Vietnam War.

[4] For clarification, we can envision a scheme which would *not* allow for the investigation of the variables discussed in Chapter 3. A scheme which only incorporated very broad changes in military technology–for example, the transition from sail to steam for propelling naval vessels–would be of little use in examining the relationship between arms diffusion and year-to-year changes in conflict or hegemony patterns at the end of the Twentieth Century.

[5] The six levels of details are nestled within one another hierarchically, i.e. diffusing a Category I innovation automatically involves diffusing innovations in Categories II through IV, and so on. The term "levels-of-analysis" is not used in order to avoid confusion with the broader use of the term in the international relations literature.

[6] See, for example, Johnson (1998).

[7] This distinction appears only for the generational level because it makes little sense to apply it at other levels. A "diversifying" meta-categorical or categorical innovation is simply another meta-categorical or categorical innovation. The distinction makes more conceptual sense at the incremental level, as incremental change can either add a new sub-system at the current level of sophistication or upgrade it to the next level. However, the very nature of incremental change mitigates against devising rigid categories to track its progression. By definition, such progression is evolutionary and "bit-by-bit" rather than stage-driven. The distinction clearly is of little use in examining continuous innovation, which is fluid and, for all intents and purposes, impossible to track at in terms of stages.

[8] While this holds true as a rule, there are some exceptions. These are discussed in the data appendices and, where relevant, in the data analysis section of the text.

[9] It is the integrated nature of these components which created the idea of a weapons "system" in the first place (van Crevald 1989; Clark 1989, 16–17).

[10] Pearson (1994, 24) provides a simple chart tracking the spread of a few categorical innovations. While interesting, as indicated above, it tells only part of a much more complicated story about the global diffusion of MTIs.

[11] For example, the T-72, Iraq's most modern tank, was a second generation MBT, while most U.S. and British tanks were third generation Challengers and Abrams. Most of Iraq's army still used first generation T-54/-55 variants, which first appeared in 1948. Similarly, Iraq's heavy surface-to-air forces were composed entirely of obsolete first and second generation systems (the Soviet SA-2, SA-3, and SA-6). Coalition SAMs featured the third generation Patriot. Finally, Iraq's air force had only a handful of fourth generation MiG-29s and Su-24Ms (about 50 aircraft out of an air force of 800). In contrast, the bulk of Coalition fighters were fourth generation F-14s, F-15s, F-16s, F-18s, Tornados, and Mirage 2000s. See Appendices B through H for details.

[12] Examples and details of these phenomena are left for the data appendices at the end of this book, which abound with references to works that express technology in generational terms.

[13] It is also clear that in complex weapons systems, shortcomings in one technical area can be overcome by advantages in another. By way of example, Soviet fourth generation fighter aircraft lack the fly-by-wire (FBW) flight controls of their U.S. counterparts, but this does not result in dramatic differences in the overall maneuverability of both groups systems. The question then becomes whether FBW controls are, in and of themselves, an "important" MTI or whether what is of real significance is whatever complex of technological advances that results in a certain level of aircraft maneuverability.

[14] For a closer examination of how weapons designations reflect the level of technological change, see Appendix A.

[15] Occasionally, analysts will describe the various incremental developmental stages of a given weapons system as "generations." Thus, the earliest versions of the MiG-21 were described as "first generation" variants, those with an improved radar as "second generation," and so on. These incremental changes are not what is meant by "generational change" in this work, because (a) earlier models can usually be physically modified to the new standard, and (b) the categories are not applicable cross-nationally or between different individual weapons systems.

[16] This becomes relevant during later data analysis, when it is assumed that intra-generational, incremental change has only a marginal effect on the path of diffusion when compared to other independent variables.

[17] Sherwin and Laurance's (1979) comment that, unlike Soviet incrementalism, U.S. generational advances lead to "step-wise" increases in weapons system cost, also stems from the unreality of Soviet-era pricing schemes under a command economy. The perception that Russian weapons are dramatically cheaper than their Western counterparts has carried over into the post-cold war era, but is not borne out by the actual prices of such weapons on the open market.

[18] The U.S. similarly keeps older equipment in service with National Guard and Reserve units, although not to the same degree as the Soviets. During the 1990s, for example, most U.S. reserve tank units were equipped with second-generation M-60

tanks, while active forces largely operated the M-1 Abrams. In contrast, active Russian units still deploy considerable numbers of *first* generation T-55s in conjunction with tanks from succeeding generations.

[19] At this point, we simply assert that the "period of interest" is the post-World War II era, from 1945 to the 1990s. A finer definition of and rationale for the study's time frame follow this section.

[20] Naval arms and land-based tactical missiles were omitted from CFE for a number of reasons. Questions about how U.S. and Soviet warships, which could be easily moved in and out of the Atlantic-to-the-Urals (ATTU) treaty-defined area, should be counted for treaty purposes would were impossible to resolve within the regional framework of the negotiations. Tactical missiles and launchers were omitted due to insurmountable verification problems. In contrast, the UNRCA lacks a verification component and imposes no numerical or categorical limitations. As a result, it is able to include both categories.

[21] For a detailed examination of the UNRCA and a comparison to CFE categories, see Laurance (1995). For a criticism of the relevance of UNRCA's reporting requirements, see Karp (1995).

[22] The UNRCA itself could also be used as a source for data on recent (post-1992) adoptions, but, since SIPRI in particular incorporates UNRCA data into its annual register, this is somewhat superfluous.

[23] The only data from IISS not available in SIPRI concerns arms acquisitions from domestic production sources. This affects a relatively small subset of adoption cases (generally speaking, the major arms producers). IISS in-service dates for weapons produced by these states can generally be checked in Jane's and other technical reference sources.

[24] By way of example, the second (1960) edition of *The Military Balance* devotes about four and a half pages to Soviet military forces and a grand total of four short paragraphs to those of the entire Warsaw Pact. Data on all Warsaw Pact naval forces is given in one sentence: "the Satellite naval forces are of little importance and only of value for local defense."

[25] In practice, excluding the Soviet and Yugoslav successor states has virtually no impact on the data. All are economically hard-pressed and have had few resources with which to purchase new MTIs since 1991. While Russia has attempted to develop a broad array of new military technologies, it has been unsuccessful at putting them into operational service. Yugoslavia/Serbia has adopted a second generation shoulder-fired SAM, and Croatia a first generation attack helicopter. These, however, took place in 1995–96, outside the data limits for the hypothesis-testing section of the project (q.v.).

[26] In cases in which conflicting adoption dates were found, I first attempted to locate a third source for the data. If no third source could be found, I used the date derived from SIPRI data.

[27] Many land-locked nations still maintain navies for riverine duties. However, the level of technology usually employed by these states is very low when compared to that of ocean-going navies.

Chapter 5
The Diffusion of Arms: Mapping the Empirical Terrain

NOW THAT I HAVE ESTABLISHED A DEFINITIONAL BASIS FOR EXAMINING the diffusion of military technological innovations (MTIs), the actual empirical analysis can move forward. To this end, it is initially useful to sketch a map of the empirical terrain over which we will be traveling. This chapter presents a summary of the MTI data gathered and draws some important conclusions about the phenomenon of arms diffusion. I am specifically interested in answering the following questions, the details of which are reserved for the analyses that follows:

(1) What are the basic patterns of arms diffusion, and are these recognizable from other realms of diffusion-of-innovations research?
(2) How fast do arms spread throughout the international system, and has this rate changed at all over time?
(3) Finally, is there a significant variance in diffusion patterns and rates among geographic regions and individual states?

Answering these questions will provide a good sense of the direction and flow of MTI diffusion across the international system. It will also allow us to examine a few propositions derived from conventional wisdom about the spread of weapons that have rarely been addressed. This will be a useful jumping off point for the hypothesis testing which I undertake in the next chapter.

THE BASIC PATTERNS OF ARMS DIFFUSION

I begin this section with two related questions. First, what are the basic patterns of global arms diffusion? Second, are these recognizable from other realms of diffusion research? These questions are important for a number of reasons. Getting an overall sense of what the spread of arms looks like graphically is a useful first step for our analysis before we move on to the use of more sophisticated methodological tools. Furthermore, as discussed in previous chapters, an extensive cross-disciplinary literature on diffusion-of-innovation processes already exists. Determining whether the spread of arms matches previously identified diffusion patterns could provide clues as to other dynamics of their spread, including possible motive factors.

Since I am interested in characterizing the spread of arms as a diffusion process, I begin this examination of the empirical data using approaches and terminology from existing diffusion-of-innovations literature. To this end, Figures 5.1 through 5.6 represent the *cumulative adopter functions* (CAFs) of the fourteen military technological innovations (MTIs) included in the data set. A CAF is simply a scatterplot in which the horizontal axis represents the time (in this case, in years) since the adoption of the initial innovation and the vertical axis represents some measure of cumulative adoption of that MTI at that time (Mahajan and Peterson 1985). The y-value for the CAF can be expressed either as the *actual number of adopters* or as the *percentage of all potential adopters* that have adopted the innovation at a given time. In these CAFs, I follow the former convention.[1] Frequently, a CAF is also simply referred to as a *diffusion curve*, and I will use the terms interchangeably. The MTIs are grouped into functional categories (i.e. tanks, aircraft, helicopters, SAMs (two groups), and ATGMs), with multiple generations of the same category of weapons appearing in the same Figure.

The x-values for the CAFs are expressed in what I term *diffusion years*. As opposed to *calender years* (1981, 1982, etc.), diffusion years represent the actual number of years that have elapsed since initial adoption of an MTI. By way of example, suppose there were two MTIs, the first of which had its initial adoption in calender year 1960 and the second in calender year 1970. MTI #1 would have its third diffusion year in 1962, while MTI #2 would have its third diffusion year in 1972. The concept of diffusion years allows us to compare the diffusion of different MTIs at identical chronological stages of their spread. In order to facilitate comparative interpretation and analysis, I have maintained a constant scale of 0 to 40 diffusion years and 0 to 100 adopters on the x and y-axes, respectively, of each Figure.

Visual inspections of Figures 5.1 through 5.6 immediately allow us to reach two preliminary conclusions about the arms diffusion phenomenon. First, the global spread of military technological innovations is a stratified and deconcentrated process. Second, the diffusion patterns of the MTIs are marked by both similarities and differences that make drawing other general judgements about the nature of the overall arms diffusion process difficult at best. I discuss each of these two findings in the following sections.

Stratification and Deconcentration. The first conclusion we can draw by visual examination of the CAFs is that arms diffusion is a stratified and deconcentrated process. Arms do not diffuse evenly across the entire international system. In fact, the international system is stratified into military haves and have-nots, with the former group accounting for better than half of the world's states.[2] Furthermore, arms diffusion is largely deconcentrated, in the sense that military innovations diffuse over chronologically long periods of time. I explore each of these in the following paragraphs.

I theoretically define the *scope* of arms diffusion as the extent to which arms spread throughout the international system. Operationally, I measure this as simply the total number of adopters of a given MTI. The maximum possible number of adopters in the data set is, by definition, 138 states (see Chapter 4). In each of the six graphs, we can see that the total number of adopters of each MTI is significantly below 138. If fact, for none of the fourteen MTIs is the total number of adopters even two-thirds of the theoretical maximum. One might argue that several of the MTIs are relatively "young" (i.e. less than fifteen years since initial adoption), and it is thus unfair to make judgements about the scope of diffusion using them as examples. But we can further operationally define the *saturation point* of an MTI's diffusion as having been reached when no new adopters for that MTI have arisen in any five- year period *after* the ten year period following its initial adoption.[3] This simply indicates the tapering off of new adoptions and final stages of the diffusion process for a given innovation. By this definition, five of the fourteen MTIs have reached their saturation point and completed or nearly completed their diffusion process. Even among these five MTIs, the average number of total adopters is 66.7, about 48% of the maximum possible number. This indicates that, for any given MTI, a significant proportion of the states we might expect in a broad sense to have the capability to adopt the innovation fail to do so. It is possible that there are some trade-offs taking place between MTIs, in the sense that states which fail to adopt one MTI may successfully adopt another one (see note 14, this chapter). However, it is clear that any single military innovation can be expected to diffuse to less than half of the states in the international system.

Another feature of the spread of arms apparent from the CAFs in Figures 5.1 to 5.6 is the relative deconcentration of the arms diffusion process. A *concentrated* diffusion process is one in which the time difference between the earliest and latest adoptions is short, or, in other words, where the rate of adoptions (number of adoptions per time period) is high. Obviously, "short" or "long" time periods and "high" or "low" rates are terms meaningful only in relation to other important variables in any diffusion study. But from the CAFs and our understanding of the construction of the time frame for this analysis, we clearly see that the diffusion of a given MTI takes a relatively long time to reach its saturation point and complete diffusion.

For the five MTIs that have reached their saturation point, the average time to complete diffusion was over 31 years. Even more amazing is the fact that three more MTIs which have *not* yet reached their saturation point are still diffusing 30 or more years since their initial adoption. To put this in perspective, arms of a given generation typically continue to diffuse after one or even two succeeding generations of weapons in the same category are well into *their* global diffusion. To use a more specific example, first generation long-range SAM systems initially deployed in the 1950s were *still* being adopted by new users in the 1990s, even after the second (from 1960) and third (from 1980) generations had made their appearance. If this pattern persists, weapons from the 1960s and 1970s will continue to spread to new states well into the second and third decade of the next century.

Diffusion Curve Shapes. I next examine the degree to which the patterns of arms diffusion were constant across the fourteen MTIs in the data set. A high degree of similarity among these patterns could provide evidence a very strong underlying diffusion process that is relatively insensitive to transitory, exogenous influences. A low degree of similarity would indicate that the underlying diffusion dynamic is relatively weak. In that case, the rate of MTI spread is either random or heavily influenced by exogenous factors. These factors could include the independent variables, which can vary from year to year, or secular changes over time.

We can see from visual examination of Figures 5.1 to 5.6 that the MTIs in the data set exhibit a variety of diffusion patterns. Most of the plots do approximate the expected S-shaped curve of other diffusion processes (Spence 1994, 78; Mahajan and Peterson 1985, 9; Rogers and Shoemaker 1971). However, the CAFs for combat aircraft (Figure 5.1), PADS (Figure 5.5), and ATGMs (Figure 5.6) are relatively steep. In contrast, the CAFs for attack helicopters (Fig. 5.2), MBTs (Fig. 5.3), and long-range SAMs (Fig. 5.4) increase at a much more gradual rate. Some curves contain noticeable "jumps," years or clusters of years in which diffusion is extremely rapid, preceded and followed by periods of more steady diffusion. For example, the first five years of Generation 3 combat aircraft diffusion (Fig. 5.1) and two periods of diffusion of Generation 2 MBTs (Fig 5.3, approximately diffusion years six and seven and 20 and 21) exhibit this pattern. Other curves, like those for Generation 3 MBTs (Fig 5.3) and long-range SAMs (Fig. 5.4), steadily increase over their entire diffusion periods, with few if any major sudden increases in adoption numbers. Finally, we can see that the relationships between the diffusion patterns of MTIs in the same weapons categories also vary. By way of example, the diffusion patterns of Generation 1 and 2 attack helicopters (Fig. 5.2) are almost identical. In contrast, those of Generations 3 and 4 combat aircraft (Fig 5.1) are markedly different, with the latter MTI diffusing much more gradually than its predecessor.

One straightforward approach for comparing these diffusion patterns is to examine the statistical relationships between the number of adopters in each individual diffusion year for each possible pair of MTIs. This can be done by simply computing the Pearson's correlations (r) for the number of new adopters in each diffusion year for each pair of MTIs.[4] The correlations provide us with measures of the strength of the relationships between the rate of increase in the number of adopters for each MTI at identical stages in those MTIs' diffusion. Strong, statistically significant values for r suggest that in identical diffusion years, different MTIs were spreading at similar rates. Weak, statistically insignificant values for r indicate that there is little relationship between the rates of spread of different MTIs in identical years of their diffusion. This is a somewhat crude measure, since it depends upon similarity in the rate of spread in *identical* years. It is insensitive to similar rates of spread in adjacent or nearby years but still within the same approximate segment of the diffusion curve. Nevertheless, the measure provides us with a first cut at the data when addressing this important, basic issue.

The r values for all fourteen MTIs are listed in Table 5.1.[5] Values significant at the .05 level are marked with an asterisk (*). Values significant at the .01 level are denoted by a double asterisk (**). Table 5.1 clearly indicates that some, but by no means all, of the MTIs share similar diffusion patterns, as defined by our test. The strength of these similarities varies considerably, however. About 12.4% of all MTI pairs (11 of 89) are significantly correlated. Further, of the pairs of innovations whose spread is significantly positively correlated, the average value of $r = .515$. With a resulting r^2 of about .27, we are still left with a considerable amount of variance (almost three-fourths) not shared by the various series. Nevertheless, the spread of all but one of the MTIs is significantly correlated with at least one, and up to three, of the other MTIs. The r^2 values range from a high of .88 to a low of .14. I conclude from these results that both the underlying diffusion dynamic and exogenous or random factors play important roles in determining how fast military innovations spread throughout the international system. This finding will prove to be important in the next chapter (Chapter 6), as it suggests that the regression analysis of each of the theoretical models detailed in Chapter 3 should include both a term to account for both the diffusion dynamic *and* any of a number of independent variables.

As Table 5.1 indicates, only Generation 1 long-range surface-to-air missiles (SAMs, MTI #7) fail to exhibit a significant relationship to at least one other MTI. Two factors may explain this finding. First, the initial long-range SAMs attained their initial operational capability (IOC) much earlier than any other MTI in the data set.[6] The IOC of first generation long-range SAMs occurred in 1953, some seven years before the beginning of the current, post-colonial international system, as defined in the previous chapter. Much of the diffusion process for this innovation thus took place during a time when international conditions (i.e. the number of states) were quite different than for the rest of the MTIs. By the time the current international system emerged in the 1960s, the second generation of long-range SAMs (MTI #8) was also already diffusing. The new states of the globe adopted second generation systems while ignoring their first generation counterparts in the same weapons category. This interpretation provides evidential support to my decision to restrict the bulk of the analysis to the post-colonial (i.e. post-1960) time frame, on the grounds that a different dynamic in the global arms production and trade system emerged during that period. It is also consistent with other findings (to be discussed later) which indicate that the 1960s and early 1970s represented a boom time for the diffusion of arms relative to other periods.

A second explanation for the exceptional status of first generation long-range SAMs may be found in two data-related factors. First, data for the first seventeen years of diffusion of this innovation are missing (see Chapter 4 for an explanation). As a result, a greater percentage of the existing data for this MTI reflects the final phases of adoption. These final phases occur when the cumulative number of adopters reaches the theoretical maximum number of adopters, and final holdouts become less and less likely to ever adopt the innovation. Graphically, it is represented by the upper "tail" of the typical S-shaped curve. We have thus been forced to omit from the analysis this innovation's early and middle years of adoption, which presumably have much higher, and potentially more variable, cumulative adopter figures. We have no way of knowing whether the diffusion pattern of MTI #7 in its earlier phases (diffusion years 1 to 17) would have matched patterns from identical time frames of other MTIs in the data set. Second, the omitted data points for first generation long-range SAMs means that a number of the other MTIs have a very constricted range of years to compare with identical years of this innovation. These shorter comparable series increase the effect that outlier and random factors have on r. In the extreme case of second-generation attack helicopters (MTI #4), there is only one diffusion year in common between the two innovations. As a result, calculating r is impossible for this pair of variables, since, with only a single overlapping year, one series is effectively a constant relative to the other.

A final angle from which to view these MTI diffusion curves is suggested in Spence (1994). Spence details a diffusion pattern commonly identified with the spread of innovations in which adopters are divided into five categories: innovators, early adopters, early majority, late majority, and laggards. *Innovators* are composed of adventurous actors, who seek to be the first to adopt new innovations. *Early adopters* are more cautious than innovators, but still well ahead of the average actor in terms of their willingness and opportunity to accept new ideas and products. Members of the *early majority* and *late majority* are deliberative in their adoption decisions, and willing to let others lead the way. Unlike early majoritarians, late majoritarians require "overwhelming pressure from their peers...to adopt anything which is different from what they have known in the past...[and] more than any of the other categories, their acceptance of any new practice is determined by basic financial considerations" (Spence 1994, 45). Finally, *laggards* require the most intense external influence to be exerted upon them before adopting an innovation. Laggards are followed only by *rejectors*, which refuse adoption under all circumstances. According to this common diffusion model, these five categories typically represent 2.5%, 13.5%, 34%, 34%, and 16% of the total population (i.e. a normal distribution), respectively, with rejectors falling outside of the distribution.

We can check to see if the diffusion patterns of the MTIs in this study fit this model. Table 5.2 displays a breakdown of the diffusion patterns of the nine MTIs from the data set. The μ and σ represent the mean and standard deviation of the number of years it took for states to adopt a given MTI. Following Spence, the classification of adopters into one of the five categories is determined by how many standard deviations their time-to-adoption is from the mean time-to-adoption for that innovation. Table 5.2 depicts the adopters which fall into each of Spence's categories as a raw number and as a percentage of the total number of adopters. Second generation attack helicopters (MTI #4), third generation main battle tanks (MTI #6), and third generation long-range SAMs (MTI #9) are not included because they are not even close to their saturation points. Since they are at early stages in their diffusion, including them in this portion of the analysis would spuriously depress the mean andstandard deviation time-of-diffusion values required for comparison with the nine fully diffused MTIs in the table. MTIs #7 (first generation long-range SAMs) and #13 (first generation anti-tank guided missiles) are omitted for the reverse reason. Because the data on early stages of these innovations' diffusion is missing, including them in the analysis at this point would tend to inflate the desired mean and standard deviation values.

Based simply upon the magnitude of thedifferences between the expected percentages (%$_E$) and the actual percentages, it is clear that none of the MTIs follows the established pattern very closely. However, we can get a more precise idea of how well the model fits our empirical data by examining a few simple measures. In Equation 5.2, I define M, the measure of fit of the model for any single MTI *j*, as:

Eq. 5.1: $$M = \sum_{i=1}^{5} |(X_{ij} - X_{ijE})/X_{ijE}|$$

where X_{ij} = the percentage of cases in the *i*th category (and $I = 1$ to 5, corresponding to Spence's five adopter categories in sequence) and X_{ijE} is the expected percentage of cases in the *i*th category. I take the absolute value of the difference of the actual and expected values to rid the equation of negative terms, since we are interested only in how far off the model is, not the direction of the error. The values thus generated for M are found in the last line of Table 5.2. The theoretical values of M can range from zero (meaning an exact correspondence of the expected and actual number of adopters in each phase of the diffusion) to 43 (that is, if 100% of adoptions took place in "innovator" phase of diffusion). Lower values of M indicate that the model describes the data very well. Higher values of M indicate that the data do not meet the expectations of the model with a high degree of accuracy.

M tells us the degree to which the data from our data set fits the standard diffusion model overall. However, it is also useful to generate a measure which indicates the fit of the standard model for each diffusion phase, in the event that that model is better at describing the behavior of the diffusion curve in some phases than in others. I thus define P_{AVG}, the average fit of the standard model for each diffusion phase across all nine military innovations in the data set, as:

Eq. 5.2: $$P_{AVG} = (\sum_{j=1}^{N} |(X_{ij} - X_{ijE})/X_{ijE}|)/N$$

where X_{ij} and X_{ijE} are the actual and expected percentages of adopters for each category across all MTIs in the table, and N is the number of MTIs in the Table (in this case, 9).

The results described in Table 5.2 reveal several interesting findings. First and most important is the fact that, for a significant portion of the innovations, the initial phases of diffusion were extremely truncated. According to the scheme, we would expect 2.5% of adoptions to take place two standard deviations or more prior to the mean time-to-diffusion. In four of the nine cases, however, the initial global adoption of the MTI took place *less* than two standard deviations from the mean. As a result, there are no values in the "innovator" category. In turn, the values for P_{AVG} for the "early adopter" category are significantly higher than expected, and demonstrate the greatest deviance ($P_{AVG} = .41$) from the predicted values, about 40% higher than the next highest P_{AVG} value (for the laggard category, where P_{AVG} = .29). As we also see from looking at the actual percentages for each MTI, the model as a whole overestimates the speed with which innovations spread. However, predictions for later stages of diffusion are much more likely to underestimate the number of adopters than those for earlier stages. This means that *early* diffusion was taking place at a much faster pace than the model would lead us to expect. Together, these observations suggest that, although arms diffusion is deconcentrated in that arms diffuse over long periods of time, arms spread throughout the first batches of adopters (the innovator and early adopter categories) relatively rapidly, or at least more rapidly than Spence's model leads us to expect.

M, the overall fit of the model to the data, varies considerably, with values from .54 to 1.76 being encountered. Unfortunately, there is little discernable pattern to the variance in M across MTIs, either across weapons category, relative unit cost, total number of adopters, or year of initial adoption (1960s, 1970s, etc.). The fit line of a scatterplot of M versus the calender year of initial adoption (Figure 5.7) indicates that, overall, the model appears to fit the data less well as time has passed. However, regressing M upon the IOC yearof each innovation using the ordinary least squares (OLS) technique yields a coefficient which is statistically insignificant at the .05 level.[7] The inability of the pure diffusion model to systematically account for the MTI diffusion patterns we have witnessed provides further justification for examining the role of exogenous forces found outside the diffusion dynamic itself in explaining the patterns by which arms spread across the globe.

THE RATE OF ARMS DIFFUSION

A second critical aspect of arms diffusion is measuring the rate at which arms spread over time. Claims and counterclaims that new weapons technologies are spreading more or less quickly, to greater or lesser numbers of states, in a given time period usually rely upon anecdotal evidence or unstated yardsticks of comparison. The purpose of this section of the chapter is to provide an empirical basis for judging the validity of such statements. Specifically, I am interested in addressing the following two questions related to this phenomenon.

(1) What is the average or baseline rate of diffusion of military technological innovations through the international system?

(2) Has this rate changed over calender (real-world) time? In particular, has the end of the Cold War marked any increase or decrease in global MTI flows? Or are there any secular changes over the entire period represented by our data?

I address each of these questions separately in the sections that follow.

The Average Rate of Arms Diffusion. We can look at the average rate of global arms diffusion from two perspectives. We could calculate the mean number of new adopters per year of an MTI over the entire course of its diffusion. This has the advantage of yielding a figure which best represents overall how fast an innovation spread over a long period of time. On the other hand, it also ignores the uneven nature of diffusion processes, the fact that the nature of interaction effects between adopters and non-adopters means that we should not expect diffusion rates to be constant across the lifespan of an MTI. On a practical note, it renders comparison of MTIs that have been diffusing for different lengths of time problematical, since the effect of later sections of the diffusion curves on the value of the mean will vary from innovation to innovation. A second, more valid approach is to divide each MTI's diffusion curve into a number of segments corresponding to the adoption phases discussed above. The mean rate of diffusion for each segment can then be independently calculated.[8] The results of the latter approach for the fourteen MTIs in our data set are summarized in Table 5.3.

Table 5.3 lists the average rate of diffusion for each MTI in three calender age-defined periods. I calculate this rate as simply the number of adopters in a given diffusion period divided by the number of years in that period. To determine the boundaries of these periods, I visually examined the diffusion curves to determine their *inflection points*, the x-values which mark the ends of the "tails" of the S-shaped diffusion curve (Mahajan and Peterson 1985, 20). For the MTIs in our data set, the two inflection points for most of the CAFs occur at between diffusion years 5 and 10, and then again between about 20 and 25. The averages of these figures (years 8 and 23) are used as the points defining the three periods: diffusion years 1–8, 9–23, and 24 and up. For MTIs that have reached their saturation point, the final period is defined from year 23 to the saturation point. For those MTIs which have not yet reached their saturation point, the final period extends to the final year for which data was available.

As Table 5.3 shows, the rate of overall arms spread during the 1960–1997 period ranged from about 1.09 new adopters per year in the early phases of diffusion to 2.50 per year in the middle phases and back down to 1.19 per year in the last phases. The range of these values for individual MTIs was considerable, running from (early) .25 to 3.13 (middle) .92 to 4.33, and (late) .56 to 2.33. The Table also shows the varying standard deviations among the three periods. Early period adoption rates are about 19% less variable than middle period adoption rates, while those for the late period are about 35% less variable. The picture that these figures paint of the spread of arms meshes with our earlier findings, and allows us to come to a few initial characterizations of the arms diffusion process.

First, these numbers provide us with a useful baseline for understanding the spread of arms during various phases of the diffusion process. On average, these MTIs have spread to anywhere between slightly over one to two-and-a-half new states per year. Diffusion at significantly higher rates than this would be considered "fast," while diffusion at lower rates can be termed "slow." The figures provide us with the yardstick necessary to judge the frequent claims that arms are spreading more or less quickly throughout the international system at various points in time, contentions that will be examined shortly, in the next part of this section of the chapter.

Second, the figures allow us to flesh out our understanding of each phase of the diffusion process. I noted earlier in this chapter that arms diffusion is relatively more concentrated that we might expect in the earliest stages of diffusion. This is evident from the finding that the standard diffusion model, which expects a normal distribution of adoption decisions, overestimates the number of states in the "innovator" category for seven of the nine fully-diffused MTIs in the data set (Table 5.2). However, we can see from Table 5.3 that the diffusion rate in this early period is *lower* than in the other two periods.[9] This confluence of results is only possible *if a small number of states are adopting MTIs rapidly relative to the overall population of states in the international system.* Such a finding adds further detail to the characterization of arms diffusion as a stratified process. The international system is not only divided strongly into military haves and have-nots. In addition, the haves themselves are concentrated into a small group of innovators who adopt MTIs much more quickly than the rest of their neighbors.

This phenomenon can be interpreted in one of at least two ways, differentiated by the identities of the states in this "innovator" category. If there is a high degree of consistency in the roster of states in this category, we must conclude that the stratification of the arms diffusion process is due to a concentration of military-technological capability in the hands of a cluster of states in the international system. In this case, for one set of reasons or another, a small number of states dominates the technological frontier of military hardware, with other states lagging various distances behind. This is the argument obliquely made by Krause (1992) in positing that a stratified arms transfer and production system is a defining feature of the larger international system in all historical periods. On the other hand, if the identities of the innovator states vary dramatically from MTI to MTI, we would be forced to attribute this clustering of "innovativeness" with respect to individual MTIs as the result of some other structural set of factors in the innovation process. In that case, states may perhaps decide to "specialize" in (or at least prioritize) certain arms categories and not others. In other words, states pick and choose the innovations which they can afford or need at specific points in time. This type of process might also be enhanced by the random impact of exogenous systemic factors upon individual states. For example, we might expect that a certain percentage of states in the international system will be engaged in interstate wars during any given period of time. Following from some of the theoretical propositions in Chapter 3, if war in fact encourages states to adopt MTIs more rapidly than they otherwise would, the warring states in any given time period might make up a high portion of the early innovators for a specific MTI. But there is no *a priori* reason to assume that the identities of this roster of warring states has a high degree of constancy over time. As a result, the identities of the early innovators could shift dramatically from MTI to MTI, depending upon who was waging war against whom at a given time. The above data cannot tell us which of these interpretations of the diffusion process is correct. To discover that, we must examine the relative "innovativeness" of individual states. I take up this task in the last section of this chapter.

Changes in Arms Diffusion Over Time. The previous section provided a clear, quantitative answer to the question of how quickly MTIs typically diffuse. The next question I seek to answer concerns the stability of these rates over time. Has the overall rate of arms diffusion remained the same over the length of time covered by the data set? Or has it increased or decreased? If one of the latter, to what degree?

Examination of the data on these MTI diffusion rates leads us to three undeniable conclusions. First, the overall rate of arms diffusion has declined significantly from the 1960s to the 1980s with each new generation of weapons. Second, as a result, and with a few exceptions, succeeding generations of armaments have been diffusing less rapidly and less widely than their predecessors. Finally, the overall impact of these trends has been an intensification of the stratification and deconcentration process in the arms diffusion phenomenon over time. I will explain in the following paragraphs how I reached these conclusions.

Refer back to Figures 5.1 through 5.6, which illustrate well these conclusions. Figures 5.1 through 5.6 show at least two generations of MTIs in each of six categories that diffused from the early 1960s into the early 1990s (with only one generation of point defense SAMs included in the data set). For three of these MTI categories (PADS, ATGMs, and attack helicopters), the rate of diffusion for the later generation appears approximately the same as that for the earlier. For the other three MTI categories, however (combat aircraft, main battle tanks, and long-range SAMs), the rate of diffusion since the 1960s of the later generations has been substantially lower than that of the earlier ones. Combat aircraft are the most dramatic example of this trend. By year 26 of their diffusion, 80 states had adopted combat aircraft of the third generation, yielding a diffusion rate of about 3.08 adoptions per year. In contrast, the number of adopters of fourth generation aircraft at a similar point in their diffusion was 54, yielding a diffusion rate of 2.08 new adoptions per year, a decline of almost 33%. Figures for tanks (from 26 to 20 adopters, a 23% decline) and long-range SAMs (34 versus 11, for a 68% decline) exhibit similarly large decreases.[10] In short, we can clearly see that newer generations of weapons system have certainly been diffusing no more rapidly, and often substantially less rapidly, than their counterparts in the previous generation.

Figures 5.8 through 5.11 provide another window on these statistics. These figures show MTIs which began diffusing in approximately the same time periods clustered together on one graph. Figure 5.8 shows innovations which began diffusing in the 1950s, Figure 5.9 those which started to spread in the early 1960s, Figure 5.10 those which started from the late 1960s and 1970s, and Figure 5.11 those from during the 1980s.

The graphs show that the steepness of the diffusion curves, which indicate the rate of arms diffusion for these MTIs, generally increased from the 1950s to the 1960s and have since been slowly dropping with every new generation of arms. Again, this clearly does not mean that every succeeding generation of arms in *every* category has diffused less rapidly that those in *every* preceding category. It is obvious from the graphs, for example, that second generation PADS from the 1970s (Figure 5.10) have spread more widely and rapidly than second generation MBTs from the 1960s (Figure 5.9). It does mean, however, that, beginning in the 1960s, the highest rates of spread of older generations of MTIs are significantly higher than the highest rates of spread of newer generations. Similarly, the lowest rates of spread have become are significantly lower as the decades have passed.

This secular downward trend can more clearly be seen in Table 5.4, where the changes in the rates of diffusion for innovations in successive generations are listed. The table shows that, as indicated previously, there have been dramatic decreases in the rate of adoption of combat aircraft, tanks, and long-range SAMs from the 1960s onward. It also indicates that attack helicopters have shared these other MTIs' declining fortunes, although the high percentages mask small drops in absolute numbers, as the diffusion rate for helicopters is considerably lower than for most other MTIs in the data set. Table 5.4 also demonstrates the dramatic *increase* in the rate of diffusion between innovations of the 1950s (Generation 1 long-range SAMs and Generation 1 ATGMs) and their succeeding generations.

Only in the cases of early period PADS and late period combat aircraft was this pattern disrupted. Regarding the latter, this is partially a statistical problem. The base of comparison for the two generations is only two data points, since Generation 4 aircraft have only been diffusing for 26 years. If we look at a somewhat larger sample of later data points by examining Figure 5.1, we can see that the slope of the curve for Generation 4 aircraft in its last eight or so years is substantially less than that for Generation 3 aircraft over the same period. We can also take the numbers at face value, however, and assume that those two final data points are significant. In that case, the simplest explanation for the late period increase is clearly that innovation periods are being drawn out in actual time by the slowing of the diffusion process. States which adopted Generation 3 combat aircraft during the initial or middle periods may be putting offadoptions until the equivalent (in calender years) of the late period. This evidence of further deconcentration of the arms diffusion process fits well with the overall impression one gets from this data, although the lack of data on similar time periods for other MTIs limits myability to see whether thisis a generalized phenomenon. The burst of diffusion of second generation PADS compared to their first generation counterparts appears to simply be an anomaly. Although both generations seem to have diffused to approximately the same extent by about their twentieth diffusion year, it simply took a longer time for widespread diffusion to begin in the case of the older generation of systems.

A final question of interest is what impact, if any, the end of the Cold War has had upon the pace of global arms diffusion. This is a difficult question to answer, for a number of reasons. First, if we take the Cold War as ending in about 1989 (with the collapse of the Berlin Wall) or 1991 (the disintegration of the Soviet Union), there are at most about a half dozen post Cold War years represented in the data set. This small sample of years does not allow for very robust analysis. The fact that the lag between orders and deliveries of modern weapons can span a period of several years (meaning that the effects of the early and mid-1990s are just now being seen) only compounds this problem. Second, as shown above, the overall trend in arms diffusion rates since the 1960s has been downward. It is therefore difficult to separate out the effects of the Cold War end from this secular downswing. One might suggest directly comparing adoption rates for identical diffusion years for the same weapons categories before and after the Cold War's end to get a sense of the trend in these figures. However, this is complicated by a host of issues, including the fact that (at least in the case of fourth generation combat aircraft) slower diffusion rates earlier may be "displacing" adoption decisions until later in the diffusion process. For example (and again, looking at Table 5.4), the adoption rate for Generation 4 combat aircraft has increased during the post-Cold War years over that for Generation 3 for several similar diffusion years. But is that because of the Cold War's end or because of the displacement effect? Separating out these different influences is extremely difficult by examining the diffusion curves using statistical methods. If the baseline number of adoptions per year for a specific period is changing, how can we say with any great precision that there are more or fewer adoptions in a given year than we should "expect?"We have no systematic way of forming an expectation under these circumstances.

One thing, however, that we *can* see by simply looking at our MTI diffusion curves is that, if there has been an independent "Cold War effect"on the diffusion process, either positive or negative, it appears to be slight. There are no significant, unexpected "flatlines" in any of the diffusion curves for the period of the 1990s that would indicate a steep drop-off in adoptions after the Cold War's termination. The diffusion of point defense SAMs (Figure 5.5) has shown little increase since 1989, but this is not substantially different than the contemporary (in diffusion years) tail end of the diffusion curve for Generation 1 PADS shown on the same figure. Likewise, the diffusion of third generation long-range SAMs (Figure 5.4) has shown little movement inthe 1990s, butthis is not substantially different thus far from the overall pattern displayed by second generation systems during a similar period in their diffusion.[11] On the other hand, there are few steep increases either that would indicate a positive relationship between the end of the Cold War and the rate of arms diffusion. Despite the attention lavishes by Hartung (1994) and others on the "flooding" of advanced U.S. tanks, aircraft, SAMs and other conventional arms into the Middle East region after the Persian Gulf War of 1991, for example, these transfers did not yield substantial increases in diffusion over an above what we might expect from prior generations of systems. In fact, one is struck more by the overall continuity of diffusion patterns of new MTIs across the Cold War and post-Cold War periods (marked by overall decline in succeeding generations of systems) than by any dramatic differences.

In reading the above analysis, one might easily concede that newer generations of weapons are spreading more slowly than older ones as time passes. However, one might then ask if the spread of older generations of MTIs is somehow compensating or substituting for the spread of newer systems, particularly after the end of the Cold War. This would complicate the contention that arms diffusion, *as an overall phenomenon*, was slowing down. One would simply be able to argue that the spread of the *newest* weapons was slower than that of *older* weapons, but not that the overall spread of *weapons* was necessarily lower.

To a certain extent, this criticism is valid. In some cases, older generations of systems are continuing their diffusion alongside newer generations. As shown in Figures 5.2 and 5.3, second generation MBTs and first generation attack helicopters, for example, have not quite entered the "tail" stages of their diffusion. As a result, current and older generation systems are spreading simultaneously in both of these categories. In the remaining twelve MTI cases, however, the older generations of systems seem to have tapped out their potential adopter bases (or reached their saturation points), and entered their terminal diffusion phases. If any additional adopters for weapons in these categories are emerging, most are choosing newest-generation systems. This, of course, does not preclude the possibility that at some point in the future, these older generation MTIs could become "active" again and find additional adopters. But experience and common sense tells us that these new adopters are likely to be few in number and thus marginal in terms of the overall adoption pattern.

ARMS DIFFUSION: REGIONAL AND STATE-LEVEL STRATIFICATION

A final descriptive question concerning the arms diffusion phenomenon concerns the level of variability of arms diffusion patternsacrossvarious geopolitical regions and individual states. Until now, I have deliberately treated arms diffusion as a global process, for all of the reasons discussed in Chapters 1 and 2. But there is an evident possibility that states and regions across the globe may exhibit sub-patterns of arms diffusion different from that of the overall systemic pattern. This section will examine some of those sub-patterns, which, as will be shown, once again reinforce the depiction of the stratified yet deconcentrated global arms diffusion dynamic.

Further Investigating Stratification. Earlier in the chapter, I noted that the process of global arms diffusion was both stratified and deconcentrated. It is *stratified* both in the sense that the world is divided into military haves and have-nots,and in the sense that, among the haves, there is a small number of states (smaller than we would expect from standard diffusion models) that adopt MTIs relatively early, followed only later by the mass of other adopters. It is *deconcentrated* in the sense that arms continue to spread for long periods of time after their initial deployment, with some MTIs diffusing for 25 to 30 years or more before the new adopter pool is finally exhausted. I left open the question of whether the identity of the states in the "early adopter" category (i.e. the haves among the haves) remains constant across all MTIs. I did note that if their identity was largely constant across most or all of the MTIs, we could argue that the "tier" structure of the arms production and transfer system noted by Krause (1992) was a good description of reality. I term this situation *tight stratification.* If not, we could argue that transitory exogenous forces tended to have a greater influence over adoption decisions. I term this situation *loose stratification.*

The purpose of this section of the chapter is to examine the data for evidence of these patterns. To do so, I first calculated the number of years it took each of the states in the data set to adopt each of the twelve MTIs for which complete diffusion data existed (excluding Generation 1 ATGMs and Generation 1 long-range SAMs). I then determined the Pearson's correlations (r) for these "time until adoption" variables across all states. The results can be found in Table 5.5. Significant positive correlations between a high number of MTI pairs would indicate that states tend to be either early, middle, or late adopters across multiple MTIs. Significant negative correlations would indicate that states that tend to adopt one MTI early tend to be late adopters of other MTIs. Correlations close to zero would indicate no relationship between the patterns of adoption for various MTIs by a single state.

Table 5.5 shows the relatively tight stratification of the arms diffusion process because of the high degree of similarity in the times it takes an individual state to adopt different MTIs. The time-until-adoption scores for each MTI are significantly positively correlated with those of an average of six other MTIs, with an average significant r value of .562. Four MTIs were significantly correlated with no less than eight others, while only three of the twelve MTIs have significant correlations with less than five other MTIs. These results suggest that, following from Krause (1992), the "position" of individual states in the global arms diffusion hierarchy has been relatively stable for most of the period from the 1960s through the 1990s. Interestingly, the three MTIs which began their diffusion in the 1980s (second generation helicopters and third generation MBTs and long-range SAMs) share the least common adoption patterns with the other nine MTIs. Significantly related to an average of only 3.6 other MTIs (versus an average of 6 for all twelve MTIs), this result may be partially statistical artifact, as there are relatively few adopters for these new innovations to compare to those of the other MTIs. It could also indicate, however, that MTI adoption patterns, i.e. the identity of the states at various tiers of the arms production and transfer system, began shifting during the 1980s.

One final piece of evidence of the tight stratification of arms diffusion isdisplayed in Figure 5.12. Until now, I have characterized the tightness of stratification solely by the average number of years it takes a state to acquire an MTI. Obviously, however, the relative military dominance of the "haves" in the arms diffusion process is enhanced not only by how early they adopt new MTIs, but also by how many MTIs they adopt. Modern weapons are synergistic, depending upon the complementary performance of numerous systems on the battlefield to achieve their full potential. It does a state little good to have the latest anti-tank missiles, for example, if that same state lacks the SAMs and fighter aircraft to defend the soldiers carrying the ATGMs from enemy air attack. Thus, the "density" of innovations adopted by a single state is also of great importance.

Figure 5.12 plots the average number of years it takes for a state to adopt a new MTI against the number of MTIs (out of the reduced 12 MTI data set) adopted by the state. In reading the graph, we can see that points in the upper left hand quadrant indicate states which adopt many MTIs and adopt them relatively quickly. I term these *high density adopters*. The farther one goes down and to the right on the graph, the longer it takes a state to adopt innovations, and the fewer MTIs the state adopts. States which are located at or near the lower right hand corner of the graph I term *low density adopters*.[12]

We can see from the graph that there are very few high density adopters, with only six states falling clearly within the area bounded by (10, 8), out of the 113 that adopted at least one MTI. Looked at from another perspective, only ten states (about 9%) managed to adopt even *half* of the twelve MTIs within ten years of their initial appearance. These figures are slightly skewed by the fact that one of the innovations (second generation attack helicopters) has only been diffusing for about a decade, and two others (second generation MBTs and third generation long-range SAMs) are less than 20 years into their diffusion patterns. Other states will presumably be adopting these innovations in due course, lifting some of the y-values for certain states depicted in the figure. Nonetheless, the overall trends depicted by the figure are clear, and demonstrate that the "have" states are marked by adoptions that are both early and span many MTI categories.

State and Regional Differences. The existence of tight stratification leads us to ask one final set of questions about arms diffusion. I have examined stratification at the level of individual states, showing that some states adopt early and often, while for most, adoptions come fewer and farther in-between. I have further shown that arms diffusion is deconcentrated, with arms spreading over long periods of time as many states wait decades before adopting new innovations. But are there any elements of these dynamics working at the regional level, as opposed to the state level?

I noted earlier (Chapter 2) that diffusion of innovations research has shown that understanding the role of "innovation leaders," early adopters whose actions often serve as a yardstick or model for the actions of others, can be important for puzzling out the patterns of diffusion across a given population. Walker (1969), for example, pointed out the critical role of regionalleadersin the diffusion of policy innovations among the American states. Can we identify the regional leaders and followers in the process of arms diffusion? And do the regions themselves fall into any sort of hierarchy or leader-follower pattern?

In order to answer these questions, we require additional measures of how innovative one state, and subsequently one region, is relative to the others. Again, such measures need to capture two dimensions of innovativeness: how many different MTIs a state adopts, and how soon it adopts them after their initial appearance. This *diffusion score*, D, should be high for early adopters of many MTIs and low for late adopters of fewer MTIs. Thus D for any state X is given by:

Eq. 5.3: $$D_X = N_X (1 - Y_{AVG} /40)$$

. . . where N_X is the total number of different MTIs adopted by state X, and Y_{AVG} is the average number of years after the initial innovation that state X adopts an MTI. The maximum number of years that it took for a single innovation in the data set to reach its saturation point (again, by definition, the point at which more than five years has passed without the addition of a new adopter) is 37. As a result, I approximate the fraction of the total "diffusion time" that has passed on average before state X adopts MTIs by $Y_{AVG}/40$. This value is subtracted from 1 to obtain larger D values for more innovative states, and smaller D values for less innovative states. For the twelve MTI data set (which I will use in the following analysis), possible values for D range from 12 (for the most innovative states) to 0 (for the least innovative states). The innovation scores generated for all 138 states using the twelve MTI data set are listed in Appendix 9 according to region. Table 5.6 summarizes this data, again according to region.

Table 5.6 clearly reveals the strong regional hierarchy of arms diffusion. Unsurprisingly, NATO/Western Europe (which includes the U.S.) and Warsaw Pact/Eastern Europe (which includes the USSR) hold two of the top three regional scores. This finding is unsurprising and confirms conventional wisdom that the superpower arms producers and the opposing blocs they led were marked by high densities of MTIs adopted early in the diffusion process. It also demonstrates that the innovation scores most likely capture our intuitive sense of the concept of military technological innovativeness quite well.

Much more surprising is just how technologically innovative the Middle East was relative to the superpower blocs, despite the fact that none of the states in the region is a major arms producer. As Table 5.6 shows, the Middle East slightly outranked the Warsaw Pact in terms of overall innovativeness, and was only about 2% behind Western Europe in the pace and breadth of its MTI acquisitions. The U.S. (D = 11.650) and Soviet Union (D = 10.475) themselves still retained a healthy margin of superiority over the Middle Eastern average (D_{AVG} = 5.08). But, for example (and as recorded in Appendix 9), the top three states in the Middle East (Israel, Saudi Arabia, and Iran) would also have ranked second, third, and fourth, respectively, if they had been located in either of these other two regions. In contrast, East Germany, the second most innovative Warsaw Pact state, would have ranked only eighth in the Middle East. Middle Eastern scores also have a somewhat lower standard deviation, indicating that MTIs were spread more evenly across Middle Eastern states. We must also note a factor which we might have expected to *depress* the Middle Easter average: the fact that at least three of the Middle Eastern states (Bahrain, Qatar, and the UAE) did not even gain independence until the early 1970s, thus making them incapable of adopting MTIs for a good portion of the period covered by the data set. We can only speculate how much higher these scores might have been had the states in question gained independence a decade earlier.

The NATO/Western Europe, Middle East, and Warsaw Pact/Eastern Europe regions are clearly far ahead of the rest of the world in terms of military innovativeness, having average scores at least 38% higher than the next most innovative region (East Asia/Pacific). Further, the 48 states in these three regions comprise just slightly over a third of the states in the data set, but account for no less than 358 of the 601 individual adoptions of MTIs recorded, or about 60%. These observations further underline the existence of a strong regional stratification of arms diffusion. But also interesting is the appearance of a clear, if sometimes weak, regional leader phenomenon present in the arms diffusion process.

I define a regional innovation leader as a state which tends to adopt a wider variety of MTIs considerably more quickly than other states in a given region. This state presumably serves as a "risk taker" that validates the utility and functionality of new military technologies. In Eastern and Western Europe, this role was obviously played by the U.S. and Soviet Union, as shown by the margin by which their diffusion scores exceed those of other states in the region. Similarly, in the Middle East, Israel can claim regional leader status.

In each of the other regions except for Africa, a weaker version of this pattern is repeated. In each region, there generally exist one or two states which have diffusion scores that would earn them at least a middle ranking in one of the "big three" regional groupings. These states lead others in their region in innovation matters by a considerable margin, and their adoption of an MTI may help spark the adoption decisions of others. In East Asia, Japan and South Korea seem to fill this role. Japan would, for example, rank #4 and South Korea would rank #8 if located in Western Europe. In South America, the regional leaders are clearly Chile and Peru, which, however, would just barely make the mid-rankings (at 15th) in Western Europe.

This pattern is even weaker in the other three regions. Their diffusion scores indicate that India and Pakistan are the leaders of the South Asian region, and would rank 8th and 11th, respectively, in Western Europe. However in their case, as in the case of Cuba (which would rank 15th), the extremely small number of states in the region and the high levels of MTI non-adoption among those states (explained at least in part by their extremely small size) make the assumption of a regional leader dynamic suspect and probably inappropriate in both cases. In Africa, the diffusion scores of the top seven states all fall within one full point of one another, creating a top tier of MTI adopters that fails to match the region leader pattern. One explanation for this may be that Africa should not be considered a single region, but rather several regions, each with its own leader-follower structure. In that case, Africa might have several regional leaders: Nigeria in West Africa, Ethiopiain the Horn region,Angola in Southern Africa, Kenya in the East, and so on.

CONCLUSIONS

I have taken a "first cut" at the MTI adoption data in this chapter and found within it a number of interesting patterns. First, I examined the patterns of MTI spread across fourteen innovations, and found the standard model for diffusion of innovations of only limited help in modeling that spread. Second, I demonstrated the global stratification and deconcentration of the spread of military technology in a number of different ways. Third, I detailed the clear decline in MTI diffusion rates since the 1960s, and demonstrated the relative constancy of that overall patterninto the thus-far brief post-Cold War period. Finally, I developed some quantitative measures for looking specifically at how far "ahead" certain adopters are of others in acquiring MTIs, and established the structure of the global hierarchy of states and regions in MTI adoption.

All of these findings have helped us to better understand the process of arms diffusion, and to place the discussion of the spread of arms on a firmer empirical footing. But they do not help us to understand what factors influence the rate of arms diffusion, or to weigh the competing theories of arms diffusion detailed in Chapter 3. I reserve that task of hypothesis testing for the following chapter.

MTI	1	2	3	4	5	6	7
1	1.000 37						
2	-.022 25	1.000 25					
3	.130 30	* .414 25	1.000 30				
4	-.353 11	.561 11	.452 11	1.000 11			
5	.199 37	.011 25	.152 30	-.273 11	1.000 37		
6	.270 17	.318 17	.023 17	-.015 11	-.155 17	1.000 17	
7	.366 27	-.249 15	-.040 20	a 1	.067 27	-.437 7	1.000 27
8	.287 37	* .439 25	.314 30	-.167 11	.272 37	.006 17	-.259 37
9	-.118 17	.260 17	-.146 17	.088 11	.309 17	-.098 17	.506 17
10	.260 28	.321 25	-.092 28	.236 11	-.106 28	* .526 17	.240 28
11	.249 33	* .490 25	.204 30	.312 11	* .378 33	.475 17	.232 33
12	.428 20	.064 20	.225 20	.438 11	-.037 20	.355 17	.576 20
13	* .468 16	-.407 11	-.008 16	a 0	** .600 23	-.982 3	.146 23
14	.095 30	.221 25	* .380 30	** .936 11	.099 30	.011 17	.386 30

MTI	8	9	10	11	12	13	14
8	1.000 37						
9	-.320 17	1.000 17					
10	.143 28	.016 17	1.000 28				
11	.174 33	* .557 17	.307 28	1.000 33			
12	-.110 20	.000 17	.056 20	.330 20	1.000 20		
13	.409 23	-.866 3	-.099 14	.337 19	-.211 6	1.000 27	
14	.021 30	.051 17	.232 28	.282 30	* .523 20	.472 16	1.000 30

Table 5.1: Correlation Values between Identical Diffusion Years for All Fourteen MTIs

Number and Percentage of Adoptions in Each Diffusion Phase											
Diffusion Phase	%$_E$	MTI#1	MTI#2	MTI#3	MTI#5	MTI#8	MTI#10	MTI#11	MTI#12	MTI#14	P$_{AVG}$
< - 2σ (innovators)	2.5	n/a	1 (1.9%)	1 (2.5%)	n/a	n/a	n/a	2 (2.5%)	1 (1.8%)	1 (1.4%)	.19
- 2σ to - σ (early adopters)	13.5	18 (20%)	5 (9.3%)	3 (7.7%)	11 (18.3%)	11 (19.3%)	9 (16.7%)	5 (6.3%)	9 (16.1%)	3 (4.2%)	.41
- σ to (early majority)	34.0	19 (21.1%)	15 (27.8%)	13 (33.3%)	13 (21.7%)	14 (24.6%)	16 (29.6%)	35 (43.8%)	10 (17.9%)	28 (39.4%)	.25
to + σ (late majority)	34.0	38 (42.2%)	23 (42.6%)	12 (30.8%)	26 (43.3%)	24 (42.1%)	20 (37.0%)	26 (32.5%)	24 (42.9%)	24 (33.8%)	.17
> + σ (laggards)	16.0	15 (16.7%)	10 (18.5%)	10 (25.6%)	10 (16.7%)	8 (14.0%)	8 (14.8%)	22 (27.5%)	14 (25.0%)	15 (21.1%)	.29
# Adopters	100	90	54	39	60	57	54	80	56	71	n/a
μ	n/a	13.7	15.4	16.9	17.9	14.1	11.6	13.4	17.0	12.4	n/a
σ	n/a	8.0	5.8	7.0	8.6	8.5	6.9	6.7	5.0	5.6	n/a
M	n/a	1.14	1.14	1.14	1.03	1.08	.54	1.58	1.76	1.62	n/a

%$_g$ = percentage of adoptions expected in each phase (from standard model)

M = fit of model from Eq. 5.1 (lower value means better fit)

P$_{AVG}$ = average fit of model for each phase (Eq. 5.2) (lower value means better fit)

μ = mean number of years before innovation adopted

σ = standard deviation of μ

Table 5.2: Fit of the Diffusion Patterns of Nine MTIs to the Standard Diffusion Model

Adoptions Per Year			
MTI	Initial Period (Yrs. 1–8)	Middle Period (Yrs. 9–23)	Late Period (Yrs. 24+)
G3 aircraft	3.13	3.47	1.30
G4 aircraft	.50	2.87	2.33
G1 helo	.38	1.73	1.63
G2 helo	.25	*1.50	n/a
G2 MBT	1.38	2.33	1.67
G3 MBT	.55	*1.40	n/a
G1 LR SAM	n/a	*.92	.56
G2 LR SAM	2.13	2.20	.80
G3 LR SAM	.50	*1.10	n/a
G1 PD SAM	1.50	2.40	.83
G1 PADS	.38	4.33	1.36
G2 PADS	1.63	*3.46	n/a
G1 ATGM	n/a	*3.38	.69
G2 ATGM	.75	3.93	.75
Average	1.09	2.50	1.19
Std. Dev.	.88	1.09	.57

Table 5.3: Average MTI Diffusion Rates, 1960–1997 (Source: Thomas W. Zarzecki/Military Technological Innovation Data Set Version 1.0)

Percentage Change in Adoptions Per Year *			
MTI	Initial Period (Yrs. 1–8)	Middle Period (Yrs. 9–23)	Late Period (Yrs. 24+)
Increases from 1950s			
G1 to G2 ATGMs	n/a	.55 (16%)	.06 (9%)
G1 to G2 LR SAMs	n/a	1.28 (139%)	.24 (43%)
Average of Increases	n/a	.92 (78%)	.15 (26%)
Decreases from 1960s			
G3 to G4 combat aircraft	-2.63 (-84%)	.60 (-17%)	1.03 (79%)
G1 to G2 attack helos	-.13 (-34%)	-.23 (**-48%)	n/a
G2 to G3 MBTs	-.83 (-60%)	-.93 (**-40%)	n/a
G2 to G3 LR SAMs	-1.63 (-77%)	-1.10 (-50%)	n/a
G1 to G2 PADS	1.25 (329%)	-.87 (-20%)	n/a
Average of Decreases	-1.31 (-63.8%)	-.40 (-35%)	n/a

* The top number is actual change in yearly number of adopters, bottom is percentage change.
** Double asterisks in the table indicate that data was available for only some of the years in that period.

Table 5.4: The Decrease in MTI Diffusion Rates from the 1950s through the 1980s

MTI	1	2	3	4	5	6
1	1.000 90					
2	.215 49	1.000 54				
3	** .733 36	** .523 29	1.000 39			
4	.467 7	* .720 8	.779 4	1.000 8		
5	* .323 52	** .620 46	** .627 27	.509 8	1.000 60	
6	.434 17	.403 18	** .941 6	.226 7	** .598 20	1.000 20
8	** .369 53	** .493 45	.319 31	.261 8	** .471 41	* .585 17
9	.531 10	.374 11	.276 6	.092 5	.249 11	.636 9
10	.156 51	** .505 38	* .515 22	* .792 7	** .483 41	** .659 17
11	** .566 65	* .359 40	** .634 34	.493 7	** .522 45	* .578 14
12	-.171 47	* .370 44	.097 24	.215 8	.095 44	.159 20
14	.173 57	** .412 47	.295 26	* .815 8	* .340 54	.352 20

MTI	8	9	10	11	12	14
8	1.000 57					
9	* .678 10	1.000 11				
10	* .384 34	.635 9	1.000 53			
11	** .462 44	** .899 8	.151 39	1.000 80		
12	.104 39	** .773 10	.192 37	.085 40	1.000 58	
14	** .453 43	.062 10	* .348 44	.110 47	.137 49	1.000 71

Table 5.5: Correlation Values between Time Until Adoption for All States, 12 MTIs

Region	D_{XAVG}	σ_D	D_{MIN}	D_{MAX}	A_N	A_R
NATO/W. Europe	5.18	2.36	1.60	11.65	20	1.00
Middle East	5.08	2.09	1.56	9.58	19	1.00
WarPac/E. Europe	5.07	2.61	.68	10.48	9	1.00
East Asia/Pacific	3.65	1.86	.75	7.20	15	.79
South Asia	2.57	2.47	.43	6.23	6	.75
South America	2.20	1.18	.50	3.55	9	.82
Latin Am./Carib.	1.62	1.62	.30	4.25	5	.45
Africa	1.39	.94	.18	3.33	30	.73
All Region Avg.	3.35	1.89	.75	7.03	14	.82

D_{XAVG} = average diffusion score for states in given region
σ_D = standard deviation of diffusion scores in region
D_{MIN} = minimum diffusion score for a state in region
D_{MAX} = maximum diffusion score for a state in rgion
A_N = number of actual adopters in region
A_R = percentage of states in region that adopt at least one MTI

Table 5.6: The Regional Hierarchy of Arms Diffusion (Source: Thomas W. Zarzecki/Military Technological Data Set Version 1.0)

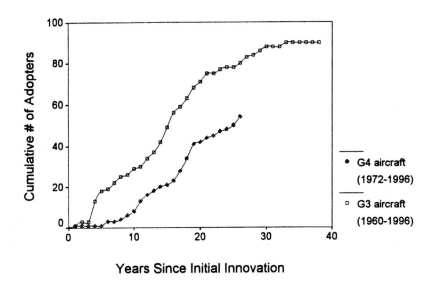

Fig. 5.1: Diffusion of Generation 3 & 4 Combat Aircraft

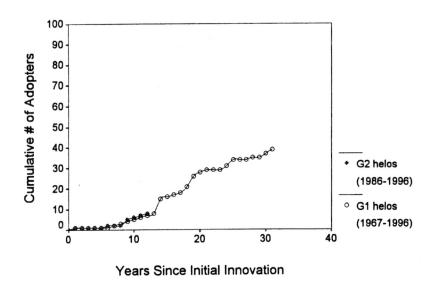

Fig. 5.2: Diffusion of Generation 1 & 2 Attack Helicopters

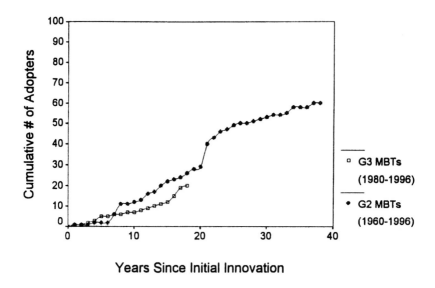

Fig. 5.3: Diffusion of Generation 2 & 3 Main Battle Tanks

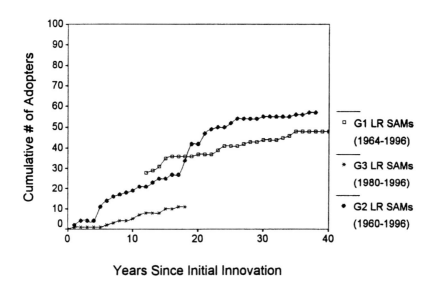

Fig. 5.4: Diffusion of Generation 1, 2, & 3 LR SAMs

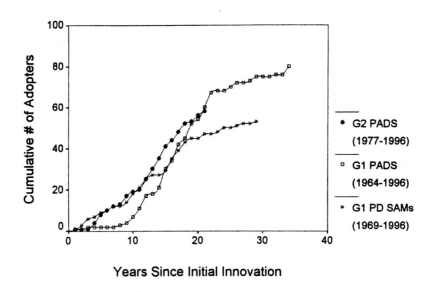

Fig. 5.5: Generation 1 PD SAMs, Gen. 1 & 2 PADs

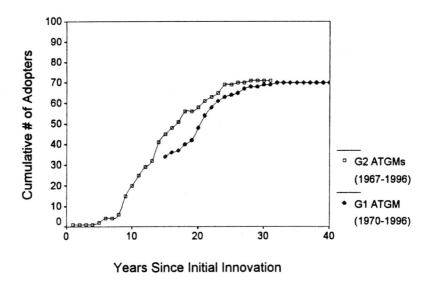

Fig. 5.6: Diffusion of Anti-Tank Guided Missiles

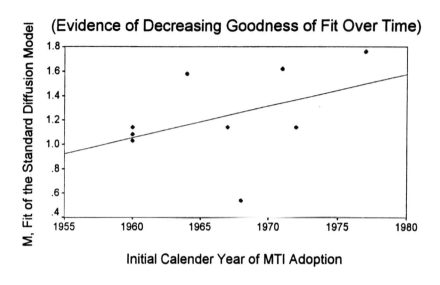

Fig. 5.7: The Fit of Standard Diffusion Model

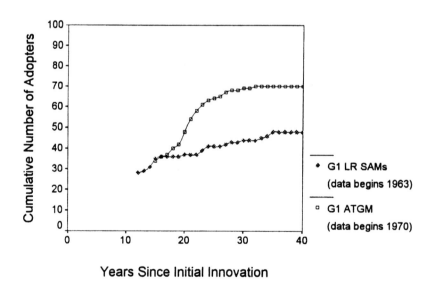

Fig. 5.8: MTIs that Began Diffusing in the 1950s

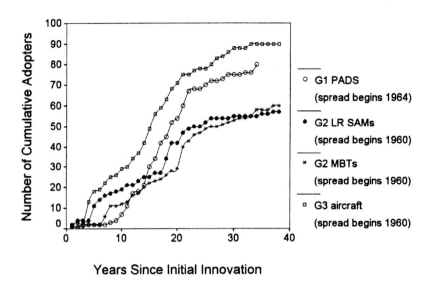

Fig. 5.9: MTIs that Began Diffusing in the 1960s

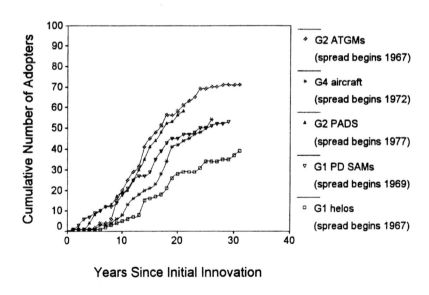

Fig. 5.10: MTIs that Began Diffusing in the Late 1960s & 1970s

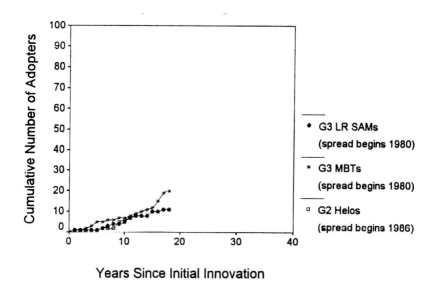

Fig. 5.11: MTIs that Began Diffusing in the 1980s

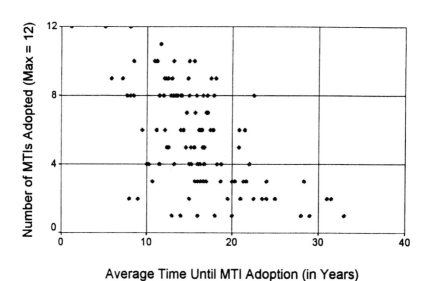

Fig. 5.12: The Stratification of Arms Diffusion

NOTES

[1] I choose to look at the raw numbers of cumulative adopters instead of percentages because the latter implies that a clear definition of a "potential adopter" exists, from which I could determine the percentage of actual adopters. But should we consider all states "potential adopters" simply because these states exist and , in some theoretical fashion, could purchase military hardware? Or should other criteria be used? At this stage of the research, it is not possible to make such distinctions in an unambiguous fashion.

[2] Actually, we can see that the percentage of global states adopting MTIs is even smaller when we realize that the 138 states covered by the data set omit several dozen smaller states that did not meet population and other requirements for inclusion. See Chapter 4 for details. When I refer to "the international system" throughout this chapter, it is with an understanding of this *caveat* in mind.

[3] An innovation's saturation point is sometimes defined in the literature as the point at which "all potential adopters have adopted" the innovation (Valente 1995, 141). This definition is frequently used in studies which pre-select for analysis only those innovations that have diffused to all adopters in a given population. I see this entire approach as somewhat tautological, for examining the saturation points of the spread of only those innovations which *have* saturation points implies that we have some concrete *a priori* criteria for what constitutes a "potential" adopter. In the case of arms diffusion, we have no *a priori* reason to believe that all the states in the data set will eventually adopt a given MTI. In fact, for the reasons discussed in the body of this chapter, we do *not* expect all states in the international system to adopt every MTI, and further *should* expect the actual number of adopters to vary from MTI to MTI. For these reasons, I have generated a more restricted definition for an MTI's saturation point, as outlined in the text.

[4] This means, in effect, that I first differenced the diffusion curve time series before computing the relevant r values. This is necessary to remove trend from these series (Kendall and Ord 1990, 37). Calculating r based on the original un-differenced series will yield strong, significant values. However, the strong autoregressive tendency of time series means that r would in this case reflect only the monotonic positive trend inherent in cumulative adopter functions. It would not register the strength of same-diffusion year relationships that we seek.

[5] In this and the following chapter, because of space constraints, I will occasionally find it necessary to refer to the fourteen innovations in the data set by number (MTI #1, MTI #2, etc.) rather than by name. These numbers are listed in Table 5.2 of Chapter 4.

[6] IOC is simply the operational deployment date of a military innovation, as defined in the previous chapter.

[7] The regression is of the form M = + YEAR + , where is the random error term. The standardized is .425 (standard error is .021), with significant only at the .254 level.

[8] A third possibility might be to consider several MTIs simultaneously, adding together and averaging the total number of adoptions of all the MTIs for each calender year. This would give us a better idea of the overall spread of military inno-

vations (plural) through the system, and build into our measure some recognition that states may make trade-offs (for example, on budgetary grounds) between the adoption of individual MTIs that are not in the same weapons category. A major problem with this approach, however, is the large number of possible MTIs a state could theoretically adopt. It would be difficult to claim with any reliability that any group of MTIs selected for such analysis encompasses all of the possible, or even significant, trade-offs a state could make regarding the acquisition of military technology. This is especially the case if one were comparing the major powers with smaller states. Among major powers, many items of military hardware are adopted (usually through indigenous development) which will never diffuse to other states, or will only diffuse to a select handful. However, collecting and using data on a large number of MTIs that represent, for example, all of the categories of major weapons systems listed in published order-of-battle and arms trade compilations could mitigate these concerns.

[9] Clearly, Table 5.3 shows that the diffusion rate for the early period is actually only slightly lower than for the late period (1.09 versus 1.19 new adopters per year). However, these figures must be seen in the light of several other factors. First, the late period is defined as encompassing adoptions which take place 24 or more years from the initial adoption. Second, the final periods for five of the fourteen MTIs extend longer than the eight years defined as the initial period for *all* MTIs. Finally, only a few of the MTIs have reached their diffusion saturation points. The result of all this is that although the rates for both early and late periods are similar in value, the total number of late period adopters is higher in absolute terms (total number of adopters per period = adoption rate x number of years in the period). We can thus conclude that arms diffusion is a relatively stratified process, as we would expect adopters in the late period to outnumber those in the early one.

[10] The years selected for comparison are the last years for which data on the newer generations are available.

[11] An interesting example of the dampening effect of the post-Cold War period could, however, be evident in what is *not* happening this case. During the mid and late1990s, there have been a spate of reports that the Russian third generation SA-10 missile would be exported to states as diverse as Hungary, Slovakia, Cyprus, Libya, Yugoslavia, Syria, Greece, Iran, and India. Problems and delays have affected all of these sales, thus depressing the number of adopters for that MTI. If these sales *had* taken place, however, when they were announced, the "jump" in the cumulative number of adopters apparent at around diffusion years 18–22 for Generation 2 systems would have been largely repeated among Generation 3 systems. It obviously remains to be seen, however, whether this will be the case.

[12] States which adopted no innovations are not depicted in the figure.

Chapter 6
Testing Models of Arms Diffusion

IN THE PREVIOUS CHAPTER, I DISCUSSED THE PHENOMENON OF ARMS DIFFU-sion using a number of different descriptive statistics. The discussion was useful in illuminating some of the basic patterns and trends in the global diffusion of arms over the last four decades, and allowed us to grapple with a few important questions concerning how fast and to whom arms diffuse. It did not, however, permit us to directly address propositions about why the rate of arms spread might differ over time derived from the five theoretical models detailed in Chapter 3. The purpose of the current chapter is to test the hypotheses derived from these five models, and thus to begin to gain better insight into what factors cause arms to spread at differing rates. In the next and final chapter of this study (Chapter 7), I will merge the results of this chapter's analysis with those discussed in Chapter 5, and discuss their combined implications for our understanding of the process of arms diffusion.

In order to test these hypotheses from Chapter 3 in a systematic fashion, we must divide the five models described in that chapter into two groups. Models 1 through 4 (realpolitik, exporting militarism, and domestic political and economic factors) make up the first group. Chapter 3 casts these first four models as conceptualizing the diffusion of arms from the perspective of the international system. In each model, the dependent variable is thus some variation of the cumulative adopter function discussed in Chapter 5, i.e. the cumulative number of adopters of a given military technological innovation (MTI) in a single year. As a result, we can analyze these four models using similar methods. The fifth model (the technological imperative) stands alone in a second group. Unlike the first four models, Model 5 argues that features of specific MTIs themselves will result in differing rates of spread. This shift in the unit of analysis requires use of a different method for investigating the hypotheses derived from Model 5. As a result, it will be discussed separately, in the final section of this chapter.

THE DIFFUSION TERM IN MODELS 1–4

As described in Chapter 3, I used theoretical Models 1 through 4 to generate nine separate hypotheses about what factors might cause variance in the rate of global arms diffusion over time. The most straightforward method of testing these hypotheses is to employ OLS (ordinary least squares) regression analysis, using some measure of the rate of arms diffusion (to be determined shortly) as a dependent variable. Because the dependent variable tracks a single phenomenon at different points in time, the method I employ is actually time series regression analysis, also referred to as transfer function analysis (Kendall and Ord 1990).

Endogenous and Exogenous Terms. As indicated in Chapter 5, we have reason to believe that both endogenous factors (i.e. those related to the interactive process of diffusion) and exogenous factors (i.e. those related to factors outside the process of communication between adopters and non-adopters) have some impact on the rates of arms diffusion. As a result, the independent variables in the regression should include both a "diffusion term" which captures the impact of this endogenous communicative process, and any of a number of other variables related directly to the nine hypotheses. From the mathematical perspective, the diffusion term(s) should be expected to capture the overall S-shape of the diffusion curve, while the other independent variables will capture any variation from the curve's expected S-shape due to the impact of other independent factors. From the conceptual perspective, the diffusion term(s) incorporate into the model the idea that there is an "underlying" rate of diffusion which can be "disturbed" by other exogenous factors, such as, for example, the occurance of civil wars or militarized interstate disputes. If, for example, the number of civil wars in the international system increases by five in one year, it can be expected to decrease the rate of arms diffusion by a certain number of adopters per year (probably after some lag). This "certain number," however, would be lower if the wars occurred in the early adoption phase of the innovation's diffusion as opposed to the mid-range phase, because of the difference in the underlying rate of adoption at those two points in time. Use of a diffusion term helps to get around the problem of arguing that a stochastic independent variable has different degrees of impact at different points in time, while still allowing for the use of basic OLS regression methods, which assumes an identical impact at all time points.

Deriving the Diffusion Term. Our first task is to generate a diffusion term which plausibly describes the arms diffusion curves shown in Chapter 5. Diffusion of innovations research, particularly as conducted by economists, has derived a number of highly complex mathematical forms to describe certain specific diffusion patterns (Mahajan and Peterson 1985). The originators of these complex functions, however, tend often to focus their aims on curve fitting rather than hypothesis testing, leaving many of their models of questionable value to this study. Instead of employing these complex logarithmic and/or differential equations, I have generated a simpler function similar to that described by Gray (1973) to model the diffusion of policy innovations among the American states. This function's analytical accuracy may be limited by its simplicity. However, the function is adequate enough to serve as the diffusion term in this study, and to at least provide a starting point for future research on arms diffusion processes.

Following Gray (1973), I derive the underlying diffusion process as follows. Let N_t be the number of adopters of an innovation at time t. Under conditions of pure diffusion (meaning that there are no exogenous forces acting on the diffusion process), the rate of innovation spread, ΔN_t, can be understood simply as some function of the current number of adopters. Thus:

Eq. 6.1: $$\Delta N_t = f(N_t)$$

where:

Eq. 6.2: $$\Delta N_t = N_{t+1} - N_t$$

When looking at the influence of diffusion in determining the spread of an innovation, it is clear that, in general, the greater the number of interactions between adopters and non-adopters, the faster the rate of diffusion, at least until the pool of potential adopters begins to be exhausted. To capture this phenomenon, we can consider N_t a function of the product of the numbers of pair relations between adopters and non-adopters. If b represents the *coefficient of diffusion* and M is the maximum possible number of adopters for an innovation, then:

Eq. 6.3: $$f(N_t) = b N_t (M - N_t)$$

Combining (6.1), (6.2), and (6.3), and decrementing the t index, we arrive at:

Eq. 6.4: $$N_t = N_{t-1} + b N_{t-1} (M - N_{t-1})$$

and finally:

Eq. 6.5: $N_t = (1 + bM) N_{t-1} - bN_{t-1}^2$

As Equation 6.4 shows, the cumulative number of adopters at time t depends upon the number existing adopters at time t-1, plus some portion (b) of the interaction between those existing adopters and remaining hold-outs $(M - N_{t-1})$. Letting $\beta_1 = 1 + bM$ and $\beta_2 = b$, we arrive at:

Eq. 6.6: $N_t = \beta_0 + \beta_1 N_{t-1} - \beta_2 N_{t-1}^2$

as the diffusion term, or diffusion terms, for our regression analysis. This expression is expected to capture the underlying S-shape of the arms diffusion curves, and allows us to carry out direct testing of the hypotheses derived from Models 1 through 4.

INDEPENDENT VARIABLES FOR MODELS 1–4

In testing each of the first four models, I employed a total of ten independent variables, one for each hypothesis plus an additional variable (described below). The operationalization of each variable is detailed in the paragraphs that follow. For each variable, I collected data for the 1960 to 1992 period, although some of the sources contain data for longer periods.

Military Conflict Frequency (Model 1). The level of interstate military conflict, WARINT, in the international system is measured by the number of interstate wars which occur in a given year. Data on this measure is derived from the Correlates of War (COW) war data base (Singer and Small 1994) by using the wars and their years of occurance listed in the data guide to compute figures for each calender year. An interstate military conflict is entered into the COW data base if it results in more than 1,000 battle deaths. This data is available from COW for the years 1816 to 1992.

Militarized Interstate Disputes (Model 1). The annual number of militarized interstate disputes, MIDS, in the international system was taken from the MIDs data set Version 2.10 described by Jones, Bremer, and Singer (1996), and maintained on the World Wide Web site of the Peace Science Society (International) at http://pss.la.psu.edu/. The original data set lists the number of MIDs for each calender year from 1816 to 1992.

Hegemony (Model 1). The level of U.S. hegemony in the international system, HEGLEV, in each calender year is also taken from the COW data set. COW's CINC (Composite Index of National Capabilities) variable captures well the multi-dimensional nature of hegemonic power. CINC includes a half dozen demographic, industrial, and military measures of national power to generate a single CINC score for a given country in a given calender year (Singer, Bremer, and Stuckey 1972). HEGLEV encompasses the U.S. share of CINC relative to the other great powers, the latter defined as the U.S., United Kingdom, USSR, France, China, and Germany and Japan (both of the last two only since 1991). Again, COW data spans the era from 1816 to 1992.

Core State GDP (Model 2). GDPCORE represents the sum of the GDP of the five core arms producing nations (the U.S., USSR, Great Britain, France, and China) in a given calender year. This figure was derived from Madisson's (1995) national GDP data base for 58 world states, including all major states, for the years 1820 to 1994. The GDP figures are in millions of constant Geary-Khamis dollars (base-year 1990), and are derived from purchasing power parity values. The data set for this study contains a single yearly value for each calender year from 1960 to 1992.

Core State Military Spending (Model 2). MILCORE represents the sum of the military expenditures of the five core arms producing nations in a given calender year. These annual figures are derived from two sources. Military expenditure data from 1960 to 1962 for each of the five core states were taken from the *SIPRI Yearbook of World Armaments and Disarmament 1968/69*, which tallies world and country-by-country figures on military expenditure from 1948 through 1968. These were then summed to create a single MILCORE figure for each calender year. Military expenditure data for the period after 1963 were taken from various annual editions of the (now-defunct) U.S. Arms Control and Disarmament Agency's *World Military Expenditure and Arms Transfers* (WMEAT) and summed. The WMEAT figures are in constant U.S. dollars, but the base dollar year changes from volume to volume. Similarly, the SIPRI figures are in constant dollars, but in a year different from those of most WMEAT figures. I thus used yearly GDP deflators taken from the World Bank's *World Development Indicators 1998* CD-ROM data set for each of the years in question to express all WMEAT and SIPRI figures in millions of constant 1982 U.S. dollars.

Democracy (Model 3). The level of democracy in the international system, DEMOS, is measured by the number of democratic states in a given year. I use the Polity III data set (Jaggers and Gurr 1995) to determine whether or not a state is a democracy. Following Gleditsch and Hegre (1997), I define a democratic state as one where the difference between the Polity III democracy and autocracy scores (DEMOC-AUTOC) is 3 or higher. After calculating this figure for each state in the data set for each year, I simply counted the number of states which met the DEMOC-AUTOC condition for each calender year. Polity III data covers the period from 1800 to 1994.

Civil Conflict (Model 3). Civil conflict, WARCIV, is measured by the number of civil wars taking place in a given year. I generated this measure

from the COW war data set in identical fashion to the measure for interstate wars, counting the number of ongoing civil wars in each calender year
for the 1960–1992 period.

World GDP (Model 4). GDPWLD is calculated from the Madisson
(1995) data set used to generate the core state GDP figures. I computed the
sum of all the national GDP figures for each calender year, entered in millions of constant 1990 dollars. Note that this data set only includes GDP
figures for 58 state of the international system, and thus the sums generated are not actual world GDP figures. Nevertheless, Madisson includes all
of the industrialized countries in his data set, plus the larger developing
world states and numerous smaller developing states. I thus argue that the
figures derived from this data set provide a very good indication of the
magnitude and direction of change in world GDP, and are valid for use in
this study.

World Military Spending (Model 4). MILWLD measures the total
world milex in millions of 1982 U.S. dollars for each calender year. MIL-
WLD data for the 1960 to 1992 period were derived in exactly the same
fashion as the MILCORE data. The WMEAT and SIPRI sources cited
above both report a single yearly figure for world milex. This figure was
standardized using the World Bank GDP deflators for the appropriate
years.

Cold War. In Chapter 5, I discussed the possible impact of the end of
the Cold War on the global arms diffusion process. In order to more systematically test this impact, it is also useful to include a COLDWAR
dummy variable in this section of the analysis. COLDWAR = 1 during the
period 1960 to 1988, and 0 from 1989–1992. Some might argue that the
Cold War did not really come to an end until the collapse of the Soviet
Union in 1991. However, for the purposes of this study, I consider the end
to have come in 1989 with the collapse of the various communist regimes
in Eastern Europe. These events signaled the de facto end of the organized
Warsaw Pact threat to Western Europe, and the choice of 1989 also allows
us to test for the Cold War's impact over more than one calender year, as
would be the case if we used 1991 as the date of that conflict's termination.

TESTING MODELS 1–4

My testing of the first four theoretical models went through three stages.
In the first stage, I used OLS regression analysis to examine the relationships between the time series of individual military innovations and individual independent variables, including the diffusion term. In the second, I
used multiple regression to test the relationships between the time series of
individual innovations and all of the independent variables simultaneously,
also including the diffusion term. Third and last, I pooled the data on all

of the military innovations and regressed this upon all the independent variables and the diffusion term. The details and justification for each of these steps is described in the following paragraphs.

Stage 1: Regression Using Individual Independent Variables. Before launching into a full-scale multiple regression, my initial goal was simply to get a general sense of two things: how the independent variables behaved in "bivariate" (excluding the diffusion term) regression analyses of the dependent variable and what the possible lag structure of any potential relationships were like. First, I wanted to see whether there were any clear, strong relationships between any of the independent variables and the rate of arms diffusion in isolation from the influence of other independent variables. These relationships might be of interest in and of themselves, even if they disappeared in the multiple regression stages of the analysis. Second, I needed some systematic way of deciding what lag structure to include in later phases of the analysis. There is a clear, real-world time delay between the decision to build or purchase military equipment and when that equipment is finally deployed. As a result, there is every reason to assume that the effect of independent political and economic variables on the dependent variable of arms diffusion will be lagged by one or more years. This factor needed to be built into the regression analysis.

I chose six of the MTIs with longer time series (Generation 3 and 4 combat aircraft, Generation 2 and 3 main battle tanks, Generation 2 long-range SAMs, and Generation 1 PADS), and, using the statistical analysis program SPSS 8.0 for Windows, regressed each of these upon each of nine independent variables separately (thus excluding the Cold War variable) at one, two, and three lags of the independent variable. For each, I included the two-part diffusion term derived in the opening section of this chapter. Hence, strictly speaking, each equation saw the dependent variable $NUMADOPT_N$ (the cumulative number of adopters of innovation N at time period t) regressed on three independent variables (the two diffusion terms and the independent variable to be tested), with four beta coefficients to be estimated. The equations were thus of the form:

Eq. 6.7: $NUMADOPT_N = $ [diffusion terms] + [exogenous variables]

or, more specifically:

Eq. 6.8: $NUMADOPT_N = \beta_0 + [\beta_1 \ NUMADOPT_{t-1} - \beta_2(NUMADOPT_{t-1})^2]$
$+ \beta_3 \ [X_n] + e_t$

where β_0 is the intercept, β_1 through β_3 are the coefficients to be estimated, e_t is a random error term, and X_n is each of the following nine variables in succeeding regression runs:

WARINT   = number of interstate wars in year t
MIDS   = number of MIDS in year t
HEGLEV   = level of U.S. hegemony in year t
GDPCORE   = total military expediture of five core states in year t
MILCORE   = total economic growth of five core states in year t
WARCIV   = number of civil wars in year t
DEMOS   = number of democracies in year t
GDPWLD   = total economic growth of world GNP in year t
MILWLD   = total military expenditure of world in year t
COLDWAR   = Cold War dummy variable (1= Cold War, 0 = no Cold War)

Most, though by no means all, arms diffusion takes place through arms transfers. I thus made the decision to test at one, two, and three lags for each variable based upon a general sense of how long it takes arms transfers to be conducted from the time of initial order to the time of delivery and deployment. For example, if a war breaks out in a given year, it is very likely that arms purchased as a result of that war (and here I mean MTIs, i.e. "new" weapons systems never before operated by that country) will arrive within less than a year to two years afterward. I have already established in Chapter 4 that for arms-purchasing countries, I have, in the absence of contradictory evidence, coded the deployment year of a given weapons system as the year after delivery. Thus, the one, two, and three year lag time appears a sensible period in which to investigate the relationship between arms diffusion and these other exogenous variables.

I separately regressed each of the six selected MTIs on each of nine independent variables, plus the diffusion terms, at lags of one, two, and three years. The results of these 162 tests provided only a few insights into the arms diffusion process. First, in most cases, the diffusion terms were statistically significant at the 95% level ($p \leq .05$, two-tailed). In a sense, this is unsurprising. It is logical to assume that, for example, in a cumulative adopter function, the best predictor of the number of adopters at time t will be the number of adopters at time t-1. In conjunction with the recurring (although not universal) significance of the second term (NUMADOPT_{t-1}^2, however, this fact indicates that the diffusion dynamic, as described by the equation derived earlier in this chapter, does a reasonably good job of describing the underlying diffusion process.

Second, while there were a number of significant relationships between independent variables and individual MTI diffusion rates, there were few discernable patterns among these relationships. Four of the six MTIs had statistically significant ($p \leq .05$, two-tailed) relationships with at least one of the independent variables at at least one of the lags. A few other independent variables approached ($p \leq .10$, two-tailed), but did not reach the 95% level of significance. No less than six of the nine independent variables were significantly related to at least one of the dependent variables.

However, only DEMOS, the number of democracies, had a significant relationship (and of approximately the same magnitude) with the diffusion rate more than one innovation (third generation combat aircraft (lag 3) and third generation tanks (lag 2)). HEGLEV, the level of U.S. hegemony, also came close to the 95% significance level in two cases (Generation 1 shoulder-fired SAMs (lag 2) and Generation 3 aircraft (lag 3)) and was significant in a third (Generation 2 long-range SAMs (lags 2 and 3)). In addition, the negative sign of the ß for both the number of democracies and the level of hegemony in all significant or almost significant cases indicated a relationship in the expected direction.[1] Nonetheless, no single variable emerged as a strong, unambiguous causal factor for arms diffusion across many or all of the innovations. And there is no reason to assume that, had different innovations been chosen from the data set, the patterns (or lack thereof) would substantially differ.

Finally, the most important result of this phase of the study was my decision to restrict the further stages of analysis to use of the third lag of the independent variables. In fully 42.6% (23 of 54) variable groupings (that is, groups of three lags for each of nine variables run for each of six MTIs), the third lag demonstrated the highest p-value for significance of any of the three lags. The respective figures for lags 1 and 2 are 29.6% (16) and 27.8% (15). In addition, 46% (6 of 13) of the independent variables that were significant at the .05 level occurred at the third lag, compared to only 15.4% (2) at the first lag and 38.5% (5) at the second. The general impression we get from looking at this data is that the higher its lag, the better job the independent variable does at predicting the rate of arms diffusion. This suggests that use of third lags of the independent variables for the next stages of this study should provide the greatest likelihood of finding significant relationships among our variables.

Stage 2: Multiple Regressions on Individual Innovations. Stage 1 provided us with useful information about the possible lag structure of the relationships between the dependent and independent variables, but little else in the way of hard evidence directed at accepting or rejecting our main theoretical hypotheses. This was acceptable, as I envisioned the first stage as solely a first cut at the data, and not the final word. The next logical step was to test the impact of all of the independent variables simultaneously on each MTI adopter function using multiple regression. The relationships uncovered in bivariate regression testing of the type in the previous section (which, again, were not strictly bivariate, given the presence of the diffusion terms) may fall apart or disappear once additional independent variables are entered into the equation. Multiple regression should thus provide a more comprehensive look at the relative predictive ability of all the independent variables in the presence of one another in the equation.

I restricted this analysis to eleven of the fourteen innovations in the data set, excluding second generation attack helicopters and the first generations of anti-tank missiles and long-range SAMs. In the latter two cases, data were incomplete for the early years of adoption. For the attack helicopters, the time series was too short, beginning only in 1986 and ending in 1992. Running the regression was impossible under such circumstances, because the number of independent variables would have been greater than the number of observations. Once again, I used the cumulative number of adopters, $NUMADOPT_N$, as the regressand in each run, and the nine independent variables plus the Cold War dummy variable as the regressors. As discussed in the previous subsection, each of the regressors were lagged three years, in order to capture the delayed effects of their impact. Once again, as previously stated in (6.7), the regressions were of the form :

Eq. 6.7: $NUMADOPT_N$ = [interactive diffusion term] + [exogenous variables]

for each of the eleven innovations. Unlike before, however, the regressions in this specific case were run as follows:

Eq. 6.9: $NUMADOPT_N = \beta_0 + [\beta_1\ NUMADOPT_{t-1} - \beta_2(NUMADOPT_{t-1})^2] +$
$$[\beta_3\ WARINT_{t-3} + \beta_4\ MIDS_{t-3} + \beta_5\ HEGLEV_{t-3} +$$
$$\beta_6\ GDPCORE_{t-3} + \beta_7\ MILCORE_{t-3} +$$
$$\beta_8 WARCIV_{t-3} + \beta_9 DEMOS_{t-3} +$$
$$\beta_{10}GDPWLD_{t-3} + \beta_{11}MILWLD_{t-3} + \beta_{12}COLDWAR] + e_t$$

with β_0 being the intercept, β_1 through β_{12} being the regression coefficients for their respective interactive terms and independent variables, e_t being a random error term, and the independent variables being the same as those on the list described in the previous subsection.

Before running this first complete model, I tested for the presence of multicollinearity among the nine independent variables by generating a bivariate matrix correlating each variable with every other variable. Although OLS regression is impossible only in situations of perfect $r = 1.0$) multicollinearity between independent variables, a high level of correlation can also create numerous problems for confidence interval interpretation (Gujarati 1995, 327). I decided as a rule of thumb to define $r \geq .7$ as "high" collinearity between two variables; in such cases about half the variance in one variable ($r^2 \geq .5$) is accounted for by variance in the other.

The matrix revealed that the four economic variables (core state GDP, core state military expenditure, world GDP, and world military expenditure) were all extremely significantly related, with r's ranging from .846 to .997 (and $p \leq .01$ in all four cases, two- tailed). Two of these (world GDP and core GDP) were also highly and significantly correlated (.714 and

.701) with the number of democracies. Upon reflection, this is perhaps unsurprising. Since the five core nations (the U.S., USSR, Britain, France, and China) make up a large percentage of the world economy, it makes sense that the direction of the world economy as a whole is highly correlated with the direction of their economies as a group. Further, since these variables are all cumulative totals with little negative fluctuation over the period under consideration, this correlation is enhanced by their simultaneous general upward trend.

Since this multicollinearity could cause serious errors in interpreting my regression results, I took two steps to deal with the problem. First, although all the economic time series may experience a simultaneous general upward trend, there is no *a priori* reason to assume that the fluctuations in that trend are collinear, particularly in relation to the noneconomic variable DEMOS, the number of democracies. I thus de-trended the four economic time series by taking the first difference of each, i.e. replacing world GDP at time *t* with the difference of world GDP at *t* and world GDP at *t* - 1, and so on. This had the effect of eliminating the high multicollinearity between the number of democracies and the four economic variables, and between the world and core state military expenditure and GDP figures. However, for the reasons cited in the previous paragraph, the high correlations between the two military variables and the two GDP variables remained. The second step I took was therefore to eliminate one of each pair of variables from the regression equation. This unfortunate but necessary step eliminates the possibility of directly testing two of the hypotheses in two different theoretical models. In order to test at least one hypothesis from each model (i.e. to avoid throwing out an entire model), however, I left core state military spending and world GDP (MILCORE and GDPWLD) in the equation. In order to test the hypotheses related to the omitted variables, some means would have to be devised to generate measures which capture the theoretical essence of their models without using core state GDP or world military spending as proxy variables. At this point, this is a task best left to future research.

The reformed regression equations thus look as follows:

Eq. 6.10; $\text{NUMADOPT}_N = \beta_0 + [\beta_1 \text{ NUMADOPT}_{t-1} - \beta_2(\text{NUMADOPT}_{t-1})^2] + [\beta_3\text{WARINT}_{t-3} + \beta_4 \text{ MIDS}_{t-3} + \beta_5 \text{ HEGLEV}_{t-3} + \beta_6\text{MILCORE}_{t-3} + \beta_7\text{WARCIV}_{t-3} + \beta_8\text{DEMOS}_{t-3} + \beta_9\text{GDPWLD}_{t-3} + \beta_{10}\text{COLDWAR}] + e_t$

The results of running this regression for each of the reduced set of eleven MTIs can be found in Table 6.1. Clearly, the results are underwhelming. The only variables significant at the .05 level are seven of the eleven first lag interactive terms, plus the number of democracies on one of the innovations (MTI #14, second generation anti-tank missiles). Not even the second part of the interactive term (NUMADOPT$_{t-1}^2$) is significant at the 95% level for any of the MTIs, although it makes the 90% level on two occasions. A handful of other variables register significance at either the .10 level or slightly above, but the results are hardly robust. There is also little consistency in even the signs of the coefficients, with, for example, six of the hegemony level coefficients being negative and five positive.

There are three ways to interpret this situation. First, the results may be accurate, and none of the variables used in the regression are significantly related to arms diffusion. Second, the model itself may be misspecified in any of a number of ways. The underlying diffusion term(s) may be an inadequate representation of the diffusion patterns found in the MTIs in the data set. The independent variables themselves may be inadequately capturing the theoretical concepts described by the models. Errors may also have crept into the data gathering and coding process. Or additional factors critical to the course of arms diffusion have been incorrectly omitted from the selection of independent variables used in the regression. A third possibility is that problems related to both the autoregressive nature of the diffusion process and the rather short time series in question are generating spurious results.

Although I have already corrected the equation for multicollinearity, autocorrelation and heteroskedasticity are still potential problems with second set of analyses. Scatterplots of the residuals of several of the regression equations versus the dependent variable indicate no glaring heteroskedastic effects. Autoregression, however, is a natural problem here stemming from the inclusion of a lagged dependent variable (i.e. the interactive term) on the regressor side of the equation. It would be possible to test and correct for suspected autocorrelation on an equation by equation basis. But another potential problem with these individual series is their limited duration. The longest series has no more that 33 data points, while the number of regressors is 10 in all cases. Some of the shorter series have just over a dozen observations. While it is possible to run regressions on such small data sets (Url and Wörgötter 1995), the results are often not very robust and the effects of sampling error magnified. The intellectual rewards for diagnosing and correcting for autocorrelation in each of these shorter series may therefore be extremely limited. As a result, I resort to pooled analysis of multiple MTIs, as described in the following section.

Stage 3: Multiple Regression Using All Innovations Simultaneously. In these eleven regression equations, the significance levels of most of the beta coefficients were extremely low, the time series were all of short duration, and there was a relatively high number of independent variables compared to the number of observations for each series. In the previous subsection, I also demonstrated our inability to detect strongly significant individual relationships between each of the independent variables and the dependent variable. All of this leads one to believe that, even if there are important links between these independent variables and the arms diffusion process, statistical difficulties stemming from the nature of the data may be preventing them from becoming apparent.

One possible solution to this problem is to pool the data and regress all eleven time series simultaneously on all of the independent variables and the interactive term. This technique dramatically expands the number of observations or time points upon which the regression results depend. Results derived from such a regression are potentially more robust and reliable and less vulnerable to sampling error. It also reduces the problem of applying statistical diagnostics and correctives to a more manageable level by allowing us to work with a single equation rather than eleven separate ones.

Once again, I used an equation of the form:

$$\text{Eq. 6.11: } NUMADOPT_{ALL} = \beta_0 + [\beta_1\,NUMADOPT_{t-1} - \beta_2(NUMADOPT_{t-1})^2]$$
$$+ [\beta_3 WARINT_{t-3} + \beta_4\,MIDS_{t-3} + \beta_5\,HEGLEV_{t-3} + \beta_6$$
$$MILCORE_{t-3} + \beta_7 WARCIV_{t-3} + \beta_8 DEMOS_{t-3} +$$
$$\beta_9 GDPWLD_{t-3} + \beta_{10} COLDWAR] + e_t$$

where $NUMADOPT_{ALL}$ is the pooled data set of cumulative adopter functions for all eleven military innovations for the 1960 to 1992 period, and all the other variables are defined as before (i.e. lag 3 values). The pooling of the eleven MTIs yields a total of 247 data points to use in the regression, dramatically expanding the extent of the data and thus potentially the validity of the statistical results.

I ran the regression once, and, because of the findings of my previous analyses, tested the results for both autocorrelation and heteroskedasticity. A scatterplot of the squared residuals versus the dependent variable revealed no substantial heteroskedasticity. I then used the Durbin-Watson *d*-statistic to calculate the Durbin *h*-statistic. Durbin's *h* is appropriate for detecting the existence of autocorrelation in regressions involving the use of one or more lagged values of the dependent variable as predictor (independent) variables in large-sample regressions (Gujarati 1985, 605).[2] The initial regression yielded an $h = 3.72$, where $-1.96 \leq h \leq 1.96$ is necessary in order to reject the null hypothesis of no autocorrelation. This indicates that, as suspected, autocorrelation was indeed a problem in this regression.

There are a number of different possible ways to solve an autocorrelation problem. One method is to assume that the autocorrelation results from an inadequate specification of the autoregressive (interactive) term in the model. This causes variance linked to structural trends in the dependent variable to be picked up by the error term, and hence produces autocorrelation. As I noted earlier in this chapter, the interactive terms suggested by Gray's (1973) research which I have used should only be considered an initial try at estimating the influence of adopter-nonadopter interaction in the arms diffusion process. These terms, however, may not be the "best" fit for describing that diffusion process.

One straightforward and common way of coming to terms with an autocorrelation problem in a first order autoregressive model of the type found here is simply to insert an additional lag of the dependent variable (in this case, $NUMADOPT_{t-2}$) into the regression calculations. The regression thus assumes the form:

Eq. 6.12: $NUMADOPT_N = \beta_0 + [\beta_1 \, NUMADOPT_{t-1} - \beta_2(NUMADOPT_{t-1})^2 + \beta_3 \, NUMADOPT_{t-2}]] + [\beta_4 WARINT_{t-3} + \beta_5 \, MIDS_{t-3} + \beta_6 \, HEGLEV_{t-3} + \beta_7 \, MILCORE_{t-3} + \beta_8 WARCIV_{t-3} + \beta_9 DEMOS_{t-3} + \beta_{10} \, GDPWLD_{t-3} + \beta_{11} COLDWAR] + e_t$

where all variables are defined as before, but the coefficients are renumbered to reflect inclusion of the new independent variable.

Insertion of this new variable assumes that the first lag autoregressive term ($NUMADOPT_{t-1}$) has failed to "absorb" or register all of the variation being caused by the interactive process. As indicated above, inclusion of another term is necessary to do so. There is no *a priori* theoretical reason to assume that $ß_1 \, NUMADOPT_{t-2}$ will necessarily remove the autocorrelated errors. However, from a statistical perspective, it often serves this purpose. From the theoretical perspective, we can explain the success of this technique by simply noting that the initial diffusion model was inadequate, did not capture the full range of variance in the dependent variable, and that additions were necessary in order to increase its fit.[3]

The results of running Equation 6.12 were very successful, as shown in Table 6.2. The Durbin *h*-statistic for Equation 6.12 is -1.03, well within the interval used accept the null hypothesis of no autocorrelation. Again, a scatterplot of the $NUMADOPT_{ALL}$ versus the squared residuals of the regression indicates no serious heteroskedasticity. All three of the diffusion terms are significant at the 99% level ($p \leq .001$), and no less than three of the independent variables–the number of democracies, world GDP, and the Cold War dummy variable–are significant at the .05 level or better. A fourth independent variable, the number of interstate wars, also approaches the 95% significance level, with $p = .075$. However, only the sign of the number of democracies is in the expected direction, showing a negative relationship between the number of democracies in the world and the level of arms diffusion. The negative relationship between the change in world GDP and arms diffusion is opposite of that expected by Model 4, and I developed no specific expectations for the impact of the Cold War on the spread of arms. The negative sign on the almost-significant number of interstate wars is also opposite of the theoretical expectation of Model 1.

Interpretation of Results and Models. The results from this final pooled regression allow us to make a number of judgements about the validity of Models 1–4. First, the results clearly do not support the hypotheses derived from the first model, Realpolitik. There is no apparent statistical relationship between either the level of U.S. hegemony or the number of militarized interstate disputes (MIDs) and the rate of arms diffusion. There may be a connection between the frequency of interstate war and the spread of arms. If so, however, wars actually *depress* the rate at which arms subsequently spread. One possible explanation for this might be that most states engage in more risky military innovation in peacetime, but spend their efforts and their budgets on personnel, ammunition, or the procurement of proven systems during wartime. In any event, the support for any relationship between interstate war and military innovation from the results of this study is limited at best.

The testing of Model 2, exporting militarism, was constrained by the need to omit one of the explanatory variables, GDPCORE, the change in total GDP of the five core arms producing states, in order to solve the multicollinearity problem. But the remaining variable, MILCORE, the total military spending of the five core states, also failed to turn up significant in the final analysis. As a result, there is little support for Model 2 in the above findings.

Model 3, domestic political factors, gained support from the very strong significance of DEMOS, the number of democracies in the international system in a given year. This variable was significant at the 99% level (p = .001), and related to the rate of arms diffusion with a ß coefficient of -.296. The steady increase in the level of global democratization thus appears to have played a significant role in reducing the overall rate of diffusion of newer generation of arms, as described in Chapter 5. Unfortunately, the same cannot be said for an increase in WARCIV, the number of civil wars in a given year, which apparently has little independent influence on the rate of arms spread.

Model 4, domestic economic factors, suffered from the same problem as Model 2, caused by the need to omit one of the two variables (world military expenditure) derived from the model's hypotheses. The remaining variable, world GDP, did prove significantly related to the rate of arms diffusion, with p = .004. However, the negative sign on the ß coefficient indicates a relationship opposite to that expected by the model. It seems that the increasing world GDP, despite freeing up additional resources for military spending, has actually resulted in a decrease in overall arms diffusion. This contrary finding might result from a redoubled emphasis during prosperous times on commerce and other economic pursuits rather than war and weaponry. This interpretation would also tie directly into the results of testing Model 3, above. In a sense, democracy, prosperity, and a reduction in arms diffusion are tied together statistically, in a manner suggested by democratic peace, liberal cooperation, and other such scholars over the years.

Finally, the Cold War dummy variable also proved surprisingly significant and negatively related to arms diffusion. This indicates that, contrary to my observations derived from the descriptive data in the previous chapter, the end of the Cold War has indeed had a role in increasing arms diffusion rates during the 1990s. With the Cold War's ß = -1.792, we can see that the Cold War's end has resulted in almost two additional new adopters of military innovations per year than would otherwise be expected from past patterns.

TESTING MODEL 5

Model 5, the technological imperative, argues that specific features of military innovations themselves have an important influence on the rate at which these innovations diffuse. The three critical features examined in Chapter 3's discussion of Model 5 were a weapon's combat effectiveness, cost, and two different production features. I will examine the validity of these hypotheses individually in the paragraphs that follow.

Combat Effectiveness. Model 5 argues that innovations with greater combat effectiveness when compared to other existing weapons should spread more rapidly that those with lesser combat effectiveness. Arguing that first generation MTIs (i.e. categorical-level innovations) yield a greater comparative level of combat effectiveness on the battlefield than MTIs of subsequent generations, I predicted in Chapter 3 that first generation systems should spread more rapidly than those of later generations.

Table 6.3 lists the average number of adopters of each innovation of a given generation in each of the three diffusion periods discussed in the previous chapter. (These periods are in "diffusion years," i.e. the number of years since an innovations initial adoption). If the combat effectiveness hypothesis were true, we would expect to find first generation innovations with substantially higher average numbers of adopters across all three periods covered in the table. Unfortunately, the data provides only limited confirmation of the expected pattern. First generation MTIs do spread faster in all diffusion periods than second generation ones, but this pattern breaks down in the third and fourth generations. The data are somewhat skewed by the very limited number of third and fourth generation MTIs in the data set (two and one, respectively), a situation which creates a quite restricted empirical basis from which to reach any firm conclusions. Unfortunately, without gathering further data, it is impossible to judge whether the upswing in diffusion rates of third and fourth generation systems stems from the identities of the specific third and fourth generation MTIs in this data set, or whether it is a broader pattern. On the positive side, the two generations for which we have the most extensive (and thus most broadly generalizeable) data do support this first hypothesis of Model 5.

Cost. The second hypothesis of Model 5 argues, simply enough, that military innovations which cost less are likely to spread more rapidly than those that cost more. Addressing this issue is complicated by the fact that specific cost data for weapons systems varies widely according to manufacturer, producing state, and a myriad of other factors, and reliable cost data is generally not available for most weapons systems. One possible way of overcoming this problem, however, is to classify weapons systems of roughly equal cost into broad cost categories, and then to examine our empirical data to see to what extent these categories are related to actual diffusion rates.

Table 6.4 shows the rate of diffusion for all fourteen military innovations in each of the three segments of the diffusion process, with the innovations ranked from highest diffusion rate to lowest diffusion rate in each period. We can compare the rankings in each of the columns with a hypothetical "ideal column," a list of MTIs ordered according to their cost. To facilitate this, I simply class each of the MTIs in the data set into one of three categories: high cost (aircraft and long-range SAMs), moderate cost (tanks, attack helicopters, and point-defense SAMs), and low-cost (anti tank missiles and shoulder-fired SAMs). I further establish the rule that, since cost typically increases with each succeeding generation of arms, later generations of MTIs should always rank higher (i.e. diffuse faster) than earlier generations in the cost list. We can thus generate two figures for each of the three columns of MTIs: the percentage of MTIs which are in the "right" rank according to their cost category (for example, PADS and ATGMs should always occupy the first four ranks in each column because they are in the low-cost category), and the percentage of generational comparisons which are in the proper order (i.e. the percentage of cases in which earlier generations rank higher than later ones).

As with the combat effectiveness variable, the expectation that cost is highly correlated with diffusion rate is only partially and weakly borne out by the data. The percentage of MTIs which fall into the rank expected if cost was a critical factor in determining diffusion rates is 41.6% for the initial period, 50% for the middle period, and only 30% for the late period. Thus, in two out of the three cases, from 60–70% of the MTIs were *not* in the order that they would be if cost was the critical factor. The situation regarding the diffusion rates of succeeding generations is somewhat better. In the initial period, 80% of the earlier generations diffuse faster than the later ones, these figures falling to 71.4% and 33% in the middle and late periods, respectively. Along both the rank and generation dimensions then, there is only moderate support for the argument that weapons system cost has greatly influenced the rate of arms diffusion in the period in question.

The U.S.-Soviet Divide. A third factor included under the technological imperative model as influencing the rate of arms diffusion is the gap between the U.S. and Soviet adoption dates of a given MTI. If the gap between these two adoption dates was longer, then diffusion was expected to be relatively slow. In order to test this hypothesis, I simply calculated that gap in time between the U.S. and Soviet adoptions of a given MTI determined the correlation (r) between these values and the diffusion rates of each MTI in each of the three adoption periods, the latter as defined in Table 6.4.

The results of this correlation did not provide strong support for the hypothesis. For none of the three time periods was the gap in U.S.-Soviet adoption dates significantly correlated with the MTI's diffusion rate at the .05 level. However, the correlation for the early period did approach the standard significance level, with p = .085 (with 12 cases). In the latter case, $r = -.518$, indicating that, as expected, as the duration of the gap went up, the diffusion rate went down. Nonetheless, the pattern detected here is not a strong one, and thus I reject this hypothesis as false.

Diversity of Innovations. The final hypothesis in the technological imperative model argues that the larger the number of different weapons systems that make up a generational grouping, the higher the rate of diffusion of that grouping. I tested this hypothesis in the same manner as the did the previous one, by correlating the number of different systems in each generation with the diffusion rates of each of the three periods shown in Table 6.4.

The results provided moderately strong support for the hypothesis. The number of different systems in a generation was strongly and significantly correlated (p = .018, $r = .621$, n = 14) with MTIs in their middle diffusion period, and almost significantly correlated with those in the early period (p = .066, $r = .546$, n = 12). The r value for the late period stood apart from the other two periods in these terms, with p = .742, $r = -.120$, n = 10. Despite the latter results, of the four hypotheses derived from the technological imperative model, the data supports this one to the greatest degree.

SUMMARY OF FINDINGS

The empirical testing of the five theoretical models which seek to explain the rate of arms diffusion conducted in this chapter has produced a better understanding of the process of the global spread of arms. These findings can be narrowed down to three critical observations, as follows.

(1) First, because of the strong and continuing significance of the interactive diffusion term in both the individual regression models and the larger pooled regression, it clearly makes sense to look at the process of the global spread of arms as a diffusion process. However, the exact form of the function which best describes this process could benefit from further investigation, a task which remains for future research.

(2) Of the five theoretical models discussed in Chapter 3, elements of domestic political factors (Model 3), domestic economic factors (Model 4), and technological imperative (Model 5) did the best jobs at predicting the rate of global arms diffusion from 1960 to 1992. The analysis in this chapter has shown that increasing numbers of democracies, increases in the growth of global GDP, and the diversity of innovations within a given generational grouping are all positively related with increased rates of arms diffusion. A first interpretation of these results suggests that non-war domestic-level factors may be more important than international systemic factors, especially those related to conflict (i.e. interstate war), in spurring or limiting the diffusion of arms. There was no apparent relationship between the rate of arms diffusion and the level of U.S. hegemony, the number of militarized interstate disputes, the number of civil wars, and the change in the level of core state military spending. There is only weak evidence of a relationship between the cost and combat effectiveness of weapons and their rates of diffusion. Finally, there may be a negative relationship between the incidence of interstate war and higher rates of arms diffusion, which is opposite of that which I expected.

(3) A final observation is that the end of the Cold War has also had a significant impact on the rate of arms diffusion. Unfortunately, I cannot determine from the testing conducted here what aspect(s) of the Cold War and the changes of the late 1980s/early 1990s were most important in helping to increase the pace of arms spread after the collapse of communism in East/Central Europe and the former Soviet Union. It also remains to be seen if this pattern will hold up as the post Cold War era lengthens and if new data points were added to the end of the arms diffusion time series in the data set.

I will reserve a more thorough discussion of the significance of these findings for our understanding of arms diffusion in the 1960–92 period, plus what they and the findings in Chapter 5 suggest to us about the future of arms diffusion for the following, concluding chapter.

	1	2	3	5	6	8	9	10	11	12	14
Laginn	1.300	1.253	1.043	.819	8.085	.503	-.495	1.081	1.226	.951	1.217
	**.000	*.012	**.007	**.009	.079	.078	.370	**.002	**.000	.368	**.000
Laginnsq	-.004	.009	7.4e-04	.005	-1.078	.006	.082	1.5e-04	-.005	.012	.002
	.070	.213	.943	.431	.082	.164	.379	.980	.141	.507	.607
Interstate Wars	-.654	.529	-.575	-.064	1.564	.662	-.034	-.737	-.198	.462	-.412
	.068	.336	.138	.900	.124	.121	.644	.059	.631	.568	.398
MIDs	-.018	.035	.014	-.001	-.108	-.008	.048	-.014	-.015	.059	.002
	.677	.556	.740	.981	.129	.874	.112	.787	.802	.519	.968
Hegemony	-.334	.247	-.540	.085	.590	-.153	-.127	-.398	-.343	.614	.196
	.172	.611	.107	.810	.124	.621	.346	.302	.353	.505	.588
Democ.	-.196	-.617	-.103	-.745	1.108	-.203	.314	.242	.032	.785	-.948
	.447	.341	.686	.079	.111	.497	.389	.506	.911	.580	*.021
Civil War	.213	.648	-.299	-.136	.701	-.015	.112	-.536	.455	-1.225	.038
	.297	.324	.344	.728	.194	.951	.563	.185	.265	.501	.913
Core Mil. Spending	-1.6e-05	-5.7e-05	8.9e-06	2.1e-06	-4e-04	-6.5e-06	-4.0e-05	6.3e-06	-2.6e-05	4.4e-04	3.1e-5
	.439	.400	.763	.948	.095	.804	.393	.830	.357	.189	.348
World GDP	-4.3e-06	8.5e-07	-1.6e-06	2.2e-06	-7e-07	-4.4e-06	3.0e-06	-5.9e-C6	-6.7e-06	1.0e-05	5.3e-07
	.097	.802	.607	.576	.484	.177	.123	.091	.061	.216	.884
Cold War	-2.270	-3.728	-1.874	-2.279	-2.764	-2.754	-.282	.323	-1.278	2.436	-3.875
	.168	.158	.279	.338	.155	.162	.532	.855	.539	.602	.076
N	29	20	25	29	12	29	12	20	28	15	25

Note: Top figure is β value; bottom figure is significance (p) value. N = number of cases.
* significant at .05 level; ** significant at .01 level

Table 6.1: Regression of Cumulative Number of Adopters on Ten Independent Variables.

Independent Variables	Parameter Estimate (ß)	Standard Error	Significance (p)
Intercept	19.440	4.398	** .000
$NUMADOPT_{t-1}$	1.322	.059	** .000
$(NUMADOPT_{t-1})^2$	-7.797E-04	.000	** .001
$NUMADOPT_{t-2}$	-.257	.064	** .000
Interstate Wars	-.209	.117	.075
MIDs	4.695E-03	.015	.756
Hegemony	-7.854E-02	.082	.337
Core Military Spending	4.570E-06	.000	.653
Civil Wars	5.445E-02	.077	.477
Democracies	-.296	.087	** .001
World GDP	-3.093E-06	.000	** .004
Cold War	-1.711	.604	** .005

* = significant at the .05 level
** = significant at the .01 level

Table 6.2: Results of Pooled OLS Regression Analysis of the Diffusion of Eleven MTIs

| Average Number of Adopters Per Year | | | | |
MTI Generation	Cases	Initial Period (Diff. Years 1–8)	Middle Period (Diff. Years 9–23)	Late Period (Diff. Years 24+)
First	6	1.82	2.51	1.12
Second	5	1.06	2.50	.78
Third	2	3.63	2.29	1.30
Fourth	1	.50	2.87	2.33

Table 6.3: Testing the Technological Imperative I: Does Weapons Generation Matter?

Initial Period (1–8 yrs.)		Middle Period (9–23 yrs.)		Late Period (24+ yrs.)	
MTI	Adoptions/Yr.	MTI	Adoptions/Yr.	MTI	Adoptions/Yr.
G3 Aircraft	3.13	G1 PADS	4.33	G4 Aircraft	2.33
G2 LR SAM	2.13	G2 ATGM	3.93	G1 Helos	1.63
G2 PADS	1.63	G3 Aircraft	3.47	G2 MBTs	1.67
G1 PD SAM	1.50	G2 PADS	3.46	G1 PADS	1.36
G2 MBT	1.38	G1 ATGM	3.38	G3 Aircraft	1.30
G2 ATGM	.75	G4 Aircraft	2.87	G1 PD SAM	.83
G3 MBT	.55	G1 PD SAM	2.40	G2 LR SAM	.80
G4 Aircraft	.50	G2 MBT	2.33	G2 ATGM	.75
G3 LR SAM	.50	G2 LR SAM	2.20	G1 ATGM	.69
G1 PADS	.38	G1 Helos	1.73	G1 LR SAM	.56
G1 Helos	.38	G2 Helos	1.50	G2 Helos	n/a
G2 Helos	.25	G3 MBT	1.40	G3 MBTs	n/a
G1 LR SAM	n/a	G3 LR SAM	1.10	G3 LR SAMs	n/a
G1 ATGM	n/a	G1 LR SAM	.92	G2 PADS	n/a

Table 6.4: Testing the Technological Imperative II: Does Weapons Cost Matter?

NOTES

[1] Thus, the greater the number of democracies, the lower the rate of arms diffusion, and the greater the level of U.S. hegemony, the lower the rate of arms diffusion.

[2] Note also that the h-statistic cannot even be effectively used to detect autocorrelation in small sample regressions with autoregressive terms of the type from the previous subsection of this chapter.

[3] For a discussion of the relationship between model fits and theoretical assumptions, see King (1989, 33–35).

Chapter 7
The Future of Arms Diffusion

S INCE THE END OF THE COLD WAR, ANALYSTS OF MANY STRIPES HAVE attempted to divine the future course of global arms diffusion, as well as the impact that such diffusion will have on military organizations and their contingency planning. These are far from easy tasks. Global turbulence (Rosenau 1998), the emergent swirl of new state and non-state actors and their complex interrelationships that increasingly determine global outcomes, makes even the basic structure of the future international system hard to see with any certainty. The role of armed forces and the military technology they employ in this complex global future is thus even less clear. Nevertheless, it is important to continue to consider the question of the future of arms diffusion, as past events (the most dramatic recent example being the U.S./U.K. bombing campaign against Iraqi weapons of mass destruction sites in December 1998) give us every reason to believe that it will be of critical future relevance to defense and foreign policy decision makers.

In this final chapter, I attempt to integrate the results of the analysis in this study with the predictions and thoughts of other strategic analysts to assess the future course of arms diffusion in the global system. In particular, I address two important, interrelated issues. First, how can we interpret the historical decline in the arms diffusion rate in light of what we know about its causes and about the evolution of the international system? Second, how should what we know about past arms diffusion inform our expectations about the diffusion of new military technologies? I address each of these questions separately in the sections that follow. In the final section of the chapter, I examine the future directions in which research on these topics should be directed.

INTERPRETING THE DECLINE IN ARMS DIFFUSION RATES

The first significant finding of this study is that the spread of new generations of military technology can in fact been interpreted as a global diffusion process. The sequential interaction and imitative behavior of adopters
and non-adopters of a given military innovation does describe an important part of the process of arms spread among the states of the world.
However, I also confirmed both that the diffusion rates of different innovations vary, and that this variance is related to other factors *not* specifically endogenous to the diffusion phenomenon

One critical dimension of this variance was demonstrated in Chapter
5: after peaking in the 1960s, the rate and extent of the diffusion of new
generations of arms has significantly declined over the past three decades.
While new weapons undoubtedly continue to spread across the globe, the
pace at which they are doing so has steadily dropped over time. This is not
a universal phenomenon across all categories of weapons systems.
However, it is an accurate description of the overall process of arms diffusion during the three-and-a-half decade period under investigation
(1960–1996). This observation casts serious doubt on the assertions of
those who claim that ever more sophisticated armaments are spreading
rapidly around the world. Throughout the period in question, there has
undoubtedly been a dramatic *quantitative* increase in the dollar value of
global arms flows, as well as of global military spending, at least until the
early 1990s. And, due to the simple pace of technological progress and the
replacement of older weapons with subsequent generations on the production line, the weapons available for export in 1999 are chronologically
newer and more sophisticated than the ones that were available in 1989 or
1979. But to say that the *rate* of spread of these weapons is greater than
those of past generations, or that the *relative newness* of the weapons
which are spreading today is greater than those in 1979 is simply not borne
out by the data at hand.

The Impact of Democracy and Wealth. How can we explain the phenomenon of declining arms spread, which seems to run counter to the conventional wisdom? In Chapter 6, I examined some theoretical explanations
for this decline by testing specific hypotheses derived from five theoretical
models. I found that increasing levels of global democracy and prosperity
throughout this period seem to have reduced the willingness and/or need
for states to procure the latest and most sophisticated armaments very soon
after their initial development. Other variables, including the frequency of
interstate and civil wars and militarized interstate disputes, the economic
status of key arms producing states, and several technological features of
the weapons themselves, seem to have little independent impact on the rate
of diffusion. It might be true, as Bassett (1999) notes, that "all wars accel-

erate industrial strategies [and] even small wars can have a profound effect on national and international defense industry thinking." However, the evidence is not strong that these wars influence systematically the flow rate of military innovations through the international system.

The democracy and wealth hypotheses, however, do not provide a complete explanation for the patterns described in Chapter 5. The results in Chapter 6 also suggest that the relationship between democracy, global prosperity, and decreased diffusion rates exists *despite* the fact that the post Cold War period seems to have been related in some unspecified way to *increased* levels of diffusion. However, the variable I used to capture the effect of the Cold War was a simple dichotomous one. As a result, we do not have a very strong sense of exactly what aspects of the Cold War's end were instrumental in influencing arms diffusion rates, or if there was some change in this dynamic over time. Despite this problem, which should be addressed more systematically by future research, we can speculatively examine the historical record for a few possible answers to the question of what specific element(s) of the Cold War international system influenced the rate of arms diffusion the most.

The Impact of the Cold War International System. As we saw from examining the diffusion patterns of weapons systems which originated in the 1950s, and comparing them to those which began to diffuse in successive decades, the appearance of the 1960s generation of military innovations created something of a boom time for arms diffusion. The innovations which first appeared in that decade spread to more states faster than those of either previous or (thus far) subsequent decades. How can we explain this arms diffusion "bulge" in the 1960s?

One possible motivating factor for this pattern was the rapid gaining of independence by dozens of new states in the 1960s and the competition for influence over these states by the competing superpower-led blocs in the context of the Cold War. Upon gaining independence, virtually all new states quickly decided that they needed to create standing militaries, either from scratch or from the remnants of guerilla armies or colonial troops left over from the pre-independence period. In either case, these new armed forces needed to be equipped with military hardware. In most cases, the U.S. and Soviet Union and/or their allies were more than willing to supply them with the latest equipment in short order. Dozens of such decisions in countries across the world led to relatively rapid arms diffusion in the immediate post-independence period.

What happened next was perhaps predictable. As the decolonization wave tapered off in the mid-1970s, its independent impact on the course of arms diffusion began to wane. And once the newly independent states possessed armed forces equipped adequately enough to carry out basic tasks, they failed to continue to innovate by automatically acquiring the next generation of MTIs when they became available. In some cases, financial resources and security concerns did not allow or warrant the purchase of increasingly costly weapons without a pressing need.[1] In many cases, however, the simple adage that "we need to have something in the way of armaments, but we don't necessarily need to have the latest or the best" seems to have carried the day. The result was a tapering off of arms diffusion rates from the 1960s through the 1980s.

An instructive example is that of Bangladesh, which gained its independence from Pakistan in 1971. Bangladesh took delivery of its first Generation 3 combat aircraft (Soviet MiG-21s) in 1974, some three years after independence and in diffusion year 15 of that MTI's spread. These jets formed the nucleus of its embryonic air force. Bangladesh has waited until 1999, however, to order a small number of fourth generation MiG-29s, in diffusion year 28 of their spread. (The actual delivery date will be even later). Similarly, Algeria received its first MiG-21s in 1966, three years after independence and in diffusion year 7 of their spread. They received fourth generation jets in 1992, diffusion year 21 of their spread.

An additional element of the Cold War dynamic possibly linked to this decline is the increasingly weak economic position of the Soviet Union in the 1970s and 1980s. Analysts have reported that the USSR began to shift its foreign military aid policies in the 1970s away from outright grants of equipment and toward sales. As Krause (1992, 121) has noted:

> Although there is a strong consensus that the Soviet drive to acquire influence and weaken the positions of the West in the non-aligned developing areas relied almost exclusively on military assistance as the most effective instrument of policy, in recent years the argument that economic forces (the pursuit of wealth) are more evident than the pursuit of power has gained considerable support. This argument is based on the observation that 'the arms now tend to be sold rather than given as bilateral aid, economic prices are often charged, credit terms have become more stringent, interest rates on loans are higher, and deposits of cash payments in hard currency are usual.'

By 1980, Soviet arms deals with oil states like Libya, Algeria, Iraq, and Saudi-financed Syria, for example, were largely conducted using hard currency, many on a "pay-as-you-go" basis (Laurance 1992, 109; Coulter, Despres, and Karp 1987). As a result, diffusion to smaller, poorer states less able to afford Soviet equipment tapered off. In addition, many of those poorer states that were receiving sizeable amounts of Soviet military aid during this period (Angola, Ethiopia, Mozambique) were also embroiled in massive civil wars that demanded large *quantities* of arms supplies, but not necessarily weapons representative of the latest technologies. These changes in Soviet export policies and behavior were not "systematic" in the sense that they were unique to one supplier (albeit a major one) in the global arms transfer and production system. As a result, they may not have been picked up by the aggregate civil war (WARCIV) and world GDP (GDPWLD) variables included in the regression runs of the last chapter. But they may still have had some impact on diffusion rates evident in the descriptive data analysis. It is an understatement to say that the collapse of the Soviet Union's foreign aid policies in the late 1980s, and the USSR itself in 1991, certainly amplified these effects.

PAST DIFFUSION AND THE SPREAD OF NEW MILITARY TECHNOLOGIES

The combination of a diffusion dynamic, the global spread of democracy and prosperity, and the geopolitical dynamics of the Cold War worked in conjunction to yield the arms diffusion patterns which I have uncovered in this study. Knowledge of these relationships is critical to our understanding of the phenomenon of arms diffusion during the period under investigation, and for the types of weapons technologies contained within the data set. In Chapter 4, I argued that the selection of the MTIs for inclusion into the data set was conducted to capture the most important aspects of the global arms diffusion process within the time frame and population of states included in the study. I also argued that the cases were typical enough to allow for broad generalizations to be made on the basis of the results derived from their analysis. As a result, this study has enhanced our overall comprehension of the arms diffusion process, and for the first time provided empirical evidence of how that process played out over the period from the 1960s to the 1990s.

Some have argued, however, that the international system has undergone massive changes in the last decade which render many such generalizations derived from the past functioning of that system of questionable relevance for understanding future events. The next question which this chapter will address, therefore, is how this information about arms diffusion helps us to more clearly understand, and perhaps even predict, the future course of the global spread of arms.

Clearly, the future course of arms diffusion may be determined by numerous factors. Here, I concentrate on discussing two critical factors whose importance is suggested partially by my findings in this study and partially from the large and growing literature on military technology. These factors are the shape and composition of the international system and the directions in which new military technologies will develop. In this section of the chapter, I first discuss current scholarly interpretations of the nature of each of these changes. I then explain how we might expect these forces to shape the future course of arms diffusion. Finally, I will then examine some recent evidence, anecdotal and otherwise, which could reflect some changes in the patterns of global arms diffusion already being wrought by both influences.

The Future of the International System. The links I have established between democracy, prosperity, and the spread of arms suggest that the wealthier and more democratic the world becomes, the slower the rate of arms diffusion we can expect. The course of arms diffusion over the next two or three decades of the coming century is therefore dependent upon the nature of political and economic developments in the international system. Unfortunately, there is no real consensus on the prospects for political change, democratization, and increasing global wealth as we head into the new millennium. In fact, two diametrically opposed schools of thought on the future of the international system–which, for simplicity's sake, I simply term the optimists and the pessimists–have emerged, each with a separate and distinct set of predictions about where the world is heading.

Optimists argue that the spread of free market capitalism and liberal democracy in the last half of the current century presage the development of a Kantian liberal international society in the coming one (Risse-Kappen 1996, Valladão 1996, Russett 1993, Fukuyama 1989). They argue that these ideological forces, which have already made warfare essentially unthinkable between any of the major Western powers, and indeed throughout Western Europe, are already and will continue to spread throughout the rest of the world's developing regions. The optimists are split on the causes of this spread. Some argue that it is the result of U.S. military, economic, and cultural hegemony at the close of the Twentieth Century. Others simply cite the exhaustion of possible ideological alternatives to liberal capitalism. Nonetheless, both camps predict that the emergence of a post-industrial information economy in the First World, and the spread of industrial modes of production to the developing world are having a profound, largely positive, and certainly transformative impact on the conduct of international affairs. According to the optimists, the combination of democratic values and capitalist modes of production will not only wipe out the last vestiges of major warfare in the international system. It will also usher in a new era of global prosperity, as free market economies unburdened by the defense expenditures which characterized so much of the preceding centuries unleash the economic force of the world's billions of consumers in new productive directions (Kiplinger 1998). Some realize that this transformation may not take place all at once, leaving the possibility of a transitional period in which the world is divided into "zones of peace" and "zones of turmoil" (Singer and Wildavsky 1993). Nonetheless, as liberal democratic capitalism engulfs larger and larger segments of the world, the "zone of peace" will grow and the "zone of turmoil" will correspondingly shrink. In the end, only the former will remain.

While optimists emphasize the integrative nature of political and economic developments in the world today, pessimists are more concerned by what they see as the growing impact of disintegrative forces upon the global body politic. Pessimists argue that the post-Cold War period has been marked by a resurgence of ethno-nationalist conflict, religious fundamentalism, and a marked decline in state sovereignty, the force which more than any other served to order world politics over the last four centuries. The economic and technological advances which optimists see as creating a new global business environment favorable to commerce and peaceful cooperation are viewed by the pessimists as the engines of political disorder, anomie (generated by the destruction of traditional social norms and patterns of living), civil strife, and environmental devastation (Smith, Lyons, and Moore 1998). Pessimists see the increasingly rapid globalization of capital, brought about by the implementation of free market norms around the world, as a key factor in weakening the national identities that have served as the glue which binds states together internally (Barber 1995). The growth in refugee flows and the seemingly interminable civil strife in numerous portions of the world underline the impact of these forces. The end result, the pessimists argue, will be an increase in the number of "failed states" like Yugoslavia, the Soviet Union, and, on a smaller scale, Somalia and Rwanda (Kaplan 1995). In these states, the central government has effectively ceased to function and civil society is overwhelmed by the forces of war, chaos, and economic and social breakdown.

The Future of Military Technology. The incredible transformations which have occurred in the international system over the last decade have arguably been matched by no less startling advances in military technology and potential nature of future warfare. It seems clear that while the rate at which arms technologies have spread throughout the globe has slowed, the pace of scientific advance in the core arms producing nations has hardly slackened. However, there seems to be less uncertainty about the foreseeable future of military technological development than there is about the precise meaning and impacts of future technological advances on the conduct of war. As with the future of the international system, an assessment of the contours of these impacts is still in serious dispute by observers from opposing intellectual camps.

Many analysts have argued that innovations in computers, communications and information technology, advanced materials, satellite and space systems, and other related fields have changed the nature of warfare, resulting in a "revolution in military affairs" (RMA). RMA advocates claim that the application of these technologies to warfare and weapons has resulted in a time-accelerated, decentralized, hyper-precise and non-linear "battlespace" which renders traditional military concepts of mass and maneuver almost irrelevant (Arquilla and Ronfeldt 1997). As a result, they argue that the future of battle rests in "information warfare," a type of conflict in which the possession and management of information about the location and activities of friendly and enemy forces and civilian information infrastructures in central to the achievement of victory (Waltz 1998). Public discussion and analysis of this hypothesized military revolution was sparked by the Gulf War of 1991, which served as a showcase for the RMA, or at least some of its key component technologies. The latter included "smart" (precision-guided) bombs and missiles, stealth technology, airborne ground surveillance radars, and other systems that provided the capability for all-weather/night high-tempo "hyperwar" operations. The ability of U.S.-led Coalition forces to inflict a tremendous defeat upon the Iraqi armed forces with relatively few casualties to themselves and the impression of incredible precision in the Coalition bombing campaign suggested that something fundamental had changed about the nature of warfare. A similar performance by U.S.-led NATO forces against Yugoslavia in 1999 further underlined this contention.

Many scholars have been quick to embrace this judgement, painting pictures of future warfare scenarios which read like something out of a science fiction novel. Inspired by the events of the Gulf War and drawing upon the insights and visions of defense scientists in a number of technical fields, Shukman (1996, xiii) describes a battlefield thirty to forty years hence populated by:

> . . . robot-soldiers the size of ants, genetically modified algae to store computer data, electronic eyes programmed to identify friend from foe, automated missiles accurate enough to hit a particularly vulnerable point on an aircraft or tank, squadrons of near-invisible solar-powered gliders poised to shoot down Scud missiles, laser-beams and super-bugs to immobilize enemy Soldiers rather than kill them, microchips which see in the dark.

Arquilla and Ronfeldt (1997, 2) also offer a still radical, if somewhat more familiar, vision of what future battlefields might look like:

> On land, there may be no fronts, because fighting may occur almost anywhere anytime in a theater. The modal size of operational units of maneuver will become quite small—perhaps below the size of the typical 700-man battalion. At sea, the need for aircraft carrier battle groups is sure to end. They will be replaced by smaller, faster, and equally capable fighting formations. The same is likely to hold for aerial warfare, which is already moving away from traditional formations, long carefully specialized in air wings of bombers and fighters. Today, the blending of the various types of aircraft in composite wings is occurring; and through stealth technology and improve-

ments in the "information packages" of air-launched missiles, the air forces of the future will be able to do much more–with less.

Obviously, the contours of such warfare would be highly dependent upon the specific set of technologies which actually make it from the laboratory to employment with fielded forces, whatever the future meaning of that last term. Nonetheless, most RMA and information warfare analysts envisioned a future in which the traditional elements of military power–the high-cost, high-visibility land, air, and sea platforms which have become so widespread in the post-World War II period–were replaced by the small, the flexible, and the constantly changing.[2]

A second school of thought questioned the wilder claims of these "technological revolutionaries" (Adams 1998). Skeptics among the conventional military establishment freely admit that the new "smart" weapons and enhanced communications and command and control systems make traditional military forces much more effective. However, they discount much of the rhetoric over the RMA as simple reformulated jargon, stressing the traditional military goals and means of fixing and destroying enemy military forces as the key goal of warfare. As one prominent military analyst has written:

> Information warfare, the latest military buzzword, is less than it appears. It's old wine in new bottles, and is pushed aggressively as a means to market proposals to research and study the new threat and then study it some more, and more . . . the moves toward this new revolution in warfare have been gradual during the last thirty years, but constant. Advances in electronics have brought us better sensors (such as thermal gun sights that can see through smoke and darkness) and much better communications. The better sensors make missiles more deadly. More powerful computers give missiles the ability to think for themselves. This results in deadly robots, of which there are several in use already. More technology has brought about miniaturization. Putting the equivalent of a laptop computer in a solider's helmet is already in the prototype stage (Dunnigan 1996, xvii).

These traditionalists stress that the hype over new forms of warfare and the weapons to fight them has been heard before, and has largely been proven inconsequential. After all, the use of smart bombs and missiles, "people sniffers" that detected the chemical trails emitted by the bodies of passing guerillas, and other "exotic" technologies were first used by the U.S. as long ago as the Vietnam War in the late 1960s and early 1970s (Dickson 1976). Yet today, we hardly think of Vietnam as a showcase for a revolution in military affairs. Military traditionalists also argue that, in addition to the focus on new forms of weaponry, the emphasis on and preparation for new forms of warfare central to the RMA/information warfare motif is also misplaced. As one RMA advocate sardonically notes, the skeptics argue that "despite the absence today (summer 1997) of a sizable conventional war, it takes only about one every decade or so to keep the notion high in people's minds that this is what war is really all about–the kind of war that matters most" (Arquilla and Ronfeldt 1997, 2).

The Implications of Structural and Technological Change on Arms Diffusion. We can see that there is no real consensus among informed observers about the path of future developments along each of the two dimensions which I have identified as critical to our understanding of the future of arms diffusion. We have full understanding of neither the kinds of weapons that will exist to diffuse (or, more precisely, which among the many emerging technologies that now exist will be weaponized and how they will fit into the dynamic of future warfare) nor the exact nature of the international system through which they might do so. But the existence of these two schools of thought along each of the two dimensions allows for the construction of a matrix of four "ideal type" future scenarios that might illuminate further debate on the topic, as shown in Table 7.1. In the paragraphs that follow, I discuss each of these scenarios in detail, describing the general nature of each, its possible impact on the type of arms that might exist, and the rate at which they would spread.

Cell I of the Table represents the confluence of the RMA advocate and the pessimist view of the international system's future. Such a world would witness a fragmented and chaotic political and economic situation combined with ready access by states, sub-state nationalist movements, and possibly terrorist and criminal groups to the latest exotic RMA technologies. This is a truly frightening future, marked by the decline of the democracy and prosperity which have been related to the suppression of arms diffusion rates in the second half of the 20th Century in conjunction with the ready access to deadly new military technologies. In such a world, arms diffusion rates could be rapid relative to those in the period of this study, although the change in the nature of the adopter population from states to sub- or non-state actors (motivated in part by the change in available technologies and in part by the collapse of the state-centric system) makes it difficult to predict just how rapid.

Cell II of Table 7.1 matches the global chaos predicted by the systemic pessimists with the more conventional military analysis of the RMA skeptics. Here, it is easy to predict a return to the increased rates of arms diffusion of the 1960s and 1970s, since we assume that the nature of military force and the tools used to apply it will not undergo radical change. As economic and political competition becomes more fierce, states will return to the means of protecting themselves which they have embraced in the past. Arms diffusion could be dampened by the increasing number of failed states which lack the infrastructure to support large, modern military forces. In sheer numerical terms, however, this could be offset by an increase in the overall number of states, as larger states fragment into smaller ones, in the manner of Yugoslavia and the Soviet Union.

Table 7.1's Cell III depicts a more comforting scenario. In this view, liberal democracy and capitalism continue their spread to all parts of the globe. Diffusion of traditional military platforms continues to decline. The advanced military technologies envisioned by the RMA advocates are developed, but the underlying peace and prosperity of the world prevents states from seeing much need to adopt them. In fact, these technologies largely remain in the hands of the United States and a few selected allies, enhancing U.S. military hegemony and allowing America to serve as the policeman of the world's few remaining trouble spots with relatively little cost in blood to itself (as in Kosovo and the Gulf). The reduction in national sovereignty, however, if it led to the emergence of powerful non-state actors like terrorist groups or criminal syndicates, could pose problems for the U.S., even in this scenario. This is particularly true if the "information warfare" strains of RMA thinking and their focus on computer crime and sabotage are accurate in their predictions.

Finally, Cell IV depicts a slightly different, and perhaps even more comforting, variant of the optimist vision. In this view, the relationships established in this study remain essentially unchanged. Democracy and wealth continue to have a negative impact on the course of the diffusion of the traditional categories of armaments. New military developments will be limited to the enhancement of existing systems, but these will increasingly find fewer and fewer markets around the world.

Examining the Evidence: Arms Diffusion in the 1990s. As previously stated, each of these scenarios is an ideal type, which may correspond to a greater or lesser degree with events as they finally do occur. The actual future will most likely incorporate some elements of each scenario; alternately, one or another of the four scenarios may predominate at different times. This final segment of this section of the chapter examines some recent events and trends in the global arms transfer and production system to assess the relevance and accuracy of each of these scenarios.

Three critical pieces of evidence about the state of the global arms transfer and production system in the late 1990s are relevant to the discussion about the future of arms diffusion. First, the decline in arms diffusion rates over the past four decades has resulted in the concentration of cutting edge traditional military power in a smaller and smaller group of states. The United States in particular thus holds a critical monopoly on many key technologies which are critical to modern military success, even (and perhaps especially) if the RMA advocates are right about future advances in military technology.

The 1999 air war against Yugoslavia demonstrated this with stunning clarity. At the conclusion of that conflict, many Western European foreign and defense policy makers realized that even they, leaders of some of the richest and most technologically advanced states on the planet, lacked access to the kinds of weapons being used by the U.S. on a daily basis over Yugoslavia. By way of example, of the nineteen NATO member states, only one besides the U.S. (Great Britain) was capable of employing long-range cruise missiles of the type being used to bombard targets in Belgrade on a nightly basis with no risk to U.S. pilots or aircraft. Only two (Britain and France) possessed airborne early warning aircraft equivalent to the U.S. AWACS, which helped direct the air battle over Yugoslavia. None operated anything approaching the U.S. fleet of JSTARS radar aircraft, used to detect movement of vehicles on the ground from long distances, or F-117 stealth fighters, which once again demonstrated their considerable ability to evade enemy radars and strike targets deep in hostile territory. The entire air war depended heavily on U.S. tanker aircraft, high-altitude reconnaissance jets, sophisticated command-and-control networks, and other high-technology systems. This observation tends to bolster the contentions of Cell III in the table (the optimist/RMA scenario).

But will this monopoly hold? A critical assumption of many who argue that RMA technologies will spread rapidly among a large number of adopters is that they are cheap and easy to use. Even states that are not wealthy, industrialized democracies will thus have access to such systems (Blair 1996, Shukman 1996). But as one author notes:

> Military revolutions occur, not as the result of deployment of a single weapon or technology, but when a set of technologies and associated operational concepts transform the nature and character of warfare *and* the relevant personnel and military organizations are able to deploy and exploit the set of technologies (Mandeles 1996, 157).

In modern warfare, military strength thus resides not in the ability of a state to master one new military innovation, but rather in the ability to net multiple innovations together in complex, synergistic fashion (Van Crevald 1989). The ability of most states in the world to master such integrative efforts is thought to be very low. Individual states might be able to assemble one or more pieces of hardware, but few if any outside the U.S. seem to be able to put enough of the pieces together to stand against a similarly integrated foe. Iraq, for example, might have had modern fourth generation fighter jets in 1991, but its long-range surface-to-air missiles were elderly, and its airborne early warning aircraft were primitive. It had some of the elements of a modern integrated military, but the U.S. and its allies could avoid these by simply attacking the weak spots in its web of systems.

A second piece of evidence regarding the current status of arms diffusion underlines the continuing importance of the interactive diffusion dynamic in the spread of arms. It seems that to a certain degree, the concentration of military power in the hands of the U.S. and a few other states is further suppressing arms diffusion rates among traditional arms categories, particularly among states which perceive themselves to be possible U.S. opponents in future conflicts. The demonstration of U.S. military power in the Gulf, Yugoslavia, and other locales has apparently convinced many states that, because of the dynamics listed under the previous point in this section, they stand little chance of directly facing the U.S. in traditional combat. They have thus eschewed the purchase of weapons in traditional arms categories, because they realize that they will never be able to acquire, integrate, and effectively operate the same diversity of weapons systems that the U.S. deploys. Instead, they have tried to acquire relatively primitive weapons of mass destruction (WMD) and inexpensive, low-technology counters to major U.S. weapons systems.

Iran is a perfect example of this phenomenon. In the early 1990s, Iran was reported to be planning a massive military build-up involving the purchase of billions of dollars of Russian conventional military equipment, including tanks, aircraft, and surface-to-air missiles. By the mid-1990s, however, few of these weapons had reached Iranian hands. Instead, Iran increasingly began spending its defense dollars on its secret nuclear weapons program, and its efforts to acquire biological and chemical weapons, as well as the ballistic missiles to carry them. None of these technologies were particularly "new" or "innovative," in a global sense. After all, modern chemical weapons made their first appearance as long ago as World War I, while nuclear weapons and ballistic missiles of the type sought by Iran can be traced back to 1945. Nevertheless, similar WMD programs blossomed in North Korea, Syria, Libya, and other "pariah" states (Klare 1995).

Given the repeated assertions of the new openness of the arms trade and the easy availability of modern weapons, the fact, for example, that none of the states mentioned above has yet deployed either a third generation long-range SAM system to counter U.S. air power or a modern Russian anti-ship missile like the SS-N-22 Sunburn to use against U.S. Navy carriers should be quite surprising. This regression to earlier, but still deadly, forms of unconventional warfare reflects both the economic and technological backwardness of non-democratic states in the post-Cold War era. As democracy and prosperity spread, the hold-outs which refuse to join in the "liberal peace" generated by such forces become less and less able to acquire the standard military means for their own protection. They are thus forced to resort to the development of less advanced "doomsday" weapons to ensure their security.[3] In this sense, we can say that the dynam-

ics of modern arms diffusion are stymieing the further spread of traditional categories of arms, preventing the spread of new RMA technologies
(since these are controlled by the major powers and cannot easily be independently developed by those most likely to need them to counterbalance
U.S. military force), and spurring the spread of older mass destruction
weapons which still pack considerable political and military punch.

This information suggests the validity of modified forms of scenarios
found in several of the cells in Table 7.1. The relevance of the
optimist/RMA advocate view (Cell III) is again verified by the realization
that RMA technologies do not seem to be spreading beyond a core set of
adopters, dominated by the U.S. Both it and the optimist/RMA skeptic
view (Cell IV) that democracy and prosperity will spread and traditional
arms diffusion decrease are darkened, however, by the realization that
recalcitrant states may resort to other, less sophisticated but equally threatening military procurement patterns. In contrast, a pessimist-style reversion
to a more fractured and conflictual international system (within which the
goals of territorial conquest, for example, could return as realistic state military aims) could result in a return to increased levels of either RMA *or* traditional military innovation, and a decrease in WMD spread.

A third and final aspect of the current global arms trade which derives
from these first two situations is the increasing complexity and unpredictability of the global military technological scene. This is a result of two
major factors. First, there is a serious oversupply problem in current global military markets. The end of the Cold War, the force drawdown and contraction of military spending among the major military powers, and the
increasing number of countries able to provide at least some sophisticated
hardware for sale have combined to increase the supply of arms at a time
in which, for the reasons listed above, overall demand is shrinking. In the
event of a crisis, this means that states, and even possibly non-state actors,
have quick and ready access to large stockpiles of modern arms on a
moment's notice. Arms diffusion is thus likely to demonstrate less long-
term "proactivity" (meaning states procuring weapons long before their
anticipated use) and more short-term unpredictability. States are likely to
wait longer to adopt major weapons systems, and more likely to upgrade
existing systems to the extent feasible. But short-term needs can be quickly filled by a very responsive and capable supply network, albeit one (as has
always been the case) greatly influenced by political factors.

Examples of this phenomenon are already numerous. Russia's threat to
supply Serbia with third-generation SA-10 SAM systems in late 1998 and
again just prior to the start of NATO's Operation *Allied Force* in March
1999, if carried out, could have seriously complicated NATO's bombing
campaign. The decision not to ship the weapons, a political move by Russia
aimed at keeping itself militarily uninvolved in the conflict, could easily

have been reversed, especially early in the crisis when NATO was unprepared to act with military force to stop the shipments. Similarly, when smaller and/or poorer states like Croatia, Eritrea, Ethiopia, Rwanda, Sierra Leone, and Sri Lanka decided at various points during the 1990s that they required advanced major weapons systems, they were able to acquire such systems quickly and with little fuss. Because more modern weapons are generally individually more lethal, it will also be easier for states to acquire the smaller numbers of these systems necessary for their security purposes. For example, Russia need not have supplied Serbia with hundreds of SA-10 complexes to enhance their air defenses substantially. A dozen would have been more than sufficient, in conjunction with existing older SAM systems, to pose a greatly-enough increased threat to NATO aircraft to change the complexion of the *Allied Force* air operation.

Second, the range of technological options open to states is growing and diversifying. This means that the arsenals of "hold-out" states (i.e. those which resist joining in the liberal capitalist peace) are more likely to be composed of a mixture of conventional and unconventional systems of varying generations, and with many more local variations than in the past. This is quite a difference from the time in which the pace of arms diffusion was largely marked by the transfer of succeeding generations of systems by the superpower suppliers to their key allies in a predictable fashion.

As I noted earlier, the incentives for the spread of nuclear, biological, and chemical WMD and their missile delivery systems are increasing. And, as the data in Chapter 5 has demonstrated, conventional arms of multiple generations in each category also continue to spread, albeit more slowly. Added to these challenges is the fact that the spread of industrial society and its technological base is making it easier for states to acquire the means for local construction and modification of military hardware. (This is true even if that same spread of industrialism decreases the overall diffusion of *deployed* weapons systems, those which we define as MTIs.) The result of all this is that such military forces are becoming ever more difficult to analyze and understand, thus increasing the difficulties encountered in planning to deter or fight them. As the number of pieces grows, it becomes more and more difficult to assemble the puzzle in a timely fashion.

The case of pre- and post-*Desert Storm* Iraq illustrates well this point. During *Desert Storm*, Iraq had assembled an arsenal of systems from at least three major (the Soviet Union, China, and France) and dozens of minor arms suppliers. Conventional weapons deployed with Iraqi armed forces represented often two or three generations of systems (for example, the air force operated second, third, and fourth generation combat aircraft). Iraq also possessed a host of WMD programs which spanned numerous lethal agents (nuclear, chemical, and biological) and delivery systems (missiles, shells, aircraft, and others). Finally, in May and June of

1998, U.S. intelligence analysts were caught by surprise when Iraq began mixing and matching various SAMs, radars, and computer support equipment to develop new air defense systems which existing U.S. electronic warfare equipment was not capable of detecting.[4] U.S. sources claimed that Iraq was very active in continuing to develop such systems.

Conclusions: Wither Arms Diffusion? The discussion of all these factors leads us to several solid conclusions about the future of arms diffusion. First, arms diffusion is and will continue to be a critical concern in the international system in general, and to U.S. policy makers in particular. While the rate of arms diffusion has slowed over the past several decades, and indications are that it may slow further, existing generations of weapons continue to spread throughout the world. This fact should and will influence military planning in the U.S. and other states for the foreseeable future.

Second, the rate and scope of the diffusion of future generations of arms will be influenced heavily by the nature of the military technologies which are developed over the coming decades. At this point in time, it is difficult to determine how fast these arms will spread, since we are still uncertain of even their identities. Indications are, however, that most of the weapons derived from existing systems will continue to spread more slowly than in the recent past, and that the U.S. and select allies will retain a monopoly on the most critical and advanced systems.

Third, tracking and analyzing arms diffusion may become more and more difficult as time passes, as the nature of the military technological threat changes. Weapons could become smaller, or changes in electronics and computerized components could come to replace changes in external features, such as the size of a tank gun, the payload of an aircraft, or the range of a missile, as most important factors in deciding military effectiveness (as RMA advocates would argue they already have). "Mix-and-match" systems pieced together by recalcitrant "pariah" states could also become more common. If these things occur, they will amplify the intelligence burden necessary to sort them all out and develop counters for them.

DIRECTIONS FOR FUTURE RESEARCH

It is clear from the results of this study that analyzing the spread of arms from the diffusion perspective is a useful and productive way of examining the spread of arms throughout the international system. In the final pages of this chapter, I address one last question related to the topic: where do we go from here? What future directions does this research suggest we explore in order to better understand the process of the spread of arms? I have identified three avenues for future investigation: improvement in the quantity and scope of the data, development of more sophisticated methodological tools for examining the diffusion process, and the asking of many questions suggested by this research.

The Data. No empirical study can be conducted without data, and the quality and quantity of data is often a crucial determinant of the success of a given piece of research. As thoroughly discussed in Chapter 4, the data set for this study was carefully assembled from a variety of sources, and designed to be as representative as possible of the general patterns of arms diffusion which occur in the world. However, as Chapter 6 especially demonstrated, the results of the analysis might have been more robust had data on the diffusion of a greater quantity and diversity of innovations been available. A number of key military innovations–most notably, naval weapons, but also tactical precision-guided missiles–were omitted from the analysis. Future research should make as strong an effort as possible to assemble additional data in these and other categories, in order to more fully capture the detail and nuance of arms diffusion in the period in question. In some cases, this may be difficult or impossible, due to the lack of reliable public data on such diffusion–here again, the case of tactical missiles comes to mind. However, the need to more fully understand the diffusion process, particularly of these weapons which many have identified as of vital importance to the modern battlefield, demands that we make the best efforts possible to include as much open-source data as we can into future analyses.

The Method. As discussed in Chapter 6, the use of a relatively simple model of the underlying diffusion curve facilitated analysis in this initial stage of research. But the diffusion of innovations literature also includes a number of more sophisticated methodological tools for examining such diffusion curves. Although there is little or no evidence to suggest that use of these methods would result in better or more valid analysis, it may be useful to incorporate some of these more sophisticated models into future research to examine their impact. In addition, examining the diffusion process using a shifting adopter base (i.e. one in which the adopter population is not constant over time) would allow us to expand dramatically the analysis of arms diffusion over greater periods of time. In addition to adding a larger number of data points to our data sets, this might also allow us to test for additional secular shifts in arms diffusion patterns. (Of course, obtaining reliable MTI adoption data for time periods before World War II might be problematic.)

Additional Research Questions. Additional data and new methodological tools would undoubtedly be useful in future studies. However, the element which must drive future research is, of course, the generation of new, interesting, and important research questions. Since the subject of arms diffusion is a new endeavor, however, there are a multitude of questions for which answers derived from systematic tests of empirical data have yet to be provided. These include, but are not limited to, the following:

- To what extent do adopters shift their diffusion score rankings over time, and what factors cause such shifts?
- Are there trade-offs being made between the adoption of one set of MTIs and another? For example, does the increased diffusion of combat aircraft have a negative impact on the diffusion of combat helicopters?
- To what extent to each of the main arms producing nations contribute to global arms diffusion? Did the U.S. or the Soviet Union do more to further the spread of arms during the Cold War? If so, why? Might this be linked to distinctions in the arms-producing process between state owned and privately-owned arms-manufacturing firms?
- What specific aspects of the Cold War had the greatest influence on arms diffusion rates?
- Can we usefully analyze arms diffusion from the state level of analysis, as opposed to the level of the international system? By disaggregating and re-analyzing the independent variables used in this study at the state level, do we still find the same relationships I uncovered here? If not, why not?
- Is there a trade-off made between the spread of new generations of weapons and the stockpiling of existing generations in state arsenals?

These are just a sample of the many questions which future research in this area could fruitfully address. Since much of background justification for the diffusion approach to the spread of arms, as well as the classification of MTIs, has already been carried out for this study, future works could be shorter and more succinct while still building upon the framework provided here.

CONCLUSIONS

The formal goals of this study were to introduce the concept of arms diffusion as a new approach to the investigation of the spread of military innovations, to derive numerous theoretical hypotheses about why arms spread, to test these hypotheses using empirical methods, and finally, to examine the implications of these findings for our understanding of the process of the global spread of arms. But the study's larger, overriding purposes were twofold. The first was to develop a new method for examining the spread of military hardware which did a better job than previous methods at explaining exactly why and how states acquire new military technology. The second was to examine the claims and counterclaims about the rate of the spread of arms using hard empirical data, and to reach some conclusions about the validity of these assertions. The reasons for this are clear: how quickly the military technological threat develops across the world today is of vital importance to military planning, arms control policy direction, and foreign policy making in general. If my work has provided a clearer picture of the spread of arms than existed before, and if that picture aids in our efforts at understanding and dealing with the phenomenon of arms diffusion in the future, that it has succeeding in achieving my original goal.

Structure of the International System

	Pessimist	Optimist
RMA Advocate	I. New actors adopt new and deadly weapons with possibly dangerous consequences	III. New technologies develop, but they are not weaponized by many states as arms diffusion remains at low levels; possible reinforcement of U.S. military hegemony
RMA Skeptic	II. Resurgence of arms diffusion along conventional lines with advanced, but still conventional weapons	IV. Continuing decline in arms diffusion rates, as seen in the 1960 to 1996 period

Table 7.1: The Possible Paths of Future Arms Diffusion.

NOTES

[1] In Chapter 6, I demonstrated that cost does not seem to be directly related to diffusion rates among weapons categories; cheap anti-tank missiles, for example, do not *necessarily* diffuse faster than expensive combat aircraft. However, cost may be an inhibiting factor in the *replacement* of existing weapons with subsequently-developed ones. The more expensive each succeeding generation of MTIs is over its predecessors, the more a state may be likely to "make due" with what it has rather than buy new systems. Upgrading of older systems in lieu of new procurement is also a possibility for these states, although the coding of the MTIs included in the data set (and as explained in Chapter 4 and in the appendices) prevents this from having an spurious impact on the results of the study.

[2] An excellent example of this type of speculation can be found in Adams (1998, 105–7).

[3] For an example of the possible utility of such weapons in operational scenarios, see the detailed analysis of Iraq's use of chemical/biological weapons for deterrence of the U.S. in Haselkorn (1999).

[4] The catalyst event was a U-2 spy plane mission which failed to detect Iraq's new Tiger Song air defense system, which mated Soviet SA-2 surface-to-air missiles with Chinese and French radars. The radars were also elevated well above the ground to make attacks by U.S. anti-radar missiles less effective (Fulghum 1998).

Appendix A
Weapon Systems Designations and Nomenclature

A KEY OBSTACLE TO DEVISING SYSTEMATIC FRAMEWORKS FOR CATEGORIZing arms technology is the often bewildering manner in which arms producers and users designate and classify military hardware. If a universally-adopted, cross-national system of technological nomenclature existed, it would be much easier to track the progression of the development of various weapons systems over time, to compare like technologies, and to develop generational categories that left little doubt as to the validity of their construction. Unfortunately, this is not the case. As a result, thus specialized knowledge of the ways in which various nations designate their military hardware is necessary. This appendix outlines some of the major areas of difficulty with this task, in the hopes of not only demonstrating the complexity of the chore at hand, but also providing the reader with adequate background information to assess the validity of the categorizations actually used in this study, as outlined in the following appendices.

Designation systems for military hardware tend to vary in six major ways: (1) between states, (2) between various arms categories, (3) between weapons producers within a given state, (4) between the various branches of the military within states, (5) over time, and (6) in idiosyncratic fashion. Each of these sources of variance creates significant challenges for identification and classification of weapons technologies, and is described in its own section below.

VARIANCE BETWEEN STATES

First of all, differences almost always arise between the arms technology designation systems of different states, even for systems in the same arms category. Two separate sets of factors create this variance: *actual* differences in naming systems, and *perceived* differences which result from the creation of *external* naming systems by outside observers. These factors will be illustrated using examples from the realm of combat aircraft.

Every state which produces its own systems in a given arms category devises an *actual* designation system which is different to varying degrees from those of other producers. U.S. and Soviet systems for classifying combat aircraft are no exceptions. Under a system adopted in 1962, U.S. combat aircraft of all services are denoted by both an alpha-numeric designator indicating the primary combat mission of the aircraft (F = fighter, A = attack, B= bomber) and the sequence number of the major design (i.e. A-6 is the 6th major attack aircraft program since the inception of the 1962 system), as well as an "official" name adopted at the time of service inception (i.e. A-6 Intruder). The first service version is typically given an "A" suffix after the numeric portion of the designator (i.e. A-6A), and subsequent versions are allotted successive letters (A-6B, A-6C, A-6D, etc.) . If a specialized variant of the aircraft is developed which adds an entirely new combat role to its basic mission description, this is recognized by the addition of a letter prefix indicating the new mission; typical prefixes include R for reconnaissance and E for electronic warfare (i.e. EA-6B). This system did not preclude the addition of new systems and equipment to an existing version which were not reflected in at least a suffix change (say, from A-6D to A-6E), but most major changes were so identified.[1]

The Soviet aircraft designation system was completely different. Soviet aircraft were identified by a prefix which indicated the design bureau (OKB) which developed the aircraft, followed by a series number indicating successive major designs from that OKB which entered active service with the Soviet armed forces. Also, for some reason, only odd designation numbers were used (generally speaking—there were a few exceptions). Thus, since 1945, the Mikoyan-Guerevich OKB, the most famous of the Soviet design firms, has produced the MiG-15, MiG-17, MiG-19, etc., up through the current MiG-35, while the Sukhoi OKB produced the Su-7, Su-9, Su-11, and so on. Unlike the U.S. system, the designations provide no clue as to the mission of the aircraft; for example, the Su-7 was a tactical bomber while the Su-9 and Su-11 were designed solely for air-to-air combat. Even more confusingly, succeeding variants of the original design were awarded letter suffixes which attempted, in a very non-standard fashion, to indicate the *nature* of the technological improvement incorporated in the variant. In the West, a guessing game about the exact meaning of certain variant suffixes often ensued among defense analysts when new sub-types were revealed by the Soviets without further explanation. To better explain this system, the Table A.1 indicates all the known variants of the Su-25 ground attack aircraft which the Soviets have unveiled since 1982, when the aircraft was first introduced.

Note that the Su-25 was not a particularly well-developed design, and thus the table represents only a fraction of the number of designations which accompany other more widely-exported or longer-lived designs, like the MiG-21 or Su-17. Not only would a decent command of the Russian language be of use for deciphering the Soviet system, but a generous amount of informed guesswork might also be helpful. Does the suffix letter B stand for *buksir* ("target"), *boyevoi* ("combat"), or, as with the Sukhoi Su-7B, *bombardirovshckik* ("fighter-bomber")? Also note that there is very little correlation between the various levels of incorporated innovations which merit the awarding of a new suffix letter. For example, the Su-25UBK is simply the export designation for the Su-25UB, and varies little from the basic aircraft. On the other hand, the Su-25T contains completely different avionics and armament and looks quite different from the basic Su-25 single-seater on which it is based. Finally, there is also very little correlation between the alpha-sequential method of U.S. aircraft labeling (F-15A, B, C, etc.) and the more *ad hoc* Soviet procedure (Su-25, K, UB, UBK, etc.). Detailed knowledge of the various technical features of each model are thus required in order to make comparison.

Because of the *actual* differences between the Soviet and U.S. designation systems, as well as a paucity of reliable information about Soviet military technology during the Cold War, the U.S. and its NATO allies imposed a *second* system for identifying and classifying Soviet military equipment.[2] This *externally-imposed* system added an additional layer of nomenclature that in some ways clarified and in some ways further muddied the waters of comparison.

The NATO Air Standards Coordinating Committee (ASCC) generated a standardized code name for each new Soviet aircraft design to appear. It then designated succeeding variants with a sequential letter suffix as they became known to the West. Names were supposedly picked only to simplify identification and reporting in operational situations and were often nonsensical, in order to avoid confusion with Western types. Fighter and attack aircraft were given names beginning with the letter "F" (Fulcrum, Foxbat, Flogger, etc.), bombers given names starting with "B" (Bison, Bear, Badger, etc.), transports names with the latter "C" (Candid, Cub, Colt), and all other aircraft names beginning with "M" (Moujik, Mongol, Maiden, etc.). Thus, the initial version of the Mikoyan-Guerevich MiG-29 to reach operational service was known as the "Fulcrum-A," the second the "Fulcrum-B," and so on.

The sequence letter bore no relation to either the Soviet name (if it was known) or to technical features of the aircraft itself. It simply represented the appearance of a new variant, whatever innovations that variant possessed that its predecessor did not. ASCC sequence letters often clustered a number of Soviet-labeled variants together under a single designation, making the Soviet designations somewhat more compatible with the U.S. system. Thus, the Soviet-designated Su-7B, Su-7BM, and Su-7BKL, three variants of a fighter-bomber with such minor differences from one another that they often served side-by-side within the same units, were all clustered together under the ASCC designation "Fitter-A."

Problems arose, however, when incomplete data led to the ASCC mislabeling variants due to poor intelligence information about Soviet designs, or simply from the fact that the Soviets would often refuse to reveal the existence of some of the more specialized variants, particularly those containing sensitive technologies. Often, ASCC designation letters were given out of sequence, if a given variant of an aircraft was "missed" by Western intelligence services and then described after subsequent variants had already appeared.[3] Changes in aircraft that were significant but not readily externally apparent (such as the addition of a new powerplant, radar, or avionics) often failed to earn a new variant name. In the mean time, relatively minor changes sometimes led to the description of a new variant. In the wake of the Cold War's end, when technical details of the Soviet military began to pour out of the East Bloc, the number of Soviet variants of long-lived aircraft like the Su-17 and MiG-25 were revealed to be larger than previously thought. Although the differences between variants were often very small, comparisons of the official NATO system and the Soviet system yield often surprising gaps in perception and labeling. Such problems have led to a situation in which it seems that the major reference sources have different, mutually incompatible designation schemes for the various models of the Su-22 strike aircraft, or that NATO has practically given up trying to sort out the multitude of variants of the Su-27 Flanker currently rolling out of Russian design bureaus.

When one adds to this situation the Chinese, French, British, Japanese, and other aircraft designation systems, it is clear that state-to-state differences pose a major challenge to developing any meta-scheme for classifying military technologies.

VARIANCE BETWEEN ARMS CATEGORIES

Even within a single state, the designation system used to identify succeeding models and various types of weapons do not necessarily translate easily between differing arms categories. This specialization derives partly from technological differences inherent in the nature of various categories of weapons. It is also partly due to the fact that institutional communities associated with various branches of warfare usually pay little heed to whether or not their designation systems are compatible with those of other communities.

An example of the former is the difference between the classification schemes of naval vessels and combat aircraft. With U.S. naval warships, succeeding designs within a given mission specialty (i.e. destroyers) are labeled as "classes" (i.e., in the US, *Spruance* class, *Kidd* class, *Arleigh Burke* class, etc.). Various major and minor updates in the designs incorporated into succeeding individual examples within the class may or may not be rewarded with a new designation.[4] In contrast, as explained above, U.S. combat aircraft generally receive a new number designator after a letter indicating their primary combat mission (F = fighter, thus the F-16 fighter succeeded the F-15 and F-14, and so on), with sub-variants marked by succeeding letters beginning with A (thus F-15A, F-15B, F-15C, and so on). Given the size and complexity difference between a single fighter aircraft and a single warship, the different schemes for identifying and classifying technological innovations (whether via the introduction of completely new systems or through improvements added to existing hardware) do not yield to simple comparison.

An example of the latter, institutional basis for variance can be found by comparing the classification scheme for ship-based naval SAMs (surface-to-air missiles) and land-based army SAMs. For the last several decades, US naval SAMs have been identified by a very different nomenclature than their land-based counterparts, with the former progressing through a series of "block numbers" (i.e. Block I, II, IIA, etc.) that follow a two-letter prefix indicating the range of the missile (thus, SM-2 (short-range missile model #2) Block IV, etc.). The latter use a "type prefix letter/type number/variant letter suffix" system similar to that for combat aircraft (i.e. the Stinger missile evolved from the FIM-92A to the FIM-92B, and so on). Although the technologies used in both arms categories are extremely similar, the bureaucratic and operational isolation of the military specialty communities which develop and use the systems has perpetuated the emergence of separate designation schemes which may or may not, depending upon the case, register equivalent levels of technological advance.

VARIANCE BETWEEN PRODUCERS WITHIN STATES

The nature of the military technological innovation process ensures that weapons systems undergo a lengthy testing and evaluation process before they enter active service with a state's armed forces, and thus weapons production firms (defense companies in the West and state design bureaus or OKBs in the former Soviet Union) often play a major role in designating and classifying military technologies. Soviet OKBs in particular internally employed a completely different designation system from the Soviet armed forces, and thus a single weapons system might have an OKB developmental name, an OKB suggested service designation, and an actual service designation throughout the course of its existence. Hence, the long-range strike aircraft called "Fencer" by NATO's ASCC was originally called the T-62 by the Sukhoi OKB, which, as it passed into operational testing, changed the name to Su-19; when it finally entered operational service with the Soviet Air Force, it was re-labeled Su-24. The Mikoyan-Guerevich firm, on the other hand, used a completely different system, which also varied from aircraft program to aircraft program.[5]

In the U.S., new variants of existing aircraft are proposed by defense companies on a regular basis, and these often have a suggested service designation (sometimes a non-standard one) attached. If the variant is rejected by the service, as many often are, the proposed designations are sometimes "skipped" in the official nomenclature sequence, in order to avoid the confusion that might result if a different variant were to use the same name as a previously canceled one. Thus, the rejected McDonnell-Douglas F-15F, G, and H paper proposals have left a gap in official sequencing between the F-15E strike and F-15I export variants of the Eagle fighter that will never be filled by actual aircraft.

VARIANCE BETWEEN MILITARY BRANCHES WITHIN STATES

Because the various branches of a state's military often have different operational needs, and also because they fiercely protect their bureaucratic turfs, their weapons designation systems are often incompatible. First, minor changes in equipment fit to an existing system are often awarded new variant names in order to reflect the difference in the operating service rather than the incorporation of major technological innovations. The designation F-16N was used by the U.S. Navy to describe its "aggressor" version[6] of the basic F-16A used by the U.S. Air Force, but this designation is non-standard to U.S. military practice under the 1962 unified system and out-of-sequence with the Air Force's variants, which only went as high as F-16E (which itself was actually only a proposed paper design); the "N" simply stood for the "Navy" version. Navy UH-46 and Marine Corps CH-46 helicopters are also basically identical, but used in different roles (one as a utility transport, and the other as an assault transport).

Second, and even more significantly, institutional proclivities sometimes engender terminological definitions which reflect deeply-held institutional beliefs and philosophies not shared by members of different military branches. A classic example of this is the tendency of the U.S. Air Force to designate attack aircraft with the "F" mission letter instead of the "A" because of the unpopularity of the battlefield air attack mission in the Air Force ranks. Thus, the F-111 and F-117 "fighters" have basically no air-to-air role or capabilities and are actually attack aircraft that typically carry only air-to-ground ordnance, yet are given the "F" mission designation and found in "Fighter Squadrons" rather than "Attack Squadrons" (which do not exist in the Air Force). Another example is the creation of a unique "F/A" mission designation for the McDonnell-Douglas Hornet to indicate to a skeptical Congress and the public-at-large that it was a true multi-role aircraft capable of undertaking both fighter and attack missions with equal skill, even though this could be said about many other aircraft in the force.[7]

VARIANCE OVER TIME

Three types of change can affect designation procedures both within states and between states over time: *deliberate systemic change, variant designation procedure change*, and *information-based change.*

Some changes are both deliberate and attempt to affect the entire system of nomenclature, and the "unified" 1962 U.S. aircraft designation system mentioned several times here is a classic example. This change was implemented during the 1960s era of defense rationalization under Defense Secretary Robert S. MacNamara, who sought to apply scientific management principles to the operational of the defense complex. Prior to 1962, each service had a completely separate system for designating its aircraft, with the Navy and Marine Corps systems involving a bewildering array of manufacturer codes, service numbers, and variant extensions that could be all-but-incomprehensible to the non-specialist, while the Air Force used a less-standardized version of the eventual unified system. When the changeover occurred (as described in previous paragraphs), aircraft which had entered service before 1962 but were still operational were given entirely new designations (for some reason, however, the F-111 escaped this, and maintained its prior designation), as well all aircraft-fired missiles, although they kept their popular names (i.e. the Intruder was still the Intruder, but its designation changed from A2F to A-6A). Such *deliberate systemic change* is rare but sweeping in its impact.

Variant designation procedure change reflects the fact that the innovation "gap" between succeeding variants of a given weapons system is not necessarily constant, and can reflect a variety of factors unrelated to the technological characteristics of the systems at hand. First, there is usually a lack of clear criteria by which the military establishments determine the extent to which an system must be modified to rate a new variant designation; as a result, the gap between sub-variants can sometimes be as great or greater than that between supposedly "new" generations of aircraft, depending on the nature and extent of the overall generational change. Again using the example of the Eagle, the F-15A and -B are virtually identical, with the only major difference between the two being the addition of a second cockpit in the latter for use in the pilot training mission. The F-15C is an upgraded version of the F-15A, featuring some new electronics and avionics systems, while the two-seat trainer F-15D is to the F-15C what the B was to the A. The F-15E, however, it a very different aircraft from the F-15A/B and F-15C/D, featuring a number of fundamental technological advances (like the digitized flight control system) absent in its predecessors. Furthermore, the gap between the E and its predecessors is far greater than that between the F-15A and F-15C.

Second, political or other factors may create an situation in which it is advantageous for an innovation to be identified either as a new weapons system or as a variant of an existing design, and thus labeled accordingly. The U.S. Navy's latest combat aircraft was designated the F/A-18E, and sold to the Congress as an evolutionary upgrade of the existing F/A-18 Hornet in order to avoid a lengthy debate over introducing a "new" weapons system into the fleet. Nevertheless, critics of the plane have claimed that it is a high-risk, complete re-design that warranted a completely new name ("F-19 Wasp" has even been suggested) (Stevenson 1993). On the other hand, the Soviets insisted during the SALT II arms control talks of the 1970s that their new bomber, known to NATO as the Backfire, was nothing more than an upgrade of the ten-year-old Tu-22 "Blinder," and was designated Tu-22M (M = *modifikatsirovanni*, "modified") to avoid considering it as a new type for the purposes of arms cuts and restrictions. After the end of the Cold War, a key Soviet aircraft designer finally admitted that the Tu-22M designation was purely a political move, and that the plane had been an entirely new design (Sweetman 1992).

Subsequent information-based change, a problem touched upon above, relates to the incomplete information possessed by the outside world of a given state's military technology, and the designation changes which take place when new information about such systems is received. This was particularly evident in the opening years of the post-Cold War period, when a flood of information about Soviet-era weapons technology was released, demonstrating flaws and shortcomings in the externally-imposed designation systems of NATO. While most of the designation mistakes were of a relatively minor nature and generally insignificant, there were a few exceptions. It was completely unknown, for example, that the Soviets had added a high-altitude bombing capability to the MiG-25 "Foxbat," an aircraft said to be a pure long-range bomber interceptor, or that the T-80 main battle tank was a direct derivative of the larger T-64 rather than its smaller successor, the T-72. In a similar fashion, information about Chinese weapons developments currently appears in fragmentary fashion in defense trade publications, mitigated only by the Chinese need to release sufficient data to attract export orders for their military wares.

But a failure to release accurate military information is hardly the sole domain of the Soviet Union and China. The top-secret U.S. "stealth fighter" was frequently identified as the "F-19" during the 1980s, since that was the next unused designation in the U.S.' sequential system. Only in

1989, was it revealed that the fighter's real designation was the F-117, termed such solely to allow the Air Force to issue a denial when asked if it was operating a secret "F-19 stealth fighter!" All states guard to varying degrees their most valuable military information, and thus an understanding of their defense technologies will always change as new information is revealed.

IDIOSYNCRATIC VARIANCE

As hinted in several places above, instances of idiosyncratic, *ad hoc* variance in military nomenclature and designation procedures also abound. The incredible variety of military technologies and their mission applications, of their domestic and export users, and of the political and institutional circumstances in which they are developed, purchased, and employed means that a host of non-systematic factors can influence the way in which they are designated.

In the immediately preceding section, the processes by which the F/A-18E and Tu-22M aircraft received their names were clearly idiosyncratic, i.e. restricted to the specific set of circumstances in which they originated and not necessarily likely to be duplicated in quite the same fashion with other systems. In one sense, the entire Soviet aircraft variant designation system was largely idiosyncratic, reflecting as it did specific technological innovations added to existing designs and the weight which a given program's chief designer gave to any one of them. For example, when a new variant of the MiG-21 was developed in the late 1960s with a reconnaissance pod, upgraded engine, and a low-level attack capability, should it have been labeled MiG-21R for reconnaissance, MiG-21F for *forsirovanniy* ("boosted," reflecting the boosted power of the engine), MiG-21B (*bombardirovshckik*, "fighter-bomber"), or simply MiG-21M (*modifikatsirovanni*, "modified")? In the end, the designation MiG-21MF was chosen, reflecting the boosted engine and lumping the other changes under the "modified" term. However, the process by which the designation was chosen depended upon no clear, unified set of criteria. Finally, the Soviet decision to term a class of ships that the West would designate light aircraft carriers as "aircraft-carrying cruisers" stemmed solely from restrictions on passing anything larger than a cruiser through Turkey's Bosphourous Straits into the Mediterranean Sea. The idiosyncratic nature of such decisions defies systematic understanding and can be assessed only through a knowledge of the specific systems in question.

Soviet Service Designation	Meaning of Suffix (If Known)	Aircraft Mission Variant
Su-25	---	basic ground attack model
Su-25K	*kommercheskiy* ("commercial")	export ground attack model
Su-25BM	*buksir misheney* ("target towing")	aerial target towing
Su-25UB	*uchebniy boyevoi* ("training-combat")	two-seat armed trainer
Su-25UBK	*uchebniy boyevoi kommercheskiy*	export two-seat armed trainer
Su-25UT	*uchebniy* + ??	two-seat unarmed trainer
Su-25UTG	*uchebniy* + ?? + *gak* ("hook")	shore-based carrier landing trainer
Su-25UBP	*uchebniy boyevoi* + *palubnyi* ("shipborne")	shipborne carrier landing trainer
Su-25T	?? ("anti-tank")	dedicated anti-tank attack model
Su-25TM	("anti-tank") + *modifikatsirovanni* ("modified")	improved anti-tank attack model
Su-25TP	("anti-tank") + *palubnyi* ("shipborne")	carrier-based anti-tank model

Table A.1: An Example of Soviet Weapons Designation Schemes: The Su-25 Aircraft

NOTES

[1] For some aircraft, particularly the F-16, the U.S. has also instituted a block number system which complements the alpha-sequential variant designation system and provides additional information about interim changes in various aircraft systems; thus F-16A Block 10, Block 15, Block 20, etc.

[2] The Soviets are not believed to have instituted a similar system for identifying NATO aircraft. As far as is known, they simply used U.S./NATO designations.

[3] For example, the MiG-23 Flogger-E, an early export derivative of the Flogger-A, was not observed by the West until after the public appearance of the Flogger-B through Flogger-D designs, which it predated by several years (Stapfer 1990, 8–9).

[4] For example, early *Arleigh Burke* class destroyers are called "Flight I" vessels, while later examples are labeled "Flight II" and "Flight IIA." The last has also been termed the *Improved Arleigh Burke* class.

[5] For example, the OKB name for the MiG-15 prototype was the I-350, for the MiG-19 it was the SM-2, and for the MiG-21 it was the Ye-7.

[6] "Aggressor" aircraft are used to simulate enemy aircraft in mock air battles with regular- service fighters.

[7] In comparison, the F-15E attack version of the Eagle air superiority fighter was not labeled the F/A-15E, even though it has a far greater attack capability than the Hornet and retains an equivalent air-to-air capability. Relabeling the F-16 as A-16 when it was tasked with the attack mission was also rejected by the Air Force, and a dual F/A designation was never considered. The Air Force simply maintains that the definition of a "fighter" aircraft is one that can carry out *both* air-to-ground and air-combat duties, and that the "A" prefix is simply definitionally unnecessary.

Appendix B
Combat Aircraft

ARMS CATEGORY

ERHAPS IN NO OTHER CATEGORY OF ARMS LITERATURE DOES ONE ENCOUNTER the concept of technological generations mentioned as frequently as in that on combat aircraft. Defense analysts commonly use the term to describe the relative capabilities of various aircraft. Defense firms themselves also often promote their wares as representing "fourth generation" or "fifth generation" aircraft technology. These terms are far from comprehensively defined in common usage. Still, enough of a consensus exists to provide a useful aid to research and classification. For the purposes of this study, I include in the category "combat aircraft" all jet-powered aircraft typically labeled as fighters, fighter-bombers, strike planes, attack planes, and interceptors, but not bombers or trainer aircraft converted for the light strike role, which belong in separate categories. In general, postwar jet combat aircraft are generally divided into four generations, with a fifth now emerging (Cook 1997, Starr 1996, Lorell, et al. 1996, Novichkov 1996, Sapfir 1991).[1]

GENERATIONAL DEVELOPMENT

Generation 1 aircraft emerged in the immediate postwar period (beginning in about 1948). The generation's signpost systems are the Soviet MiG-15 and U.S. F-86 Sabrejet. Compared to wartime designs (the British Meteor, German Me.262 *Schwalbe*, and U.S. P-80), the swept-wing low-drag design of these jets allowed them to fly higher and faster than ever before. Subsequent limited developments in engines and aerodynamics allowed these jets to just barely break the sound barrier on an operational basis.

Generation 2 designs comprise the first jets capable of maintaining supersonic or better speed in level flight. They continued the trend of increased size, operating altitude, and overall system complexity (Friedman et al. 1985, 113). Systems considered as belonging to this generation include the American "century series" (the F-100, F-101, F-102, F-104, F-105, and F-106), Soviet designs like the MiG-19 and Su-7, and European planes like the French Super Mysteré. Optimized for high-altitude interception of enemy bombers and nuclear attack missions, they began entering active service in 1954.

Generation 3 systems arrived during the early 1960s. They represented the apex of the quest for speed and altitude, additional increases being seen as operationally unimportant (Friedman et al. 1985, 113). Better engines allowed for heavier aircraft that carried larger radars and the first radar-guided missiles. Many aircraft in this generation did not initially carry the cannon which equipped virtually every combat aircraft design since before World War II, as close-range aerial combat was thought to be obsolete. Later Generation 3 designs also saw the first operational use of variable-geometry airfoils ("swing wings") that promised better aircraft performance across the flight envelope. Avionics featured innovations like radars that could detect targets flying beneath their own altitude (so-called look-down capability) and inertial navigation systems (INS) that improved navigation over long distances.

Generation 4 systems were developed to rectify many of the operational shortcomings of their third generation predecessors. Combat experience from wars in the Middle East and Southeast Asia demonstrated that short-range combat continued to be a mainstay of modern air combat. Generation 3 aircraft lacked the maneuverability and weapons to engage in such combat effectively. Fourth generation systems thus enhanced maneuverability through a variety of methods: leading and trailing edge wing flaps, blended wing designs, variable geometry engine inlets, thrust-to-weight ratios in excess of unity, fly-by-wire flight controls, light-weight composite (non-metal) structural materials, and inherently unstable airframe design. Pulse-Doppler radars capable of detecting and engaging extremely low-flying targets (look-down/shoot-down systems (LD/SD)) also became standard. Attack avionics compatible with the latest generation of precision-guided munitions (PGMs) and precision navigation systems are also fourth generation features. Finally, the increased cost of such complex systems meant that the single-mission aircraft of the past would have to be replaced by those capable of carrying out a variety of missions on the battlefield, and most of the aircraft in this generation are consequently multi-role machines.

A fifth generation of systems is now emerging that combines stealth design features, new super cruise engines that allow for extended operation at Mach 1+ speeds without the use of afterburner. This includes the U.S. F-22, Eurofighter Consortium EF-2000, and French Rafale, none of which have yet entered service.

SYSTEMS

Generation 3 contains a large number of systems representing the diversity of approaches and mission specializations being explored with the technology of the time. The lighter end of the fighter spectrum is represented by a number of single-engine designs. These include the Soviet MiG-21 Fishbed, French Mirage III/5 and Mirage F.1, Israeli Kfir, and U.S. F-5E, while those geared for the attack mission include the U.S. A-7 Corsair II, British Jaguar, French Etendard IVM and Super Etendard, and Japanese F-1. A step up the weight ladder brings one to the U.S. F-4 Phantom II, Soviet MiG-23/-27 Flogger, MiG-25 Foxbat, and Su-17/20/22 Fitter, the Chinese J-8 Finback, and Swedish AJ.37. The heaviest systems include the swing-wing Soviet Su-24 Fencer and U.S. F-111 Aardvark strike aircraft.[2]

The signpost systems for this generation are the U.S. F-4 Phantom, the Soviet MiG-21 and MiG-23, and the French Mirage III. Peebles (1995, 220) writes that:

> . . . comparisons between the F-4 and the MiG-21 indicated that, on the surface, they were evenly matched...when [the two fought], the results were a draw—the F-4 would win some fights, the MiG-21 would win others. There were no clear advantages . . .

. . . although the former was much larger, heavier, and had a better radar. The MiG-23, with its variable-geometry wings, larger size, and more powerful radar, was seen by the Soviets as a "half-generational" step up from the MiG-21. Still, as Gunston (1986b, 20) writes,

> To a first approximation, the MiG-23 is rather like a Soviet equivalent of the F-4 Phantom. It has roughly the same level of technology, roughly the same capabilities as a fighter, and a generally similar level of performance...[its radar] is clearly broadly comparable to the Westinghouse AWG-10 used in some Phantoms, both in bulk and operating modes.

Israel military officials have categorized it as little improvement over the MiG-21 in most respects, despite its sequentially higher designation number (Cockburn 1984, 230).

The MiG-21's performance was also described as "roughly equal to that of the Mirage III" by Israeli sources, with the latter being outperformed at higher altitudes but having a longer range. Similarly, "while the F-4 is not as maneuverable as the MiG-21 or Mirage, it was fast, [and] had twice the range" of the latter pair (Nordeen and Nicole 1996, 184, 198, 238). The Mirage F.1 was a later development, but still "roughly comparable with U.S. F-4 Phantoms" (Davis 1996, 29). Lacking the advanced radar and other features of Generation 4 aircraft, it is firmly a Generation 3 system, having a similar relationship to the Mirage III as the MiG-23 does to the MiG-21.[3] The Chinese J-8 is based on MiG-23 technology provided to China by Egypt (Allen et al. 1995, 225), and is roughly equivalent to an F-4 in sophistication.[4] The MiG-25 is a very specialized design, optimized for the extreme high-speed/high-altitude interception mission, and its design parameters are quite different from the other aircraft in this generation. Nevertheless, its avionics and electronics suite, overall design, and weapons fits also place it in the third generation rather than the fourth.[5]

In a manner that would repeat itself in the following generation, the designers of Western Generation 3 aircraft like the Mirage III and F-4 discovered that while capable, their aircraft were expensive and often difficult to maintain. As a result, they designed lighter counterparts (similar in size to the MiG-21) that maintained critical Generation 3 features of the heavier jets while reducing cost and size significantly. The resulting "high-low" mix of systems yielded a plethora of additional aircraft types either geared for a more limited range of missions, or destined for the export market. The F-5E Tiger II was a single-engined fighter which supplemented the F-4, and was in fact used to simulate the MiG-21 in mock combat with other U.S. fighters, being equal to the MiG in most respects (Cordesman 1983, 87). Similarly, the Mirage 5 was a simplified version of the Mirage III, and the Israeli Kfir is basically an unlicenced copy of the Mirage 5 with numerous Israeli systems and the J-79 engine of the F-4 Phantom (Gunston 1986a, 177).

Whereas the F-4/-5, MiG-21/-23, and Mirages were optimized for air combat, the second cluster of similar systems in this generation was geared toward the attack role, even though the aircraft retained some air-to-air capabilities. The A-7 Corsair II was to the F-4's attack role what the F-5E was to its fighter role: a less costly version that kept all of its best features for that single role but omitted the others considered non-essential to the primary task (in this case, a radar, a second engine and pilot, and radar-guided air-to-air missiles). The Japanese F-1 and Franco-British Jaguar both had a similar relationship with the F-4s exported to those countries as well.[6] The Etendard IV/Super Etendard series of French light carrier attack jets had a similar relationship to the Mirages, while the Soviet Su-17 swing-wing attack jet omitted the air-to-air features of the MiG-23 swing-wing fighter but still belongs in the same generation (Sweetman 1982, 187).

The final cluster of systems in this generation includes two very similar aircraft, the F-111 and the Su-24. The Su-24 has been described as an "F-111 lookalike" (Taylor 1986, 89), a "clear counterpart to the F-111"

(Zaloga 1989, 213), or "similar to the F-111 in all major respects" (Cockburn 1984, 233; Hartcup 1993, 202). Unusually, both straddle the divide between third and fourth generation systems. While all variants feature the swing wings, static inlets, and conventional airframe characteristic of other third generation designs, only the latest models have the sophisticated terrain-following radars (TFR), attack avionics, and other internal systems which make them "almost new aircraft" conceptually similar to the fourth generation Tornado (Gunston 1986a, 274). In this study, for reasons of conceptual coherence, the final major variant of each design (the Su-24M and F-111D/F) is considered a fourth generation system, although this has almost no impact on the data or subsequent analysis.[7]

Generation 4 is comprised of twelve systems: the U.S. F-14 Tomcat, F-15 Eagle, F-16 Fighting Falcon, F/A-18 Hornet, Soviet MiG-29 Fulcrum, MiG-31 Foxhound, and Su-27 Flanker, French Mirage 2000, Swedish JA.37 Viggen, the Anglo-German-Italian Tornado, and late models of the Soviet Fencer (Su-24M) and U.S. Aardvark (F-111D/F).

Descriptions of the unity of this generation in the defense technology literature are many and unambiguous. Allen et al. (1995, 140) writes that "the United States began introducing fourth-generation fighters (the F-14, F-15, F-16, and F-18) in the mid-1970s, whereas the Chinese are only now starting to operate equivalent systems (such as the Su-27) some two decades later." Taylor (1986, 86–7) writes that ". . . [the MiG-29, MiG-31, and Su-27] represent a new generation of Soviet fighters;" that ". . . [the MiG-29] can be judged as the Soviet equivalent of the U.S. F-16;" and that ". . . the Sukhoi Su-27 Flanker is the Soviet equivalent of the [F-15 Eagle] and has a radar with lookdown/shootdown and track-while-scan comparable in performance to the F-15's AN/APG-63." Zaloga (1989, 214) observes that ". . . the MiG-29 was developed in the early 1970s as a counterpart to the F-16 and F-18 . . . and shares a very similar configuration [to the latter plane]." Belyakov and Marmain (1994, 323) writes that "the [MiG-29] was intended to counter a trio of American fighters developed during the 1960s and 1970s: the F-15, F-16, and F-18." Gunston (1986a, 27, 204) notes that the MiG-29 is a "close parallel" to the F/A-18, the Su-27 is an "equivalent" to the F-15, the F-14 is the "naval contemporary" of the F-15, and the MiG-31 "has an advanced lookdown/shootdown radar with track-while-scan, a radar comparable with that fitted to the U.S. F-14 Tomcat."[8] Finally, a Soviet engineer even went so far as to publicly admit that "without the F-15, there would never have been a Su-27. Without the F-16, there would never have been a MiG-29" (Lambeth 1996, 237).

The Tornado contains many features common to other fourth generation systems, but is optimized for long-range strike. Similar to the aforementioned late-model Su-24M and F-111D/F, its IDS (Interdictor/Strike) variant was designed to drop heavy bomb loads, including precision-guided munitions (PGMs), in poor weather and darkness, and contains the most advanced navigation and targeting sensors available during the 1980s, including FLIR (Forward Looking Infrared Radar) pods, TFR (Terrain Following Radar), and advanced electronic countermeasures (ECM).[9] An ADV (Air Defense Variant) also exists, and, as a long-range stand-off interceptor with a powerful look-down/shoot-down radar, is similar in conception to the F-14 or MiG-31.

ADOPTER LISTS

GENERATION 3 (90 ADOPTERS)

1.	Afghanistan	MiG-21 (1967); Su-17 (1983); MiG-23 (1985)
2.	Albania	J-7 (1973)
3.	Algeria	MiG-21 (1966); Su-17 (1978); MiG-23 (1979); MiG-25 (1980)
4.	Angola	MiG-21 (1977); MiG-23 (1984); Su-17 (1985)
5.	Argentina	Mirage III/5 (1973); Super Etendard (1982)
6.	Australia	Mirage III/5 (1964); F-111 (1975)
7.	Bahrain	F-5E (1986)
8.	Bangladesh	MiG-21 (1974); J-7 (1990)
9.	Belgium	Mirage III/5 (1971)
10.	Brazil	Mirage III/5 (1973); F-5E (1976)
11.	Bulgaria	MiG-21 (1963); MiG-23 (1978); MiG-25 (1982); Su-17 (1985)
12.	Burkina Faso	MiG-21 (1988)
13.	Cambodia	MiG-21 (1986)
14.	Chile	F-5E (1977); Mirage III/5 (1981)
15.	China	J-7 (1968); J-8 (1986)
16.	Colombia	Mirage III/5 (1974)
17.	Congo	MiG-21 (1989)
18.	Cuba	MiG-21 (1963); MiG-23 (1978)
19.	Czechoslovakia	MiG-21 (1963); MiG-23 (1978); Su-17 (1985)
20.	East Germany	MiG-21 (1963); MiG-23 (1980); Su-17 (1985)
21.	Ecuador	Jaguar (1980); Mirage F.1 (1980); Mirage III/5 (1983)
22.	Egypt	MiG-21 (1963); MiG-23 (1974); Mirage III/5 (1974); Su-17 (1975); F-4 (1980); J-7 (1981)
23.	Ethiopia	F-5E (1975); MiG-21 (1978); MiG-23 (1978)
24.	Finland	MiG-21 (1963)
25.	France	Mirage III/5 (1961); Etendard IVM (1962); Jaguar (1973); Mirage F.1 (1974); Super Etendard (1979)
26.	Gabon	Mirage III/5 (1979)
27.	Greece	F-4 (1972); A-7 (1976); Mirage F.1 (1976)
28.	Guinea	MiG-21 (1989)
29.	Honduras	F-5E (1988)
30.	Hungary	MiG-21 (1963); MiG-23 (1980); Su-17 (1985)
31.	India	MiG-21 (1964); MiG-23 (1981); MiG-25 (1982); Jaguar (1982)

32. Indonesia	MiG-21 (1965); F-5E (1981)
33. Iran	F-4 (1972); F-5E (1974); J-7 (1993)
34. Iraq	MiG-21 (1964); Su-17 (1975); MiG-23 (1977); MiG-25 (1981); Mirage F.1 (1982); J-7 (1984); Super Etendard (1985)
35. Israel	Mirage III/5 (1963); F-4 (1970)
36. Japan	F-4 (1974)
37. Jordan	F-5E (1976); Mirage F.1 (1983)
38. Kenya	F-5E (1978)
39. Kuwait	Mirage F.1 (1977)
40. Laos	MiG-21 (1978)
41. Lebanon	Mirage III/5 (1969)
42. Libya	Mirage III/5 (1972); MiG-23 (1977); Mirage F.1 (1979); MiG-21 (1980); MiG-25 (1980); Su-17 (1981)
43. Madagascar	MiG-21 (1980)
44. Malaysia	F-5E (1976)
45. Mali	MiG-21 (1986)
46. Mexico	F-5E (1983)
47. Mongolia	MiG-21 (1979)
48. Morocco	Mirage F.1 (1978); F-5E (1981)
49. Mozambique	MiG-21 (1978)
50. Myanmar	J-7 (1992)
51. Nigeria	MiG-21 (1977); Jaguar (1985)
52. North Korea	MiG-21 (1966); MiG-23 (1986)
53. North Yemen	F-5E (1980); MiG-21 (1980); Su-17 (1981)
54. Oman	Jaguar (1980)
55. Pakistan	Mirage III/5 (1969); J-7 (1989)
56. Peru	Mirage III/5 (1975); Su-17 (1978)
57. Poland	MiG-21 (1963); Su-17 (1975); MiG-23 (1980)
58. Portugal	A-7 (1982)
59. Qatar	Mirage F.1 (1985)
60. Romania	MiG-21 (1963); MiG-23 (1982)
61. Saudi Arabia	F-5E (1975)
62. Singapore	F-5E (1980)
63. Somalia	MiG-21 (1975)
64. South Africa	Mirage III/5 (1964); Mirage F.1 (1977)
65. South Korea	F-4 (1973); F-5E (1975)
66. South Yemen	MiG-21 (1973); MiG-23 (1980); Su-17 (1980)
67. Spain	Mirage III/5 (1970); F-4 (1972); Mirage F.1 (1976)
68. Sri Lanka	J-7 (1992); Mirage III/5 (1996)
69. Sudan	MiG-21 (1971); F-5E (1983); MiG-23 (1988); J-7 (1996)
70. Sweden	AJ.37 (1971)
71. Switzerland	Mirage III/5 (1967); F-5E (1979)
72. Syria	MiG-21 (1967); Su-17 (1974); MiG-23 (1975); MiG-25 (1981)
73. Taiwan	F-5E (1975)
74. Tanzania	J-7 (1975)

75. Thailand   F-5E (1979); A-7 (1996)
76. Tunisia   F-5E (1985)
77. Turkey   F-4 (1974)
78. Uganda   MiG-21 (1976)
79. UAE   Mirage III/5 (1974)
80. U.K.   F-4 (1969); Jaguar (1974)
81. U.S.   F-4 (1961); A-7 (1966); F-111 (1968); F-5E (1973)
82. USSR   MiG-21 (1960); MiG-23 (1970); Su-24 (1970); Su-17 (1971);
                    MiG-25 (1972)
83. Venezuela   Mirage III/5 (1974); F-5E (1979)
84. Vietnam (N)   MiG-21 (1966); Su-17 (1982)
85. Vietnam (S)   F-5E (1974)
86. West Germany   F-4 (1971)
87. Yugoslavia   MiG-21 (1963)
88. Zaire   Mirage III/5 (1975)
89. Zambia   MiG-21 (1982)
90. Zimbabwe   J-7 (1987)

GENERATION 4 (54 ADOPTERS)

1. Algeria   Su-24M (1992)
2. Australia   F/A-18 (1986)
3. Bahrain   F-16 (1991)
4. Belgium   F-16 (1980)
5. Bulgaria   MiG-29 (1990)
6. Canada   F/A-18 (1983)
7. China   Su-27 (1993)
8. Cuba   MiG-29 (1990)
9. Czechoslovakia MiG-29 (1989)
10. Denmark   F-16 (1981)
11. East Germany   MiG-29 (1988)
12. Egypt   F-16 (1983); Mirage 2000 (1987)
13. Finland   F/A-18 (1996)
14. France   Mirage 2000 (1985)
15. Greece   F-16 (1989); Mirage 2000 (1989)
16. Hungary   MiG-29 (1994)
17. India   MiG-29 (1985); Mirage 2000 (1986)
18. Indonesia   F-16 (1990)
19. Iran   F-14 (1977); MiG-29 (1990); Su-24M (1994)
20. Iraq   MiG-29 (1988); Su-24M (1991)
21. Israel   F-15 (1977); F-16 (1981)
22. Italy   Tornado (1982)
23. Japan   F-15 (1982)
24. Jordan   F-16 (1997)
25. Kuwait   F/A-18 (1992)
26. Libya   Su-24M (1990)

27. Malaysia   MiG-29 (1996)
28. Netherlands   F-16 (1980)
29. North Korea   MiG-29 (1989)
30. Norway   F-16 (1981)
31. Pakistan   F-16 (1984)
32. Peru   Mirage 2000 (1988)
33. Poland   MiG-29 (1989)
34. Portugal   F-16 (1995)
35. Romania   MiG-29 (1990)
36. Saudi Arabia   F-15 (1983); Tornado (1988)
37. Singapore   F-16 (1989)
38. South Korea   F-16 (1987)
39. Spain   F/A-18 (1987)
40. Sweden   JA.37 Viggen (1979)
41. Switzerland   F/A-18 (1997)
42. Syria   MiG-29 (1988); Su-24M (1990)
43. Taiwan   F-16 (1997)
44. Thailand   F-16 (1989)
45. Turkey   F-16 (1988)
46. UAE   Mirage 2000 (1990)
47. U.K.   Tornado (1982)
48. U.S.   F-14 (1972); F-111D/F (1972); F-15 (1974); F-16 (1979);
                    F/A-18 (1983)
49. USSR   MiG-31 (1982); Su-24M (1983); MiG-29 (1984); Su-27
                    (1986)
50. Venezuela   F-16 (1984)
51. Vietnam (N)   Su-27 (1997)
52. West Germany   Tornado (1982)
53. Yemen (S/U)   MiG-29 (1994)
54. Yugoslavia   MiG-29 (1990)

DIFFUSION OF GENERATION 3 COMBAT AIRCRAFT

1960	USSR	1
1961	France, U.S.	3
1962		3
1963	Bulgaria, Cuba, Czechoslovakia, East Germany, Egypt,	
	Hungary, Israel, Poland, Romania, Yugoslavia	13
1964	Australia, Finland, India, Iraq, South Africa	18
1965	Indonesia	19
1966	Algeria, North Korea, Vietnam (N)	22
1967	Afghanistan, Switzerland, Syria	25
1968	China	26
1969	Lebanon, Pakistan, U.K.	29
1970	Spain	30
1971	Belgium, Sudan, Sweden, West Germany	34
1972	Greece, Iran, Libya	37

1973	Albania, Argentina, Brazil, South Korea, South Yemen	42
1974	Bangladesh, Colombia, Japan, Turkey, UAE, Venezuela, Vietnam (S)	49
1975	Ethiopia, Peru, Saudi Arabia, Somalia, Taiwan, Tanzania, Zaire	56
1976	Jordan, Malaysia, Uganda	59
1977	Angola, Chile, Kuwait, Nigeria	63
1978	Kenya, Laos, Morocco, Mozambique, Oman	68
1979	Gabon, Mongolia, Thailand	71
1980	Ecuador, Madagascar, North Yemen, Singapore	75
1981		75
1982	Portugal, Zambia	77
1983	Mexico	78
1984		78
1985	Qatar, Tunisia	80
1986	Bahrain, Cambodia, Mali	83
1987	Zimbabwe	84
1988	Burkina Faso, Honduras	86
1989	Congo, Guinea	88
1990		88
1991		88
1992	Myanmar, Sri Lanka	90
1993		90
1994		90
1995		90
1996		90
1997		90

column on right = cumulative number of adopters

DIFFUSION OF GENERATION 4 COMBAT AIRCRAFT

1972	U.S.	1
1973		1
1974		1
1975		1
1976		1
1977	Iran, Israel	3
1978		3
1979	Sweden	4
1980	Belgium, Netherlands	6
1981	Denmark, Norway	8
1982	Italy, Japan, West Germany, U.K., USSR	13
1983	Canada, Egypt, Saudi Arabia	16
1984	Pakistan, Venezuela	18
1985	France, India	20
1986	Australia	21
1987	South Korea, Spain	23
1988	East Germany, Iraq, Peru, Syria, Turkey	28

1989	Czechoslovakia, Greece, North Korea, Poland, Singapore, Thailand	34
1990	Bulgaria, Cuba, Indonesia, Libya, Romania, UAE, Yugoslavia	41
1991	Bahrain	42
1992	Algeria, Kuwait	44
1993	China	45
1994	Hungary, Yemen (S)	47
1995	Portugal	48
1996	Finland, Malaysia	50
1997	Jordan, Switzerland, Taiwan, Vietnam	54

column on right = cumulative number of adopters

NOTES

[1] Sapfir (1991, 199) clearly delineates the four generations, listing "swept-wing jet[s]" (F- 86, MiG-15) as the first generation, "supersonic fighter[s]" (F-100, MiG-19) as the second, "swing-wing" jets (F-111, Su-24) as the third, and "new generation" fighters as the fourth (F-14/15/16/18, MiG-29, Su-27). Nordeen and Nicole (1996, 156) consider the MiG-15 and F-86 "second generation jets," counting the wartime jets as the first generation, but the difference is semantic, and most start generational counting with the first postwar systems.

[2] A pair of Soviet interceptors, the Su-11 Fishpot and Su-15 Flagon, could also be considered Generation 3 systems, but they have never been exported, and were preceded into service by other Soviet third generation aircraft, making their influence on the data set nil (Gunston 1986a, 271).

[3] Kolodziej (1987) notes that the Mirage F.1 lost the four-nation European fighter competition to the fourth generation F-16 in the 1970s due to its inferior technical features.

[4] Starr (1996, 60) equates the J-7 (MiG-21) with the F-4 and the J-8 Finback with an "upgraded" (i.e. late model) F-4. Since the J-8 is derived from MiG-23 technology, it meshes well with the classification of all four aircraft (F-4, J-8, MiG-21/J-7 and MiG-23) belonging in the same technological generation.

[5] Sweetman (1982, 189) also describes the MiG-31 as the "next generation" replacement for the MiG-25. Since the MiG-31 is generally accepted to be a fourth generation aircraft, this would place the MiG-25 into the third.

[6] Gunston (1986a, 225) notes that the Mitsubishi F-1's predecessor (the T-2) "bears more than a passing resemblance to the Jaguar," and both share the Jaguar's twin Adour engines. (Gunston, 1985: 51) notes that the F-1 is "almost indistinguishable from the Jaguar." The Super Etendard also barely bested a navalized Jaguar for the French Navy's attack plane requirement (Gunston 1986a, 134). Berman (1978, 45) also terms the Jaguar "similar" to the attack version of the MiG-23.

[7] Since no late-model F-111s were exported, and the clearly fourth generation F-14 preceded the F-111D/F into service by a year or two, the latter's classification as a fourth generation system has no impact on the data. Similarly, late model Su-24s appeared only after the arrival of the fourth generation MiG-31 in the Soviet inventory. Only two of the adopters of the Su-24M improved model (Algeria and Libya)

failed to purchase other clearly fourth generation systems first, rendering its effect on the data minimal as well.

[8] While similar comparisons involving the Mirage 2000 and JA.37 Viggen are less frequent due to their lower visibility in global air forces, their systems closely match those of the other fighters (look down/shoot-down radar, etc.), and thus are categorized as fourth generation systems.

[9] Gunston (1986a, 274) notes that the "all-around capability of the [late-model Su-24 and Tornado] is uncannily similar."

Appendix C
Attack Helicopters

ARMS CATEGORY

AFTER WORLD WAR II, THE DEVELOPMENT OF THE MILITARY HELICOPTER as a transport, liaison, and utility vehicle proceeded apace. However, given the dangerous environment in which helicopters operated, it was not very long before crews began carrying makeshift weaponry to suppress ground fire and neutralize other threats. Despite this, military planners did not began to envision the development of dedicated attack helicopters, also known as helicopter gunships, optimized for carrying air-to-surface weapons and providing fire support to ground forces, until the mid-1960s. While virtually any helicopter can carry some form of armament, and, in fact, many utility models have been converted to the gunship role, only the dedicated attack helicopter features the combination of heavy weapons, special targeting avionics, and protective armor to allow it to operate in the presence of high concentrations of ground-based enemy air defenses.

GENERATIONAL DEVELOPMENT

Compared to their utility model cousins, Generation 1 attack helicopters featured slimmer fuselages to provide minimal targets to enemy defenders during head-on attacks and heavier armor to absorb enemy fire. They also had side-mounted weapons pylons for carrying rockets and missiles and nose-mounted turrets for machine guns, cannon, and grenade launchers. In the U.S., Italian, and Soviet cases (the only producers of Generation 1 systems), the two-person crew rode in stepped, tandem pilot and gunner cockpits. The larger Soviet attack helicopters also featured rear compartments for troop carriage. Upgrades to these basic machines added more advanced missiles and missile aiming systems over time, but the systems maintained their basic configurations.

Generation 2 systems featured much heavier armor than their predecessors, made possible by, among other things, the emergence of more powerful engines capable of lifting heavier loads. The biggest advances, however, came with the addition of integrated target acquisition and designation systems that added night/all-weather fighting capabilities that far surpassed anything possessed by the earlier generation. When equipped with even more advanced anti-tank guided missiles (ATGMs), the Generation 2 attack helicopters became powerful dedicated tank hunters as well as extremely useful for providing basic air support.

SYSTEMS

Generation 1 attack helicopters comprise the U.S. AH-1 Cobra, the Soviet Mi-24 Hind, and the Italian A.129 Mangusta. Zaloga (1989, 105) calls the Mi-24 the "counterpart" of the AH-1, although the former's design philosophy (incorporating a troop compartment in addition to its air-to-ground weapons) results in a "bulkier," faster, and "much more massive" helicopter. Ryan (1995, 28–34) also claims that the AH-1 is the "closest competitor" to the Mi-24, and an analysis of the technical features of both (Gunston and Spick 1986, 104–5, 142–3) shows the basic similarities. All three share the same tandem cockpit/gunner forward layout, narrow fuselage, and employ similar weapons, including a nose-mounted turret and stub wing pylons for carrying anti-tank missiles and other ordnance. These three (plus the Apache, which is clearly a second-generation system) were the only systems identified by name as "attack helicopters" under the provisions of the Conventional Forces in Europe Treaty, signed by the members of NATO and the Warsaw Pact in 1990.

Generation 2 attack helicopters consist of the U.S. AH-64 Apache, Russian Ka-50 Hokum and Mi-28 Havoc, should the last ever see service. Most sources clearly equate the Russian and U.S. systems in this generation. Sources claim, for example, that "[Ka-50 and Mi-28] have an air-to-air and a ground support mission capability similar to the U.S. Apache," that the Mi-28 is "similar in concept and appearance to the AH-64 Apache" (Mellinger 1995, 179, 207), or that the Mi-28's "general configuration is similar to that of the slightly smaller U.S. Army AH-64A Apache, and it has broadly similar applications" (Taylor 1993, 77). Zaloga (1989, 165) also calls the Apache and Havoc the "next generation of attack helicopter," after the Cobra/Hind (first) generation.

ADOPTER LISTS

GENERATION 1 (39 ADOPTERS)

1. Afghanistan   Mi-24 (1979)
2. Algeria   Mi-24 (1980)
3. Angola   Mi-24 (1985)
4. Bahrain   AH-1 (1996)
5. Bulgaria   Mi-24 (1980)
6. Cuba   Mi-24 (1983)
7. Czechoslovakia   Mi-24 (1980)
8. East Germany   Mi-24 (1974)
9. Ethiopia   Mi-24 (1981)
10. Greece   AH-1 (1987)
11. Hungary   Mi-24 (1980)
12. India   Mi-24 (1984)
13. Iran   AH-1 (1975)
14. Iraq   Mi-24 (1977)
15. Israel   AH-1 (1976)
16. Italy   A.129 (1990)
17. Japan   AH-1 (1985)
18. Jordan   AH-1 (1986)
19. Libya   Mi-24 (1980)
20. Mongolia   Mi-24 (1991)
21. Mozambique   Mi-24 (1985)
22. Nicaragua   Mi-24 (1985)
23. North Korea   Mi-24 (1986)
24. Pakistan   AH-1 (1982)
25. Peru   Mi-24 (1984)
26. Poland   Mi-24 (1980)
27. Sierra Leone   Mi-24 (1996)
28. South Korea   AH-1 (1978)
29. South Yemen   Mi-24 (1980)
30. Sri Lanka   Mi-24 (1997)
31. Sudan   Mi-24 (1991)
32. Syria   Mi-24 (1984)
33. Taiwan   AH-1 (1994)
34. Thailand   AH-1 (1990)
35. Turkey   AH-1 (1991)
36. U.S.   AH-1 (1967)
37. USSR   Mi-24 (1972)
38. Vietnam (N)   Mi-24 (1985)
39. Zaire   Mi-24 (1997)

GENERATION 2 (8 ADOPTERS)

1.	Egypt	AH-64 (1994)
2.	Greece	AH-64 (1996)
3.	Israel	AH-64 (1991)
4.	Netherlands	AH-64 (1997)
5.	Saudi Arabia	AH-64 (1994)
6.	UAE	AH-64 (1994)
7.	U.S.	AH-64 (1986)
8.	USSR	Ka-50 (1995)

DIFFUSION OF GENERATION 1 ATTACK HELICOPTERS

1967	U.S.	1
1968		1
1969		1
1970		1
1971		1
1972		1
1973	USSR	2
1974	East Germany	3
1975	Iran	4
1976	Israel	5
1977	Iraq	6
1978	South Korea	7
1979	Afghanistan	8
1980	Algeria, Bulgaria, Czechoslovakia, Hungary, Libya, Poland, South Yemen	15
1981	Ethiopia	16
1982	Pakistan	17
1983	Cuba	18
1984	India, Peru, Syria	21
1985	Angola, Japan, Mozambique, Nicaragua, Vietnam	26
1986	Jordan, North Korea	28
1987	Greece	29
1988		29
1989		29
1990	Italy, Thailand	31
1991	Mongolia, Sudan, Turkey	34
1992		34
1993		34
1994	Taiwan	35
1995		35
1996	Bahrain, Sierra Leone	37
1997	Sri Lanka, Zaire	39

column on right = cumulative number of adopters

DIFFUSION OF GENERATION 2 ATTACK HELICOPTERS

1986	U.S.	1
1987		1
1988		1
1989		1
1990		1
1991	Israel	2
1992		2
1993		2
1994	Egypt, Saudi Arabia, UAE	5
1995	USSR	6
1996	Greece	7
1997	Netherlands	8

column on right = cumulative number of adopters

Appendix D
Main Battle Tanks

ARMS CATEGORY

P RIOR TO THE LATE 1940S, TANKS WERE GENERALLY CLASSIFIED ACCORDING to their weight, with light, medium, and heavy tanks being used by all the major military powers. The postwar main battle tank (MBT) grew out of the heavy gun tanks of the World War II period. Threats from a plethora of anti-tank weapons of varying calibers and ranges had increased. There was also a need to protect against at least the indirect effects of nuclear blasts and radiation expected to be a feature of any major war. These both led to a drive for heavier armor, and thus larger guns to penetrate the armor of similarly-equipped opposing tanks (Hartcup 1993, 112).[1] All tank designs represent a compromise between the need for mobility, armor protection, and firepower on the battlefield (Dunnigan 1996). Since 1945, tank capabilities in all three areas have significantly increased. Still, individual designs may emphasize one quality at the expense of another. When compared to U.S. and other Western designs, for example, Soviet tanks tend to be smaller and lighter (and thus theoretically harder to detect and destroy), with larger guns. However, they feature less armor protection for the crew.[2]

GENERATIONAL DEVELOPMENT

Generation 1 MBTs generally featured larger guns than their World War II predecessors. They also had heavier armor and wider tracks for increased cross-country mobility. They began to appear in 1948, with the Soviet T-54/-55 (with a 100 mm gun) and U.S. M-47/-48 Patton (with a 90 mm gun). Later incarnations, like the Soviet T-62 (an evolutionary development of the T-55 with a smoothbore 115 mm gun) arrived into the early 1960s.[3]

Generation 2 systems featured three main improvements over the preceding generation. First, more powerful engines led to increased weights, thicker steel armor, and larger guns, from 105 mm up to 125 mm caliber. Second, advances in gun technology fostered attempts to integrate anti-tank guided missiles (ATGM) into the main gun apparatus. The Soviets had the greatest success in this area. It was hoped that a guided anti-tank round would increase gun accuracy, reduce the number of rounds needed on average to score a single hit on an enemy tank, and allow engagements at longer ranges. The Soviet Union also introduced automatic main gun loaders to replace one of the tank's crew. The reduction in necessary space inside the tank led to an overall smaller silhouette and thus a smaller target for enemy gunners. Third, designers began to introduce more sophisticated aiming and detection systems for the main gun. Earlier Generation 2 models were equipped with infrared searchlights and gun stabilizers. Later ones sported laser-rangefinders and gunlaying computers. Generation 2 systems began to enter service about 1960.

Generation 3 systems currently represent the latest in MBT design. The most significant innovations have been in the areas of armor and fire-control. Previous MBT generations featured cast and welded steel chassis and turrets. Third generation systems feature composite armors made from layers of synthetic materials, including ceramics, plastics, carbon fiber, depleted uranium (DU), and other exotic substances. These can almost double armored protection without equivalent increases in overall weight (Hartcup 1993, 121). These tanks also possess advanced integrated fire-control systems (FCS) for their main guns. These include laser-rangefinders and advanced thermal and optical sights that allow for firing on the move, in poor weather conditions, and at night.

SYSTEMS

Generation 2 is comprised of the U.S. M-60, Soviet T-64 and T-72, British Chieftain and its derivatives, German Leopard 1, French AMX-30, Israeli Merkava, Japanese Type 74, Swiss Panzer 61, Italian OF-40, Swedish S-Tank, and Chinese Type 69–III.

According to Friedman et al. (1985, 133), "during the 1960s, the NATO nations developed and deployed a new generation of MBTs," centered around the M-60, Leopard 1, and AMX-30, after the collapse of a Franco-German-Italian effort to create a common NATO tank in the late 1950s led to the development of three similar, parallel national projects to meet the same requirements.[4] Since the OF-40 "incorporates some components of the Leopard 1 and physically resembles the German tank"

(Gelbart 1996, 33, 57), it also belongs in this generation. All four, plus the Merkava and the Japanese Type 74, use the same 105 mm main gun, and have very similar systems and performance. The British decided to equip the Chieftain with a 120mm gun, closer to the size of Soviet tanks' main weapon, but all the export derivatives (Khalid, Vickers Mk.1/3, Vijayanta) used a standard 105 mm barrel, and it is in most ways similar to others Generation 2 tanks. Similarly, Israel's Merkava was built only when a request to purchase Chieftain was refused (Gelbart 1996, 33). Gelbart (1996, 62) also writes that "the Japanese Type 74 is a clear generation ahead of its predecessor," the Type 61 similar to the earlier U.S. M-48, and the Type 74 itself can thus be seen as a generational equivalent to the M-60.

Foss (1992, 24) writes that "in many respects, the T-64 MBT was the most advanced MBT in the world when it entered production in the mid-1960s," indicating that it was a generational leap over the existing Soviet tanks, and Bitzinger (1991,15) also claims equivalency between the T-64 and M-60.[5] Dunnigan (1996, 64) notes that the M-60 and T- 72 have approximately the same amount of armor protection, with the latter having a more powerful, larger caliber 125mm gun.[6] Cordesman (1997, 125) writes that the M-60 "lacks a decisive technical superiority over the T-72," also indicating a measure of technological parity. Cockburn (1984, 200) claims that the M-60 is "better than the T-54, T-55, and T-62, but slightly inferior to the T-64 and T-72." Although it did not see widespread service, the U.S. did have an M-60 variant (the M-60A2) which could launch a guided missile from its main projectile in the same manner as the T-64 and T-72. The Chinese Type 69–III (also called the Type 80 or Type 88) is similarly designed in the Soviet style, and clearly labeled a "second generation MBT" by one authority (Foss 1992, 6). Finally, Schneider (1991) says that the T-72 is directly comparable to the Chieftain, AMX-30, Leopard I, and M-60A1.

Generation 3 systems include the U.S. M-1 Abrams, Soviet T-80 and T-90, British Challenger, German Leopard 2, French Leclerc, Italian Ariete, Israeli Merkava 3, Japanese Type 90, and the South Korean Type 88 Rokit.

Gelbart (1996, 115) claims that the Challenger, Leopard 2, M-1 Abrams, Leclerc, and the Merkava 3 are candidates for "the best MBT on the market," clearly identifying them as generational equivalents, while Garrett (1989, 61) says the same about the M-1, Challenger, and Leopard 2. Gelbart also writes (1996, 59) that Ariete was developed "to meet an Italian requirement for a Leopard 1 and M-60 replacement," both second generation tanks. The Challenger, Leclerc, and Abrams have competed fiercely for contracts with several Middle Eastern nations in the 1990s (Kuwait, Saudi Arabia, the UAE), and the technical differences between them are considered minimal (Cordesman 1997, 129). The Merkava 3's armor is considered "comparable to Chobham," the armor devised for use on the Challenger and which served as the pattern for armor on the M-1 and Leopard 2, two parallel designs necessitated by the collapse of the joint German-U.S. MBT-70 project that both ended up sharing the same 120 mm gun.[7] Zaloga (1989, 103) also identifies the Abrams, Challenger, and Leopard 2 as representing a "new generation of tanks." The Japanese Type 90 and South Korean Type 88 share the advanced armor and integrated FCS of the others, and therefore can also be classified as third generation (Ogorkiewicz 1996, 111).

Initial Pentagon reports that the T-80 was equivalent to the M-1 (and therefore justified the latter's development by the U.S. Army) were contested by a number of analysts (Sapfir 1991, 48; Messinger 1985, 31; Cockburn 1984) who claimed that the T-80 was no more than a minor upgrade of the T-64/-72. This is now known to be somewhat in error, as shown in several recent publications. Gelbart (1996, 85) notes that the Soviet Union did "not appear to place the same level of trust in ceramic, laminated armor as do Western manufacturers of modern MBTs," and this, combined with the Soviet penchant for smaller, lighter tanks, means that the design philosophy behind the T-80/-90 family has resulted in a somewhat differently-engineered machine. Nevertheless, the T-80 does feature advanced ceramic armor around the turret (Foss 1992, 15), a large-caliber 125 mm gun, and integrated FCS of other third generation tanks, and was designed to counter M-1s, Challengers, and Leopard 2s on the European battlefield.[8] It also retains the autoloader and gun-fired ATGMs not found on the Western tanks, and is powered by a gas turbine engine similar to that of the Abrams. Dunnigan (1996, 64) rates the armor protection and firepower of the T-80 as comparable with the early M-1 Abrams, and the derivative T-90 with the upgunned M-1A1. Russian sources themselves also compare the T-80 very favorably with other third generation MBTs.[9]

ADOPTER LISTS

GENERATION 2 (60 ADOPTERS)

1.	Algeria	T-72 (1980)
2.	Austria	M-60 (1967?)
3.	Australia	Leopard 1 (1977)
4.	Bahrain	M-60 (1988)
5.	Belgium	Leopard 1 (1969)
6.	Bulgaria	T-72 (1980)
7.	Canada	Leopard 1 (1979)
8.	Chile	AMX-30 (1982)
9.	China	Type 80 (1993)
10.	Cyprus	AMX-30 (1989)
11.	Czechoslovakia	T-72 (1980)
12.	Denmark	Leopard 1 (1977)
13.	East Germany	T-72 (1980)

14. Egypt   M-60 (1982)
15. Ethiopia   M-60 (1975)
16. Finland   T-72 (1987)
17. France   AMX-30 (1967)
18. Greece   AMX-30 (1972); Leopard 1 (1984); M-60 (1991)
19. Hungary   T-72 (1980)
20. India   Chieftain/Vijayanta (1966); T-72/Ajeya (1982)
21. Iran   M-60 (1967); Chieftain (1972); T-72 (1991)
22. Iraq   T-72 (1980); Chieftain/Khalid (1981)
23. Israel   M-60 (1971); Merkava 1 (1980)
24. Italy   M-60 (1966); Leopard 1 (1972)
25. Japan   Type 74 (1976)
26. Jordan   M-60 (1978); Chieftain/Khalid (1982)
27. Kenya   Vickers Mk.2 (1980)
28. Kuwait   Vickers Mk.1 (1971); Chieftain (1979); T-72 (1991)
29. Libya   T-72 (1980)
30. Morocco   M-60 (1990)
31. Netherlands   Leopard 1 (1970)
32. Nigeria   Vickers Mk.3 (1984)
33. North Yemen   M-60 (1980)
34. Norway   Leopard 1 (1971)
35. Oman   M-60 (1981); Chieftain (1983)
36. Pakistan   Type 80 (1993)
37. Poland   T-72 (1980)
38. Portugal   M-60 (1993)
39. Romania   T-72 (1980)
40. Qatar   AMX-30 (1978)
41. Saudi Arabia   AMX-30 (1973); M-60 (1978)
42. Sierra Leone   T-72 (1996)
43. South Korea   M-60 (1973)
44. South Vietnam   M-60 (1973)
45. Spain   AMX-30 (1974); M-60 (1993)
46. Sudan   M-60 (1982)
47. Sweden   S-Tank (1967)
48. Switzerland   Panzer 61 (1966)
49. Syria   T-72 (1981)
50. Taiwan   M-60 (1996)
51. Thailand   M-60 (1992)
52. Tunisia   M-60 (1984)
53. Turkey   Leopard 1 (1983); M-60 (1993)
54. UAE   AMX-30 (1981); OF-40 (1982)
55. UK   Chieftain (1963)
56. US   M-60 (1960)
57. USSR   T-64 (1967); T-72 (1973)
58. Venezuela   AMX-30 (1974)
59. Yugoslavia   T-72/M-84 (1985)
60. West Germany   Leopard 1 (1966)

GENERATION 3 (20 ADOPTERS)

1. China   T-80 (1996)[10]
2. Cyprus   T-80 (1997)
3. Egypt   M-1 Abrams (1991)
4. France   Leclerc (1993)
5. Israel   Merkava 3 (1990)
6. Italy   Ariete (1996)
7. Japan   Type 90 (1992)
8. Kuwait   M-1 Abrams (1995)
9. Netherlands   Leopard 2 (1983)
10. Oman   Challenger (1996)
11. Saudi Arabia M-1 Abrams (1994)
12. South Korea   Type 88 Rokit (1986)
13. Spain   Leopard 2 (1996)
14. Sweden   Leopard 2/Panzer 87 (1995)
15. Switzerland   Leopard 2/Strv. 121 (1988)
16. UAE   Leclerc (1995)
17. UK   Challenger (1984)
18. US   M-1 Abrams (1982)
19. USSR   T-80 (1984)
20. West Germany Leopard 2 (1980)

DIFFUSION OF GENERATION 2 MAIN BATTLE TANKS

1960	U.S.	1
1961		1
1962		1
1963	U.K.	2
1964		2
1965		2
1966	India, Italy, Switzerland, West Germany	6
1967	Austria, France, Iran, Sweden, USSR	11
1968		11
1969	Belgium	12
1970	Netherlands	13
1971	Israel, Kuwait, Norway	16
1972	Greece	17
1973	Saudi Arabia, South Korea, Vietnam (S)	20
1974	Venezuela, Spain	22
1975	Ethiopia	23
1976	Japan	24
1977	Australia, Denmark	26
1978	Jordan, Qatar	28
1979	Canada	29
1980	Algeria, Bulgaria, Czechoslovakia, East Germany, Hungary, Iraq, Kenya, Libya, North Yemen, Poland, Romania	40

1981	Oman, Syria, UAE	43
1982	Chile, Egypt, Sudan	46
1983	Turkey	47
1984	Nigeria, Tunisia	49
1985	Yugoslavia	50
1986		50
1987	Finland	51
1988	Bahrain	52
1989	Cyprus	53
1990	Morocco	54
1991		54
1992	Thailand	55
1993	China, Pakistan, Portugal	58
1994		58
1995		58
1996	Sierra Leone, Taiwan	60

DIFFUSION OF GENERATION 3 MAIN BATTLE TANKS

1980	West Germany	1
1981		1
1982	U.S.	2
1983	Netherlands	3
1984	U.K., USSR	5
1985		5
1986	South Korea	6
1987		6
1988	Switzerland	7
1989		7
1990	Israel	8
1991	Egypt	9
1992	Japan	10
1993	France	11
1994	Saudi Arabia	12
1995	Kuwait, Sweden, UAE	15
1996	China, Italy, Oman, Spain	19
1997	Cyprus	20

column on right = cumulative number of adopters

NOTES

[1] The term "main battle tank" did not enter the military lexicon until the 1960s. The concept itself, however, had been around for some time (Hartcup 1993, 117).

[2] Sapir (1991, 49) notes that "if we compare from generation to generation, Soviet tanks tend to be lighter than their Western counterparts [and]...are similar to the French AMX-30 and to Swiss tanks."

[3] Since their initial adoption falls well outside the time scope of this analysis, the first generation MBTs are mentioned here only for the sake of completeness and are not entered into the data base.

[4] Friedman et al. (1985, 134) initially writes that this is "reckoned to be the third generation since the introduction of tanks in 1918," apparently lumping all tanks deployed between World War I and the 1960s into a single generation! Later on the same page, however, the authors divide the post-1945 tanks into three generations for each superpower bloc (T-54/-55, T-62, and T-64 for the Soviets, and M-48, Chieftain, and Challenger/Leopard 2 for NATO). The latter scheme is taken to more accurately represent "generations" in the sense used throughout this study, although I argue in the main text of this appendix for a slightly different breakdown of the systems.

[5] The T-64 was initially equipped with a 115 mm gun, but this was changed to a 125 mm model (identical to that of the T-72) later in the T-64's design life.

[6] Dunnigan (1996, 64) omits consideration of the T-64 in his table, probably because it is historically a poorly known system that was used only by Soviet forces and has never been exported. Foss (1992, 24) indicates that the T-64 was revolutionary for its time, and that the T-72 was a somewhat simplified subsequent design that shared many of the former's better technical features; Simpkin (1984, 43) also writes that "there now seems little doubt that T-64 and T-72 were more or less contemporary solutions to the same general staff requirement." On these grounds, they are here considered part of the same generation, geared towards facing the same generational array of Western threat tanks (M-60, Leopard 1, Chieftain, etc.), with the T-64 being the initial innovation.

[7] The M-1 initially carried a 105 mm gun as an interim measure; later examples featured a 120 mm gun equivalent to that of the Challenger and Leopard 2.

[8] For a more complete discussion/comparison of the T-80 and modern Western tanks like the M-1 Abrams, see Zaloga (1989, 99–106).

[9] For a detailed Russian comparison, see Shishlevskiy (1995).

[10] *The Military Balance 1996–1997* does not list China as a T-80 operator, although other sources indicate that it imported a large number of tanks from Russia in the 1990s, and at least two (Foss 1995; SIPRI 1996) confirm a Chinese purchase of 200 T-80s. Also see Gill and Kim (1995, 64).

Preface to Appendices E, F, and G

GROUND-BASED SURFACE-TO-AIR MISSILES (SAMs) COME IN A WIDE VARI-ety of sizes, weights, ranges, and guidance systems. Because of this, discerning distinct arms categories within this broad grouping of systems is a daunting task. Consideration of various technical and operational features, however, yields a four-fold categorization of these systems: (1) *long-range SAMs*, which are usually tasked with protecting fixed or strategic targets behind the forward edge of the battle; (2) *point defense SAMs*, short-range, mobile weapons meant to provide close-in defense of key installations and protect troops engaged in direct combat with enemy forces; (3) *shoulder-fired PADS* (portable air defense systems), light missiles capable of being fired by a single soldier; and (4) *vehicle PADS*, which incorporate missiles similar to those used in shoulder-fired systems, but mount a number of firing canisters on a mobile platform.

The operational criteria for these arms categories are listed in Table A.2. In classifying individual systems, a weapon was placed into one of these categories if it met at least two of the criteria listed. In the majority of cases, systems meet all three requirements. For several reasons, this study will incorporate data from only three of these four categories, omitting vehicle PADS from consideration. First, while these missiles' launchers are vehicle-mounted like most battlefield SAMs, the missiles themselves are usually just boosted versions of shoulder-fired systems. The elimination of the need to make them light enough to be human-portable may allow them to be somewhat larger, and thus longer-ranged, but does not otherwise dramatically increase missile size or lethality.[1] Second, the SAMs in this category share infrared guidance systems similar or identical to the PADS from which they are derived. In this, their performance is much closer to PADS than to battlefield SAMs, which are almost exclusively radar-guided weapons. Last, adding the vehicle-mounted PADS to the data set would cover little empirical terrain not already accounted for by PADS themselves. In the case of virtually every adopter of the few systems in this category, the shoulder-fired version of the weapon was adopted prior to the vehicle-mounted version. As a result, if the two categories were merged, the initial adoption dates for the system would not change.

Each of the remaining three categories of SAM will be treated as a separate innovation, with successive technological generations. Long-range SAMs are covered in Appendix E, point defense SAMs in Appendix F, and shoulder-fired PADS in Appendix G.

Category	Max. Range (mi.)	Weight (lbs.)	Max. Altitude[2]	U.S. Examples
PADS	<4	<40	very low	Stinger
Vehicle PADS	<7	40 to 100	very low	Avenger
Point Defense	4 to 10	100 to 500	low	Chaparral
Long-Range	over 10	over 1,000	medium-high	Patriot

Table A.2: Surface-to-Air Missile Category Characteristics

NOTES

[1] There are five operational systems in this category. The U.S. Avenger is a vehicle-mounted Stinger PADS. The Russian SA-9 Gaskin and SA-13 Gopher use missiles similar to the SA-7 *Strela*. The Russian SA-19 uses a version of the SA-16 and SA-18 *Igla*. Finally, the Chinese Anza uses the shoulder-fired HN-5. A number of other PADS, like the British Starstreak, can be mounted on mobile chassis (in that case, the Alvis Spartan armored personnel carrier), but the combined system is not given a new name.

[2] Exact figures given for effective maximum and minimum altitude often vary considerably (for examples, compare those cited for Soviet missiles in Dunnigan (1993, 204–5) and Taylor (1993, 81–3)). As a result, I simply group altitudes into three categories representing where the missile was designed to operate and is most effective, based on Dunnigan's estimates. "Very low" means the weapon operates optimally at from 0 to about 5,000 meters, "low" from 10–100 minimum to about 12,000 meters maximum, and "medium-to-high" from 50–300 minimum upwards to 100,000 maximum. Not all missiles in each category share the same minimums and maximums, but all fall roughly within the given ranges.

Appendix E
Ground-Based Surface-to-Air Missiles I: Long-Range SAMs

ARMS CATEGORY

ALLIED BOMBING OF GERMANY IN WORLD WAR II WAS CARRIED OUT from successively higher altitudes to avoid thickening German anti-aircraft artillery (AAA) and fighter defenses. To counter this, Germany attempted to develop ground-launched, radar-guided rockets to intercept bombers. These first surface-to-air missiles (SAMs) could not be made operational in time to stave off Germany's defeat. However, the rocket technologies captured after the war provided a foundation for the initial generation of SAMs deployed by the other major powers. Advances in electronics miniaturization made succeeding generations of missiles smaller, more maneuverable in flight, and more mobile on the ground. As a result, the primary category of long-range SAMs had by the 1960s split into a number of sub-categories. Each was optimized for specific roles and missions. Despite this, however, the long-range heavy SAM (defined here as a weapon with a maximum range in excess of 10 miles and a weight of 1,000 pounds or more) still figures prominently in the air defense of many nations. The use of the Patriot missile in Operation *Desert Storm* attests to the weapon category's continuing importance.

GENERATIONAL DEVELOPMENT

Generation 1 SAMs were large, heavy weapons designed to intercept hostile aircraft at long distances from the launcher. The launchers themselves were actually only one component of a SAM fire unit. The unit also included multiple radar, control, support, and transloader (reloading) vehicles at each launch site. The support equipment for some SAMs was so complex and the missiles themselves so large that the sites were essentially stationary. These SAMs were relegated to protecting fixed targets like cities and military bases. In others, the SAM system was technically mobile, in that the launchers and support equipment could be packed up and moved in a convoy of rather vulnerable vehicles. In practice, however, these also tended to operate from fixed, prepared sites. Typically, Generation 1 SAMs were linked to large air defense networks. These networks used surveillance radars to direct coordinated missile and aircraft defenses against high-altitude attacks (in some cases in excess of 100,000 feet) by massed bomber formations. By later standards, their monopulse radio command (RC) guidance systems were relatively easily spoofed through a combination of electronic countermeasures (ECM) and evasive flight tactics.

Generation 2 long-range SAMs corrected several shortcomings of the Generation 1 systems. First, aircraft could nullify the threat of the first generation SAMs by flying under their minimum effective operating altitude or even beneath their radar horizon. Designers thus realized that the next generation of systems had to be more flexible and capable of operating at medium as well as high altitudes.[1] Second, advances in the miniaturization of electronics and other components allowed for the development of smaller missile systems. These were more portable than their larger, heavier predecessors, although still tied to a host of external support vehicles. These were the first truly mobile SAMs. Their launchers capable of being mounted on tracked or wheeled chassis which could periodically move them to better avoid being located and destroyed by enemy aircraft. Third, new continuous wave (CW) semi-active radar homing (SARH) guidance systems replaced relatively vulnerable RC/monopulse seekers. This was particularly true for terminal phase guidance. Optical tracking could also be added for use in particularly heavy ECM conditions. Due to a combination of size reduction, aerodynamic improvements, and electronics advances, missiles themselves became more nimble. They were thus less easy for aircraft to evade by "jinking," making rapid changes of flight direction which could break the lock of the airborne missile's seeker head.

Generation 3 systems employed advances in a number of technological areas, particularly computers and radar, to expand the capabilities of the long-range SAMs even further. First, the development of new phased array radar systems linked to track-via-missile (TVM) guidance sets allowed for greater seeker accuracy at higher speeds. Target aircraft thus had less time to employ countermeasures. Inherent missile resistance to ECM and other countermeasures was also tremendously improved. Second, the range of potential targets has expanded. The U.S. and the Soviet Union claiming that their third generation SAMs have the capability to intercept not only medium-to-high altitude aircraft, but also low-flying aircraft, cruise missiles, and even the re-entry vehicles from ballistic missile warheads (Taylor

1993, 82; Crabtree 1994, 164). Last, advances in propellant and engine technology have allowed third generation systems to combine the high mobility of the second generation with the longer ranges of the first.

SYSTEMS

Six systems comprise the first generation of long-range SAMs: the British Bloodhound Mk.1, the Chinese HQ-2, the Soviet SA-1 Guild and SA-2 Guideline, and the U.S. Nike-Ajax and Nike-Hercules.

SA-1 Guild and SA-2 Guideline were the Soviet Union's first operational SAMs. The SA-1 operates only from fixed sites in the USSR and has never been exported. The more portable SA-2, perhaps the quintessential first generation SAM system, is about a third lighter than SA-1. It shares a similar aerodynamic layout, performance, and RC guidance system (Bonds 1982, 214). China reverse-engineered SA-2s received from the Soviets and created the HQ-2 (NATO CSA-1 Guideline). These HQ-2 is virtually identical to the original system.

The U.S. paralleled these Soviet developments with the Nike series of SAMs. The Nike-Ajax had an essentially fixed-site launcher, and relied on a complex web of facilities for support. Taylor and Taylor (1972, 47) write that the original SA-2 "was similar to the first generation U.S. Nike-Ajax in many design features and probably had a comparable performance." Nike Hercules was a bigger, longer-ranged weapon that used four boost motors instead of the single one on Ajax. It shared the same basic RC guidance system of the Ajax, as well as its electronic sophistication and aerodynamic principles, but was designed to be somewhat more portable.

The Bloodhound was the first postwar British SAM system. It underwent a lengthy gestation period from conception to deployment, and, as the last first generation system to become operational, it featured more advanced semi-active radar homing (SARH). Despite this, however, it's initial Mk.1 version shares the broad features of other first generation systems. These include long range, large size, low mobility, an easily-jammed monopulse radar seeker, and poor low-level performance (Hartcup 1993, 48; Taylor 1990, 10–13). The Bloodhound Mk.2 was a completely reworked system, and is considered below as part of the second generation (Taylor and Taylor 1972, 19).

The second generation of SAMs is composed of nine systems: the British Bloodhound Mk.2 and Thunderbird, the Soviet SA-3 Goa, SA-4 Ganef, SA-5 Gammon, SA-6 Gainful, and SA-11 Gadfly, and the U.S. HAWK.

The cornerstone systems in this generation, accounting for the vast majority of worldwide diffusion, are the HAWK, SA-3, and SA-6.[2] All three are mobile missile systems with terminal SARH guidance geared toward medium and lower-altitude engagements. All were seen as medium-altitude counterparts to first generation systems (HAWK to the Nikes and SA-3/-6 to the SA-1/-2) that would fill in gaps in lower-level air defenses. SA-3 is considered "Russia's early counterpart" (Taylor and Taylor 1972, 45; Taylor 1993, 81) or "equivalent" (Donnelly et al., p. 60) to the U.S. HAWK, fulfilling much the same role (JWS, 1969–1970), although it has older monopulse radar guidance instead of the HAWK's more modern CW system.[3] SA-6 is equated either with HAWK itself or the upgraded IHAWK (Improved HAWK), with SA-3 being comparable to the original model. Cordesman (1985, 12) writes that SA-6 is "somewhat similar to Improved HAWK," a second source (JWS, 1969–1970: 67) reports that the two are "roughly comparable," and Crabtree (1994, 109) says they are "generally assessed as equivalent." Finally, Taylor and Taylor (1972, 41) claim that SA-6 "is somewhat larger than the American HAWK . . . but almost certainly fulfils a similar role by providing a rapid-reaction defence against aircraft flying at low and medium altitudes."

The SA-4 Ganef is similar technologically to the SA-6, but has a longer range and higher operational altitude (Taylor 1993, 81). Dunnigan (1993, 208) contrarily describes it as the "Russian equivalent of the Nike-Hercules," although its technical features do not bear this out. In any event, it was exported to only a few states. As a result, whether classified as first or second generation, it will have no impact on the data. The SA-11 Gadfly is a more advanced complement to SA-6, with somewhat better performance figures for most operational parameters. It has progressively replaced both SA-4s and SA-6 in Soviet service (Taylor 1993, 82). Despite this, it can use the same guidance radar as the SA-6 and is not interoperable with a phased array set, a key mark of a third generation system. It is probably roughly equivalent to a late model IHAWK in terms of overall sophistication, and is considered a very advanced second generation system. The SA-5 is a throwback system, a SARH guided SAM with all of the other characteristics of a first generation system (extreme range, massive size, fixed launcher, low maneuverability, etc.) (Bonds 1982, 215). Like the SA-4, however, with only a few export purchasers, the SA-5 will have no effect on the data whether considered first or second generation.

Finally, the vastly upgraded capabilities of the British Bloodhound Mk.2, with its improved low-level performance, increased mobility (although nowhere near that of the self-propelled systems like SA-6 or HAWK), and more accurate CW SARH guidance place it in the second generation.[4] The British Thunderbird filled the same role as the U.S. Hawk for tactical Army air defense.

Finally, four systems fall into the fourth generation of long-range SAMs: the Taiwanese Skybow, the Soviet SA-10 Grumble and SA-12 Gladiator/Giant, and the U.S. Patriot.

Patriot was designed to replace the HAWK in U.S. Army service, and is the definitive third generation SAM. Patriot has a phased array radar with TVM guidance, advanced ECCM, and limited ATBM (anti-tactical ballistic missile) and low-to-high altitude interception capabilities. The Taiwanese Skybow (*Tien Kung*) is reportedly a copy of the Patriot, and has been described as a "Patriot-type" weapon.

The Soviet SA-10 and SA-12 are both variants of the same basic missile, the S-300, which has been described as "Russia's counterpart to the U.S. Army's MIM-104 Patriot" (Taylor 1993, p. 82). Being larger, however, they have much longer ranges than Patriot or Skybow.

ADOPTER LISTS

GENERATION 1 (48 ADOPTERS)

1.	Afghanistan	SA-2 (1967)
2.	Albania	HQ-2 (1967)
3.	Algeria	SA-2 (1967)
4.	Angola	SA-2 (1986)
5.	Australia	Bloodhound Mk.1 (1962?)
6.	Belgium	Nike-Ajax (????); Nike-Hercules (1963)
7.	Bulgaria	SA-2 (1964)
8.	China	SA-2 (1958?); HQ-2 (1966?)
9.	Cuba	SA-2 (1962)
10.	Czechoslovakia	SA-2 (1964)
11.	Denmark	Nike-Ajax (????); Nike-Hercules (1963)
12.	East Germany	SA-2 (1964)
13.	Egypt	SA-2 (1964)
14.	Ethiopia	SA-2 (1979)
15.	France	Nike-Ajax (????); Nike-Hercules (1963)
16.	Greece	Nike-Ajax (1960); Nike-Hercules (1960)
17.	Hungary	SA-2 (1964)
18.	India	SA-2 (1966)
19.	Indonesia	SA-2 (1962)
20.	Iran	HQ-2 (1987)
21.	Iraq	SA-2 (1963)
22.	Italy	Nike-Ajax (????); Nike-Hercules (1963)
23.	Japan	Nike-Ajax (????)
24.	Libya	SA-2 (1976)
25.	Mozambique	SA-2 (1987)
26.	Netherlands	Nike-Ajax (????); Nike-Hercules (1963)
27.	North Korea	SA-2 (1967)
28.	North Yemen	SA-2 (1982)
29.	Norway	Nike-Ajax (????); Nike-Hercules (1964)
30.	Pakistan	HQ-2 (1985)
31.	Peru	SA-2 (1976)
32.	Poland	SA-2 (1964)

33. Romania   SA-2 (1964)
34. Somalia   SA-2 (1975)
35. South Korea   Nike-Hercules (1966)
36. South Yemen   SA-2 (1980)
37. Spain   Nike-Hercules (1975)
38. Sudan   SA-2 (1972)
39. Sweden   Bloodhound Mk.1 (????)
40. Syria   SA-2 (1968)
41. Taiwan   Nike-Hercules (1960)
42. Turkey   Nike-Ajax (1956); Nike-Hercules (1960)
43. U.K.   Bloodhound Mk.1 (1958)
44. U.S.   Nike-Ajax (1953); Nike-Hercules (1958)
45. USSR   SA-1 (1953); SA-2 (1958)
46. Vietnam (N)   SA-2 (1965)
47. West Germany   Nike-Ajax (????); Nike-Hercules (1963)
48. Yugoslavia   SA-2 (1964)

GENERATION 2 (57 ADOPTERS)

1. Afghanistan   SA-3 (1980)
2. Algeria   SA-6 (1981); SA-3 (1982)
3. Angola   SA-6 (1981); SA-3 (1982)
4. Bahrain   HAWK (1996)
5. Belgium   HAWK (1964)
6. Brazil   HAWK (1978)
7. Bulgaria   SA-3 (1977); SA-6 (1977); SA-4 (1983); SA-5 (1990)
8. Cuba   SA-3 (1978); SA-6 (1983)
9. Czechoslovakia   SA-3 (1977); SA-4 (1977); SA-6 (1977); SA-5 (1990)
10. Denmark   HAWK (1965)
11. East Germany   SA-3 (1977); SA-4 (1977); SA-6 (1979); SA-5 (1988)
12. Egypt   SA-3 (1970); SA-6 (1973); HAWK (1983)
13. Ethiopia   SA-3 (1978)
14. Finland   SA-3 (1980); SA-11 (1998)
15. France   HAWK (1968?)
16. Greece   HAWK (1966)
17. Guinea   SA-6 (1984)
18. Hungary   SA-6 (1977); SA-3 (1981); SA-4 (1984); SA-5 (1991)
19. India   SA-3 (1978); SA-6 (1978); SA-5 (1992)
20. Israel   HAWK (1964)
21. Iran   HAWK (1965); SA-5 (1991); SA-6 (1997)
22. Iraq   SA-3 (1973); SA-6 (1978)
23. Italy   HAWK (1965)
24. Japan   HAWK (1964)
25. Jordan   HAWK (1978)
26. Kuwait   HAWK (1978); SA-6 (1980)
27. Laos   SA-3 (1985)
28. Libya   SA-3 (1975); SA-6 (1976); SA-5 (1986)

29. Mali	SA-3 (1982)
30. Mozambique	SA-3 (1977)
31. Netherlands	HAWK (1964)
32. North Korea	SA-3 (1985); SA-5 (1988)
33. North Yemen	SA-5 (1994)
34. Norway	HAWK (1989)
35. Peru	SA-3 (1978)
36. Poland	SA-3 (1977); SA-6 (1977); SA-4 (1981); SA-5 (1988)
37. Romania	SA-6 (1978)
38. Saudi Arabia	HAWK (1967); Thunderbird (1967)
39. Singapore	Bloodhound Mk.2 (1972); HAWK (1982)
40. Somalia	SA-3 (1975); HAWK (1983)
41. South Korea	HAWK (1966)
42. South Yemen	SA-3 (1980); SA-6 (1980)
43. Spain	HAWK (1969)
44. Sweden	HAWK (1964); Bloodhound Mk.2 (1964)
45. Switzerland	Bloodhound Mk. 2 (1964)
46. Syria	SA-3 (1972); SA-6 (1973); SA-5 (1984)
47. Taiwan	HAWK (1961)
48. Tanzania	SA-3 (1980); SA-6 (1980)
49. Thailand	HAWK (1970)
50. UAE	HAWK (1984)
51. U.K.	Thunderbird (1960?); Bloodhound Mk.2 (1964)
52. U.S.	HAWK (1960)
53. USSR	SA-3 (1961); SA-5 (1966); SA-6 (1967); SA-4 (1969); SA-11 (1980)
54. Vietnam (N)	SA-3 (1973); SA-6 (1980)
55. West Germany	HAWK (1964)
56. Yugoslavia	SA-3 (1977); SA-6 (1978)
57. Zambia	SA-3 (1980)

GENERATION 3 (11 ADOPTERS)

1. Bulgaria	SA-10 (1990)
2. China	SA-10 (1994)
3. Israel	Patriot (1991)
4. Japan	Patriot (1986)
5. Kuwait	Patriot (1996)
6. Netherlands	Patriot (1989)
7. Saudi Arabia	Patriot (1994)
8. Taiwan	Skybow (1987)
9. U.S.	Patriot (1985)
10. USSR	SA-10 (1980); SA-12 (1986)
11. West Germany	Patriot (1990)

DIFFUSION OF GENERATION 1 LONG-RANGE SAMs

Total of 20 adoptions by 1963 (exact dates uncertain): Australia, Belgium, China, Cuba, Denmark, France, Greece, Indonesia, Iraq, Italy, Japan, Netherlands, Norway, Sweden, Taiwan, Turkey, West Germany, U.K., U.S., USSR

1964	Bulgaria, Czechoslovakia, East Germany, Egypt, Hungary,	
	Poland, Romania, Yugoslavia	28
1965	Vietnam (N)	29
1966	India, South Korea	31
1967	Afghanistan, Albania, Algeria, North Korea	35
1968	Syria	36
1969		36
1970		36
1971		36
1972	Sudan	37
1973		37
1974		37
1975	Somalia, Spain	39
1976	Libya, Peru	41
1977		41
1978		41
1979	Ethiopia	42
1980	South Yemen	43
1981		43
1982	North Yemen	44
1983		44
1984		44
1985	Pakistan	45
1986	Angola	46
1987	Iran, Mozambique	48

column on right = cumulative number of adopters

DIFFUSION OF GENERATION 2 LONG-RANGE SAMs

1960	U.S., U.K.	2
1961	Taiwan, USSR	4
1962		4
1963		4
1964	Belgium, West Germany, Israel, Japan, Netherlands, Sweden,	
	Switzerland	11
1965	Denmark, Iran, Italy	14
1966	Greece, South Korea	16
1967	Saudi Arabia	17
1968	France	18
1969	Spain	19
1970	Egypt, Thailand	21
1971		21
1972	Singapore, Syria	23

1973	Iraq, Vietnam (N)	25
1974		25
1975	Libya, Somalia	27
1976		27
1977	Bulgaria, Czechoslovakia, East Germany, Hungary, Mozambique, Poland, Yugoslavia	34
1978	Brazil, Cuba, Ethiopia, India, Jordan, Kuwait, Peru, Romania	42
1979		42
1980	Afghanistan, Finland, South Yemen, Tanzania, Zambia	47
1981	Algeria, Angola	49
1982	Mali	50
1983	50	
1984	Guinea, UAE	52
1985	Laos, North Korea	54
1986		54
1987		54
1988		54
1989	Norway	55
1990		55
1991		55
1992		55
1993	55	
1994	North Yemen	56
1995		56
1996	Bahrain	57

column on right = cumulative number of adopters

DIFFUSION OF GENERATION 3 LONG-RANGE SAMs

1980	USSR	1
1981		1
1982		1
1983		1
1984		1
1985	U.S.	2
1986	Japan	3
1987	Taiwan	4
1988		4
1989	Netherlands	5
1990	Bulgaria, West Germany	7
1991	Israel	8
1992		8
1993		8
1994	China, Saudi Arabia	10
1995		10
1996	Kuwait	11
1997		11

column on right = cumulative number of adopters

NOTES

[1] The low/very low altitude, short-range air defense role was handled by point defense SAMs (see Appendix 6), shoulder-fired weapons (Appendix 7), and more traditional anti-aircraft artillery.

[2] HAWK is an acronym standing for "Homing All-the-Way Killer," and is thus capitalized.

[3] Crabtree (1994, 108) has a somewhat different assessment than Taylor and Taylor (1972) or Taylor (1993), writing that "technologically, the [SA-3] was only slightly more advanced than the [SA-2], utilizing built-in Electronic Counter-Countermeasures (ECCM) and a two-stage solid-fueled rocket." Dunnigan (1993, 208) goes even further, saying that there is "no Western equivalent" to the SA-6, and downplaying the capabilities of the SA-3. Given the weight of other evidence, however, I consider both SA-3 and SA-6 as second generation systems in this study.

[4] One source directly states that "Bloodhound Mk.2 is a second-generation mobile anti- aircraft guided weapon" (JWS 88–89, p. 183).

Appendix F
Ground-Based Surface-to-Air Missiles II: Point Defense SAMs

ARMS CATEGORY

WHILE HEAVIER, LONG-RANGE SAMs COULD BE VERY EFFECTIVE against enemy aircraft, ground troops could only benefit from this protection if they operated within the SAM's maximum engagement range. Unfortunately, most of the larger long-range SAMs like the SA-2 were effectively fixed-site weapons. Although they could be packed aboard their transport vehicles and moved, this was a time-consuming process that left them open to attack while they were in transit. Even smaller models like the HAWK and SA-3 required a host of separate radar and command vehicles that were also vulnerable to enemy attack. This rendered them unsuitable for extreme forward deployment with the potentially highly mobile troops they were supposed to defend. Since their positions were more or less fixed for considerable periods of time, they were also vulnerable to location and destruction by enemy forces. Finally, the size and weight of these weapons made them incapable of engaging aircraft beyond some minimum range and beneath a minimum altitude which the missile needed to achieve sufficient velocity for maneuvering. If an aircraft could sneak past the SAM's minimum engagement zone, it could attack the launchers and radars with relative impunity.

Point defense SAMs were developed to overcome all of these problems. First, these missiles were meant to be deployed right on the battlefield, providing ground troops with direct, short-range (less than 10 miles) protection against enemy air attacks. The missiles' small size (typically no more than ten or less feet long and weighing less than 500 pounds) meant that a number of them (typically two to six) could be mounted for instant use on a single armored vehicle chassis. The chassis, containing the launchers, radar, and other guidance systems, and providing some protection for the missile operators, formed a so-called "autonomous fire unit" that required little or no external support. Typically, a few of these vehicles would be deployed with each mechanized or armored unit to provide an organic air defense capability not linked to the unit staying within range of the larger SAM sites. Second, their size and low cost also meant that these weapons could be employed in large numbers. This, combined with their high mobility, made it difficult for an enemy to hunt down and destroy all or even a majority of them in the opening stages of a battle, as might be done with large, less mobile weapons. Finally, point defense SAMs filled in the short-range air defense gap, providing low-altitude point defense against incoming aircraft that would be difficult or impossible with longer-range weapons. Because of this capability, many were even mounted on non-armored chassis or on towed platforms and used to defend high-value installations not on the forward edge of the battlefield. When paired with longer-range missiles in air defense complexes, point defense SAMs created a layered defense that protected vital targets against aerial attacks from all altitudes and ranges.

GENERATIONAL DEVELOPMENT

Generation 1 point defense SAMs embody the features mentioned above. They are short-range (<10 miles), light (<500 pounds) missiles mounted either on armored vehicles for forward deployment or on small towed trailers for close-in defense of fixed sites. The guidance method is variable, with infrared, optical, and radar all possibilities.

A second generation of point defense SAMs may be emerging, as the replacements for the first generation systems begin to enter service. These include the Russian SA-15 Gauntlet and the U.S. ADATS. Since the technical distinctions between these and the first generation systems are still not fully known, only the first generation is considered here.

SYSTEMS

Ten systems comprise the first generation of point defense SAMs: the British Tigercat and Rapier, the Chinese HQ-61, the French Crotale and its derivatives, the Franco-German Roland, the Italian Aspide, the Japanese Type 81 Tan-SAM, the Soviet SA-8 Gecko, and the U.S. Chaparral and Sparrow.

Tigercat, a naval SAM quickly mounted on a towed launcher for land-based use, was the initial innovation in this weapons category. Tigercat is broadly comparable to earlier models of other systems in this generation, but its further development was abandoned in favor of Rapier, which replaced it in British service. Hartcup (1993) directly states that the Rapier, Crotale, Roland, and Chaparral were all direct "rivals" that had between them divided up the Western market for low-level SAMs in the 1970s. The Japanese Type 81 Tan-SAM, "similar in appearance to British Rapier" (JWS 88–89, 174), was also developed during the 1970s as a competitor to these systems (Drifte 1986, 68). When it first appeared in 1975, the SA-8 was almost immediately described as the "the direct counterpart to the Franco-German Roland missile" (Clawson and Kaplan 1982, 177; Menaul 1980, 217), resembling Roland in many respects. Crotale variants have been marketed under different names for various customers, including Cactus (South Africa), Shahine (Saudi Arabia), and FM.80 or HQ-7 (China).

A second cluster of systems in this category involves those similar to or derived from the Sparrow missile family. These are somewhat larger than the other point defense SAMs, and geared more toward the defense of fixed installations from unarmored launchers. The AIM-7 Sparrow was originally designed as an air-to-air missile (AAM), but the U.S. developed the RIM-7E ground-based SAM variant in the 1970s. AIM-7/RIM-7 was sold to Italy, and became the basis for the Aspide family of SAM/AAM systems. Sparrow and/or Aspide was then copied by the Chinese and served as the basis for the HQ-61. While these weapons are not usually compared to the first group in the literature because of the difference in launcher mode, their size, range, mission, and level of sophistication are broadly similar.

ADOPTER LISTS

GENERATION 1 (53 ADOPTERS)

1.	Algeria	SA-8 (1980)
2.	Angola	SA-8 (1984)
3.	Argentina	Tigercat (1971); Roland (1983)
4.	Australia	Rapier (1979)
5.	Bahrain	Crotale (1992)
6.	Brazil	Roland (1978)
7.	Chile	Crotale (1984)
8.	China	HQ-61 (1986); FM.80 (1990?)
9.	Colombia	Sparrow (1984)
10.	Cuba	SA-8 (1992)
11.	Cyprus	Aspide (1995)
12.	East Germany	SA-8 (1986)
13.	Ecuador	SA-8 (1997)
14.	Egypt	Crotale (1980); Sparrow (1985); Aspide (1986); Chaparral (1987)
15.	Finland	Crotale (1994)
16.	France	Crotale (1977); Roland (1978)
17.	Greece	Sparrow (1986); SA-8 (1995)

18. Guinea	SA-8 (1984)
19. India	Tigercat (1973); SA-8 (1984)
20. Indonesia	Rapier (1986)
21. Iran	Tigercat (1969); Rapier (1973); FM.80 (1994)
22. Iraq	Roland (1983); SA-8 (1983)
23. Israel	Chaparral (1974)
24. Italy	Aspide (1985)
25. Japan	Type 81 (1983)
26. Jordan	Tigercat (1970); SA-8 (1984)
27. Kuwait	SA-8 (1985); Aspide (1994)
28. Libya	Crotale (1975); SA-8 (1982)
29. Malaysia	Rapier (1991)
30. Morocco	Chaparral (1980); Crotale (1980)
31. Nigeria	Roland (1985)
32. Oman	Rapier (1977)
33. Pakistan	Crotale (1978)
34. Poland	SA-8 (1984)
35. Portugal	Chaparral (1989)
36. Qatar	Tigercat (1971); Rapier (1984); Roland (1988)
37. Saudi Arabia	Crotale (1981)
38. Singapore	Rapier (1978)
39. South Africa	Crotale (1973); Tigercat (1975); SA-8 (1988)
40. Spain	Aspide (1987); Chaparral (1987); Roland (1987)
41. Switzerland	Rapier (1984)
42. Syria	SA-8 (1980)
43. Taiwan	Chaparral (1978)
44. Thailand	Aspide (1989); Crotale (1994)
45. Tunisia	Chaparral (1981)
46. Turkey	Rapier (1985)
47. U.A.E.	Crotale (1979); Rapier (1979)
48. U.K.	Tigercat (1970); Rapier (1975)
49. U.S.	Chaparral (1971); Roland (1982); Rapier (1985)
50. U.S.S.R.	SA-8 (1975)
51. Venezuela	Roland (1987)
52. West Germany	Roland (1979)
53. Zambia	Rapier (1972); Tigercat (1979)

DIFFUSION OF GENERATION 1 POINT-DEFENSE SAMs

1969	Iran	1
1970	Jordan, U.K.	3
1971	Argentina, Qatar, U.S.	6
1972	Zambia	7
1973	India, South Africa	9
1974	Israel	10
1975	Libya, USSR	12
1976		12

1977	France, Oman	14
1978	Brazil, Pakistan, Singapore, Taiwan	18
1979	Australia, UAE, West Germany	21
1980	Algeria, Egypt, Morocco, Syria	25
1981	Saudi Arabia, Tunisia	27
1982		27
1983	Iraq, Japan	29
1984	Angola, Chile, Colombia, Guinea, Poland, Switzerland	35
1985	Italy, Kuwait, Nigeria, Turkey	39
1986	China, East Germany, Greece, Indonesia	43
1987	Spain, Venezuela	45
1988		45
1989	Portugal, Thailand	47
1990		47
1991	Malaysia	48
1992	Bahrain, Cuba	50
1993		50
1994	Finland	51
1995	Cyprus	52
1996		52
1997	Ecuador	53

column on right = cumulative number of adopters

Appendix G
Ground-Based Surface-to-Air Missiles III: Shoulder-Fired PADs

ARMS CATEGORY

SHOULDER-FIRED SAMS, ALSO CALLED PORTABLE AIR DEFENSE SYSTEMS (PADS) or infantry SAMs, were introduced in the mid-1960s. PADS typically weigh under 15 kg and have a range of 6 km or less. Their primary feature is the ability to be operated by a single soldier. Many, however, are usually fired from portable mounts that decrease the workload necessary for their operation. PADS give the infantry a light, extremely short-range weapon capable of engaging low-flying aircraft and helicopters. PADS' flexibility provides many advantages over the large, vehicle-mounted SAMs which were previously the only missile defense available to ground forces. PADS are relatively cheap, can be produced in vast numbers, and easily deployed without much logistic support. Conversely, their small size is also the source of many limitations. PADS generally lack lethality, due to their small warhead. Many PADS also lack the sophisticated electronics necessary to avoid jamming and spoofing by target aircraft that is found on other, larger SAMs.

GENERATIONAL DEVELOPMENT

Generation 1 infantry SAMs featured unreliable guidance systems that were readily spoofed by attacking aircraft. Five of the six systems in this generation sported a nose-mounted infra-red (IR) sensor only sensitive enough to home in on the hot jet exhaust of their targets. As a result, they could only be fired at an aircraft from behind, i.e. usually only after it has dropped its ordnance on its targets. These are hence often referred to as "tail-chase" or "revenge" weapons (Menaul 1982). These early IR seekers could also be easily defeated by the dropping of flares or violent aircraft maneuvers that turn the tailpipe away from the approaching missile seeker and cause it to break its lock.

A sixth system, the British Blowpipe, featured a manual command-to-line-of-sight (MCLOS) guidance system.[1] After firing, the infantry soldier had to guide the Blowpipe toward its target with a thumb-operated joystick. This is easy task against a fast-moving, maneuvering aircraft. In practice, it effectively limited the Blowpipe to engaging only slow-moving subsonic aircraft (Watson and Dunn 1984). Blowpipe's guidance system does allow the missile to be fired at an aircraft from any aspect angle. However, in combat conditions, Blowpipe can be defeated by a burst of cannon fire from an attacking aircraft that breaks the operator's concentration and forces him to take cover. Even under optimal conditions, it requires an extremely high level of operator training to be even moderately effective.

In short, as one source notes, although first generation PADS are simple and easy-to-use, they have "severe shortcomings, to the point of being just a morale-raiser" to the infantry on the ground (Bonds 1983, 244).

Generation 2 advances increased the lethality and accuracy of PADS through a number of technical means. Generation 1 systems were essentially considered mere infantry confidence-builders with only limited actual destructive value. Generation 2 thus placed emphasis on designing replacements that could actually reliably shoot down enemy aircraft, and from any angle (hence the term "all-aspect" weapons) rather than simply from the rear (Bonds 1983, 249). This impetus led designers in several directions as far as guidance systems were concerned, with weapons employing much improved IR, optical/radio-command, and laser-guidance all seeing operational service. The kill probability (number of missiles fired per enemy aircraft destroyed) of this generation of missiles increased dramatically over that of Generation 1, as demonstrated by their success in the 1982 Falklands Islands conflict and in Afghanistan after 1986, versus the very low success rate of first generation systems in the 1973 Arab-Israeli war and in Vietnam (Menaul 1982, 216; Walters 1995).

The British Starstreak is the first system in an emergent third generation of PADS, entering service in 1995 (Nash 1995). Unlike first and second generation PADS, Starstreak is hypersonic, reaching speeds of up to Mach 4.5 after launch. Starstreak also features an advanced warhead design that is expected to significantly improve its lethality.

SYSTEMS

Generation 1 systems comprise the British Blowpipe, Chinese HN-5, Pakistani Anza- 1, Soviet SA-7 Grail and SA-14 Gremlin, and the U.S. FIM-43 Redeye.

Virtually all sources indicate that SA-7, SA-14, Anza-1, HN-5, and Redeye are almost identical to one another, share a common design lineage, and are generational equivalents in the technological sense. Chadwick and Caffrey (1991, 53) write that "the SA-7 is reported to be a copy of the [Redeye] . . . [it] is an early heat-seeker, and is only effective when fired at a target moving away from the launcher," and Messenger (1985, 81), Menaul (1982, 216), and Foss (1996) also describe the two weapons as extremely similar. HN-5 is an SA-7 copy, reverse-engineered from missiles acquired by China on the black market during the late 1970s or early 1980s (Karniol 1997a). Anza-1 is a Pakistani copy of the HN-5 (Hussein 1989, 298). The Soviets introduced the SA-14 Gremlin (Russian *Strela-2*) in the late 1970s. This was a somewhat improved version of the SA-7 (*Strela-2*), which "reportedly introduces a more sensitive IR detector, but still lacks full forward-aspect capability, and, thus, does not quite compare" with missiles of the succeeding generation (Friedman 1997, 404).[2] Blowpipe is discussed above in detail. Although it has a nominal all-aspect capability, its severe limitations place it in the first generation along with these other IR-guided systems.

Generation 2 systems include the British Javelin and Starburst, Chinese QW-1 Vanguard, French Mistral, Japanese Type 91 Kin-SAM, Pakistani Anza-2, Soviet SA-16 Gimlet and SA-18 Grouse, Swedish RBS-70, and U.S. FIM-92 Stinger.

The majority of these weapons (Anza-2, Stinger, Mistral, Vanguard, Kin-SAM, SA-16, and SA-18) feature a greatly improved IR seeker as the chosen technical solution to the problem of improving accuracy and lethality. The British Javelin replaces the Blowpipe's MCLOS guidance with a SACLOS (semi-automatic to line-of-sight) system. A Javelin operator need only keep the target aircraft in his sights while the guidance system automatically guides the missile to the designated target. Javelin thus maintains Blowpipe's all-aspect capability but removes its greatest limitation, its manual guidance. The Swedish RBS-70 pioneered the use of laser-homing SACLOS guidance, which provided a basically un-spoofable all-aspect engagement capability.[3] Finally, Starburst is a version of Javelin that incorporates similar laser guidance.

The literature clearly describes these systems as generational equivalents. Walters (1995a) describes Mistral as the "French equivalent of Stinger." Foss (1991) says that SA-16/-18 are "roughly comparable" to Stinger and Mistral.[4] Foss (1996) later equates Stinger to the Chinese

Vanguard. Anza-2 is derived from both Stinger and Vanguard technologies (JLBAD 97–98). We can also categorize these SAMs as second generation by the systems they replaced in service. Redeye was replaced by Stinger in the U.S. and the RBS-70 in Sweden. The U.K. replaced Blowpipe with Javelin. Russia replaced the SA-7 and SA-14 with SA-16 and SA-18.[5] China is replacing HN-5 with Vanguard. Finally, Pakistan has begun to replace Anza-1, HN-5, and Redeye with Anza-2. All nine missiles are capable of effective all-aspect engagements, a key feature of the second generation.

ADOPTER LISTS

GENERATION 1 (80 ADOPTERS)

1. Afghanistan   SA-7 (1978)
2. Algeria   SA-7 (1979)
3. Angola   SA-7 (1977); SA-14 (1988)
4. Argentina   Blowpipe (1982); SA-7 (1982)
5. Australia   Redeye (1975)
6. Bangladesh   HN-5 (1997)
7. Botswana   SA-7 (1982)
8. Bulgaria   SA-7 (1974); SA-14 (????)*
9. Burkina Faso   SA-7 (1984)
10. Burundi   SA-7 (1997)
11 Cambodia   SA-7 (1988)
12. Canada   Blowpipe (1975)
13. Chad   Redeye (1984)
14. Chile   Blowpipe (1984)
15. China   HN-5 (1985)
16. Cuba   SA-7 (1977); SA-14 (1987)
17. Cyprus   SA-7 (1985)
18. Czechoslovakia   SA-7 (1975); SA-14 (????)*
19. Denmark   Redeye (1975)
20. East Germany   SA-7 (1975); SA-14 (1990)
21. Ecuador   Blowpipe (1977)
22. Egypt   SA-7 (1973)
23. El Salvador   SA-7 (1992); SA-14 (????)
24. Ethiopia   SA-7 (1978)
25. Finland   SA-7 (1979); SA-14 (1987)
26. Ghana   SA-7 (1997)
27. Greece   Redeye (1981)
28. Guinea   SA-7 (1984)
29. Guinea-Bissau   SA-7 (1980)
30. Guyana   SA-7 (1982)
31. Hungary   SA-7 (1978); SA-14 (1990)
32. India   SA-7 (1983); SA-14 (????)*
33. Iran   SA-7 (1978); HN-5 (1986); SA-14 (????)
34. Iraq   SA-7 (1975); HN-5 (????); SA-14 (1988)

35. Israel	Redeye (1976)
36. Jordan	Redeye (1978); SA-7 (1986); SA-14 (????)*
37. Kuwait	SA-7 (1980)
38. Laos	SA-7 (1985)
39. Libya	SA-7 (1979)
40. Malawi	Blowpipe (1980)
41. Mauritania	SA-7 (1982)
42. Mongolia	SA-7 (1986)
43. Morocco	SA-7 (1978)
44. Mozambique	SA-7 (1978)
45. Myanmar	HN-5 (1995)
46. Nicaragua	SA-7 (1985); SA-14 (1987)
47. Nigeria	Blowpipe (1982)
48. North Korea	SA-7 (1973); HN-5 (1984?); SA-14 (1987)
49. North Yemen	SA-7 (1981); SA-14 (1997)
50. Oman	Blowpipe (1983); SA-7 (1988)
51. Pakistan	Anza-1 (1989); HN-5 (1989); Redeye (1990)
52. Peru	SA-7 (1981); SA-14 (????)*
53. Poland	SA-7 (1974); SA-14 (????)*
54. Portugal	Blowpipe (1984)
55. Qatar	Blowpipe (1985); SA-7 (1997)
56. Romania	SA-7 (1978)
57. Rwanda	SA-7 (1997)
58. Saudi Arabia	Redeye (1980)
59. Sierra Leone	SA-7 (1984)
60. Somalia	SA-7 (1985)
61. South Africa	SA-14 (1988); SA-7 (1989)
62. South Korea	Redeye (1989)
63. South Yemen	SA-7 (1980)
64. Sudan	SA-7 (1980); Redeye (1991)
65. Sweden	Redeye (1971)
66. Syria	SA-7 (1973); SA-14 (1988)
67. Tanzania	SA-7 (1980)
68. Thailand	Redeye (1982); Blowpipe (1983); HN-5 (1989)
69. Turkey	Redeye (1985)
70. Uganda	SA-7 (1978)
71. UAE	Blowpipe (1992); SA-7 (????); SA-14 (????)*
72. U.K.	Blowpipe (1974)
73. U.S.	Redeye (1964)
74. USSR	SA-7 (1966); SA-14 (1978)
75. Vietnam (N)	SA-7 (1972); SA-14 (????)*
76. West Germany	Redeye (1974)
77. Yugoslavia	SA-7 (1979); SA-14 (????)*
78. Zaire	SA-7 (1991)
79. Zambia	SA-7 (1980)
80. Zimbabwe	SA-7 (1982)

* = SA-14 adoption uncertain

GENERATION 2 (58 ADOPTERS)

1. Argentina   RBS-70 (1985)
2. Austria   Mistral (1994)
3. Bahrain   RBS-70 (1980); Stinger (1988)
4. Belgium   Mistral (1992)
5. Botswana   Javelin (1993); SA-16 (1994)
6. Brazil   Mistral (1997); SA-18 (1997)
7. Bulgaria   SA-16 (1989)
8. Canada   Javelin (1991); Starburst (1997)
9. Chad   Stinger (1988)
10. Chile   Javelin (1990); Mistral (1991)
11. China   QW-1 (1997)
12. Cuba   SA-16 (1996)
13. Cyprus   Mistral (1990)
14. Czechoslovakia SA-16 (1989)
15. Denmark   Stinger (1994)
16. East Germany   SA-18 (1989)
17. Ecuador   SA-18 (1997)
18. Egypt   Stinger (1991)
19. Finland   SA-16 (1988); Mistral (1991); SA-18 (1996)
20. France   Stinger (????); Mistral (1988)
21. Greece   Stinger (1990)
22. Hungary   SA-16 (1989)
23. India   SA-16 (1991)
24. Indonesia   RBS-70 (1983)
25. Iran   RBS-70 (1986); Stinger (????); SA-16 (????)
26. Iraq   SA-16 (1990)
27. Ireland   RBS-70 (1980)
28. Israel   Stinger (1992)
29. Italy   Stinger (1985)
30. Japan   Stinger (1985); Type 91 (1991)
31. Jordan   SA-16 (1992)
32. Kenya   Mistral (1991)
33. Kuwait   SA-18 (1996); Starburst (1996)
34. Malaysia   Javelin (1990); Starburst (1996)
35. Mexico   RBS-70 (1995)
36. Netherlands   Stinger (1986)
37. Nicaragua   SA-16 (1988)
38. North Korea   SA-16 (1993)
39. Norway   RBS-70 (1982); Mistral (1993)
40. Oman   Javelin (1989)
41. Pakistan   RBS-70 (1984); Stinger (1985); Anza-2 (1995)
42. Peru   SA-16 (1994); Javelin (1996)
43. Qatar   Stinger (1988); Mistral (1993)
44. Saudi Arabia   Stinger (1985); Mistral (1992)
45. Singapore   RBS-70 (1981); Mistral (1995); SA-16 (1997)

46. South Korea	Javelin (1987); Stinger (1989); Mistral (1994); SA-18 (1997)
47. Spain	Mistral (1991)
48. Sweden	RBS-70 (1977)
49. Switzerland	Stinger (1994)
50. Tunisia	RBS-70 (1980)
51. Turkey	Stinger (1991)
52. UAE	RBS-70 (1981); Mistral (1991); SA-16 (1992)
53. U.K.	Stinger (1982); Javelin (1985); Starburst (1992)
54. U.S.	Stinger (1981)
55. USSR	SA-18 (1981); SA-16 (1986)
56. Vietnam (N)	SA-16 (1993)
57. West Germany	Stinger (1994)
58. Yugoslavia	SA-16 (1996)

DIFFUSION OF GENERATION 1 SHOULDER-FIRED SAMs

1964	U.S.	1
1965		1
1966	USSR	2
1967		2
1968		2
1969		2
1970		2
1971	Sweden	3
1972	Vietnam (N)	4
1973	Egypt, Syria, North Korea	7
1974	Bulgaria, Poland, U.K., West Germany	11
1975	Australia, Canada, Czechoslovakia, Denmark, East Germany, Iraq	17
1976	Israel	18
1977	Angola, Cuba, Ecuador	21
1978	Afghanistan, Ethiopia, Hungary, Iran, Jordan, Morocco, Mozambique, Romania, Uganda	30
1979	Algeria, Finland, Libya, Yugoslavia	34
1980	Guinea-Bissau, Kuwait, Malawi, Saudi Arabia, Sudan, Tanzania, South Yemen, Zambia	42
1981	Greece, North Yemen, Peru	45
1982	Argentina, Botswana, Guyana, Mauritania, Nigeria, Thailand, Zimbabwe	52
1983	India, Oman	54
1984	Burkina Faso, Chad, Chile, Guinea, Portugal, Sierra Leone	60
1985	China, Cyprus, Laos, Nicaragua, Qatar, Somalia, Turkey	67
1986	Mongolia	68
1987		68
1988	Cambodia, South Africa	70

1989	Pakistan, South Korea	72
1990		72
1991	Zaire	73
1992	El Salvador, UAE	75
1993		75
1994		75
1995	Myanmar	76
1996		76
1997	Bangladesh, Burundi, Ghana, Rwanda	80

column on right = cumulative number of adopters

DIFFUSION OF GENERATION 2 SHOULDER-FIRED SAMs

1977	Sweden	1
1978		1
1979		1
1980	Bahrain, Ireland, Tunisia	4
1981	Singapore, UAE, U.S., USSR	8
1982	Norway, U.K.	10
1983	Indonesia, Thailand	12
1984	Pakistan	13
1985	Argentina, Italy, Japan, Saudi Arabia	17
1986	Iran, Netherlands	19
1987	South Korea	20
1988	Chad, Finland, France, Nicaragua, Qatar	25
1989	Bulgaria, Czechoslovakia, East Germany, Hungary, Oman	30
1990	Chile, Cyprus, Greece, Iraq, Malaysia	35
1991	Canada, Egypt, India, Kenya, Spain, Turkey	41
1992	Belgium, Israel, Jordan	44
1993	Botswana, North Korea, Peru, Vietnam (N)	48
1994	Austria, Denmark, Switzerland, West Germany	52
1995	Mexico	53
1996	Cuba, Kuwait, Yugoslavia	56
1997	Brazil, China	58

column on right = cumulative number of adopters

NOTES

[1] This is identical in principle to the MCLOS guidance sets used in first generation anti- tank guided missiles, q.v.

[2] A few early reports credited SA-14 with all-aspect performance, but these are now known to have been in error. See Friedman, et al. (1985: 150), which mis-describes the SA-14 as "comparable to the U.S. Stinger" and Taylor (1993, 82). Compare this to Nash (1995, 87), who writes that "the SA-14 is the closest relation to SA-7," while SA-16 is "a generation apart."

[3] See "Creation of a Missile System" (1991).

[4] This series of Soviet SAMs entered service in 1983 with the *Igla* (9M39), followed by the modified *Igla-1* (9M13) in 1986. These were identified out of order by NATO observers, the latter receiving the numerically earlier designation SA-16 Gimlet and the older missile the designation SA-18 Grouse. Since their performance and technical features of both are very similar, they are considered part of the same generation by this study, and the designation error should not affect the data (Foss 1991, Karniol 1997b).

[5] Although the SA-14's performance is better than that of the SA-7, it never completely replaced the latter in the Soviet and Warsaw Pact armed forces. It was apparently produced in more limited numbers. It seems to have been an interim system, introduced to bridge the gap between the SA-7's obsolescence and the introduction of the SA-18 in the early 1980s.

Appendix H
Anti-Tank Guided Missiles

ARMS CATEGORY

WORLD WAR II SAW THE WIDESPREAD USE OF SEVERAL CATEGORIES OF anti-tank weapons. Tank destroyers were low-mobility, relatively lightly armored vehicles with large caliber high-velocity anti-tank guns, often of very limited traverse. Towed direct-fire anti-tank guns (ATG), like the famous German 88 mm, were also widely used. By the middle of the war, however, the increasing price of these vulnerable weapons led to a search for new anti-tank systems that combined low cost, wide-deployability, and high lethality against modern armor (Forty 1983, 142). Systems like the wartime U.S. bazooka and German *Panzerfaust* shoulder-fired anti-tank rockets (ATR) were cheap and easily operated by a single infantry soldier. However, they were light, unguided, direct-fire systems of very short range that placed their operators dangerously close to enemy guns and treads.

These shortcomings and the increasing thickness of armor on succeeding generations of postwar main battle tanks (MBTs, see Appendix 4) forced military planners to consider new approaches to anti-tank warfare. By the late 1950s, arms producers began to field a new category of armor-destroying system: the anti-tank guided missile (ATGM). ATGMs were slightly larger than the ATRs they supplemented, and often required a stand-alone mount for firing. Despite this, they were still less costly than specialized anti-tank vehicles. In fact, they could themselves be mounted on armored personnel carriers (APCs) or other platforms, like helicopters, for greater mobility should the need arise. Since the weapons were guided, they could be used with accuracy over longer ranges than direct-fire ATRs. This afforded infantry the ability to seek protection further away from their armored targets. Using a firing mount other than the human shoulder also allowed for the development of larger projectiles with bigger warheads to defeat thicker armor. This became of critical importance with the quadrupling of average armor thickness by the third generation of MBTs which emerged in the 1980s.

GENERATIONAL DEVELOPMENT

The development of ATGMs has passed through two distinct generations since the 1950s, this division being widely recognized and identified as such by a variety of sources. The definition of a third generation is still a matter of debate.

Generation 1 ATGMs are identified by their so-called MCLOS (manual command to line-of-sight) guidance systems. The missile operator fixes the target in the system's sights, fires the missile, and must steer it to the target via a joystick. Steering instructions are passed from the operator to the missile via a number of potential means, most commonly a thin wire which unspools as the missile flies toward the target. Weapons which use this method are termed "wire-guided". Wire-guidance has a number of flaws, not least of which is the fact that it requires the operator to steer the missile to its target for upwards of ten seconds, often under enemy fire. Operationally, this has proven to be a major demand. In battle, tank gunners that detected the flash of a missile firing were usually able to bring the location under fire within a few seconds. This disrupts the missile operator from his task and causes the missile to veer wildly off course.

Generation 2 systems were designed to overcome this shortcoming through the use of SACLOS (semi-automatic command to line-of-sight) guidance. Unlike MCLOS systems, a SACLOS system requires only that the operator keep the aiming sights fixed on the target. A computer in the launcher then automatically steers the missile toward the target. Because this is much easier, Generation 2 systems achieve much higher hit probabilities than Generation 1 systems under operational conditions. While most Generation 2 systems are wire-guided, a number of key weapons use laser-homing to achieve greater flexibility and longer ranges.

Three different conceptions of the third generation of ATGMs exist. The first, which emerged in the early 1980s, saw the U.S. AGM-114 Hellfire as the spearhead of the new generation. This is used by Cordesman (1983), Dunnigan (1996), and IWD (1980). While Hellfire is powerful missile, however, its guidance is clearly SACLOS, albeit using a semi-active laser (SAL) rather than the more common wire-guidance. Hellfire shares its SAL guidance with the Russian AT-8, AT-10, and AT-11. A major difference of these systems over their contemporaries is the ability for remote lasers (i.e. lasers not on the launch platform) to designate targets for the missile. While this might be described as a "fire-and-forget" capability (see below), a human somewhere must still maintain a lock on the target for the missile to work, even if the person is not co-located with the launch platform. For this reason, these weapons are classified here as second generation systems.

A second conception, from the early 1990s, sees a pair of developmental ATGMs, the European TRIGAT and MACAM-3, as the first examples of a new generation. These feature the new ACLOS (automatic command to line-of-sight) guidance system. Continuing the drive toward missile/operator independence, ACLOS requires only that the operator acquire the target before launching. Once fired, the missile seeks out the target on its own, free of the need for operator assistance. This true fire-and-forget system allows for a single operator to attack several targets in rapid succession without worrying about the guidance of the previously-launched missiles. It is expected to provide a quantum leap in hit probabilities. This is the conception used in Adelman and Augustine (1990, 75) and Norris (1996). Even if this conception is used, however, no systems in this category will be operational for a number of years.

The third, most recent conception classifies a number of new Israeli-designed missiles as the avatars of a new generation. A trio of Israeli ATGMs, the NTD/Dandy, NTG/Gill, and NTS/Spike, use fiber-optical guidance (FOG) and an innovative flight profile to strike tanks on their thinly-armored tops instead of their heavily-armored fronts and sides. Similar U.S. designs are also in development. These are very new weapons (NTS/Spike was only officially announced in 1997), and few details are available, but some sources have christened them third generation systems.[1] Even if we accept this, these weapons have just begun to diffuse (being only in service with Israel and the Netherlands), and are thus too new to be included in the data set.

SYSTEMS

The first generation of ATGMs is composed of 14 systems, developed and produced by 9 different states: the Argentine Mathogo; the British Vigilant and Swingfire; the Chinese HJ-73; the French SS.10, SS.11, and Entac; the West German Cobra/Mamba; the Italian Mosquito; the Japanese KAM-3D; the Soviet AT-1 Snapper, AT-2 Swatter, and AT-3 Sagger; and the Swedish RB.53 Bantam.

Second generation ATGMs include 21 systems from 8 different states: the Chinese HJ-8 Red Arrow; the French Harpon, HOT, and Eryx; the Franco-German Milan; the Soviet AT-4 Spigot, AT-5 Spandrel, AT-6 Spiral, AT-7 Saxhorn, AT-8 Songster, AT-9, AT-10 Stabber, and AT-11 Sniper; the

Israeli MAPATS; the Japanese KAM-9; the South African ZT-3; the Swedish RBS.56 BILL; and the U.S. Shillelagh, TOW, Dragon, and Hellfire.

Since the distinctions between first and second generation ATGM systems are so unambiguous, a lengthy literature review of system comparisons is not necessary. Examples of the use of these generational categories can be found in Adelman and Augustine (1990, 75), Cordesman (1983, 70–1), Dunnigan (1996, 187–8), IWD (1980, 109–13), Norris (1996), and *International Defence Review Special Series* (1980, 87–89).

ADOPTER LISTS

GENERATION 1 (70 ADOPTERS)

1. Afghanistan *   AT-1 (1963); AT-3 (1977)
2. Algeria *   AT-3 (1975)
3. Angola *   AT-3 (1976)
4. Argentina   SS.11 (1970); Cobra (1970); Bantam (1977); Mathogo (????)
5. Australia   Entac (1975)
6. Bahrain   SS.11 (1987)
7. Belgium   SS.10 (????); SS.11 (1967?); Entac (1967?); Swingfire (1977)
8. Brazil   SS.11 (1975); Cobra (1977)
9. Bulgaria   AT-1 (????); AT-2 (????); AT-3 (????)
10. Canada   SS.11 (1974?); Entac (1975?)
11. Chile   SS.11 (1976); Cobra (1980)
12. China   AT-3 (1981); HJ-73 (1981)
13. Colombia   SS.11 (1976)
14. Cuba *   AT-1 (1962); AT-2 (????); AT-3 (1981)
15. Czechoslovakia   AT-1 (????); AT-2 (????); AT-3 (????)
16. Denmark   Cobra (????)
17. East Germany   AT-1 (????); AT-2 (????); AT-3 (????)
18. Egypt   AT-1 (1964); AT-2 (????); AT-3 (1973); Swingfire (1980)
19. Ethiopia *   AT-3 (1978)
20. Finland   SS.11 (1967?); Vigilant (1967?)
21. France   SS.10 (1957?); Entac (1958?); SS.11 (1963)
22. Greece   Cobra (1968); SS.11 (1977?)
23. Hungary   AT-1 (????); AT-2 (????); AT-3 (????)
24. India *   Entac (1970); SS.11 (1970); AT-3 (1982)
25. Indonesia   Entac (1969)
26. Iran   SS.11 (1971); Entac (1975); Swingfire (1975); AT-3 (1991)
27. Iraq   SS.11 (1971); AT-3 (1977); AT-2 (1981)
28. Israel   SS.10 (1956); Cobra (1963); Entac (1964); SS.11 (1964); AT-3 (1976)
29. Italy   Cobra (1973?); Mosquito (1973?); SS.11 (1973?)
30. Japan   KAM-3D (1964)
31. Kenya   Swingfire (1979)

32. Kuwait	Vigilant (1963); SS.11 (1976)
33. Lebanon	Entac (1975); SS.11 (1975)
34. Libya	Vigilant (1973); AT-3 (1976); SS.11 (1976); AT-2 (1981)
35. Malaysia	SS.11 (1980)
36. Mongolia *	AT-1 (1973)
37. Morocco	Cobra (1979); Entac (1981); AT-3 (1993)
38. Mozambique	AT-3 (1978)
39. Netherlands	?
40. Nicaragua	AT-3 (1985); AT-2 (1989)
41. Nigeria	SS.10 (????)
42. North Korea *	AT-3 (1977); AT-1 (1985?)
43. North Yemen	Vigilant (1978)
44. Norway	Entac (1975?)
45. Pakistan	Cobra (1967); HJ-73 (????)
46. Peru *	SS.11 (1976); Cobra (1983)
47. Poland	AT-1 (????); AT-2 (????); AT-3 (????)
48. Portugal	SS.11 (1977)
49. Romania	AT-1 (????); AT-2 (????); AT-3 (????)
50. Saudi Arabia	Vigilant (1965); SS.11 (1976)
51. Somalia	AT-3 (1976)
52. South Africa	Entac (1975); SS.11 (1977)
53. South Yemen	AT-2 (1982); AT-3 (1982)
54. Spain	Cobra (1976); SS.11 (1976)
55. Sudan *	Swingfire (1983)
56. Sweden	SS.10 (????); SS.11 (1964?); Bantam (1965)
57. Switzerland	Entac (????); Mosquito (????); Bantam (1967)
58. Syria	AT-1 (????); AT-2 (????); AT-3 (1973)
59. Turkey	Cobra (1965); SS.11 (1969)
60. Uganda	SS.11 (1974); AT-3 (1975)
61. UAE	Vigilant (1973); SS.11 (1976)
62. U.K.	SS.10 (????); SS.11 (????); Vigilant (1964?); Swingfire (1969)
63. U.S.	Entac (????); SS.10 (????); SS.11 (1960?)
64. USSR	AT-1 (1961?), AT-2, AT-3
65. Venezuela	SS.11 (1977)
66. Vietnam (N) *	AT-3 (1972)
67. West Germany	SS.10 (????); SS.11 (1965?); Cobra (1960)
68. Yugoslavia	AT-1 (1974); AT-3 (1974)
69. Zaire *	AT-1 (1977)
70. Zambia	AT-3 (1982)

States marked with an * may also use AT-2, but since it was not the first Generation 1 system in their inventories, it has no effect on the data. Rwanda, Sierra Leone, and Sri Lanka operate Mi-24s and may also operate AT-2, but there is no evidence for this at the time. SS.11 also includes AS.11 air-launched variant users.

GENERATION 2 (71 ADOPTERS)

1. Algeria	Milan (1982); AT-4 (1982); AT-5 (1982)
2. Angola	HOT (1990)
3. Australia	Milan (1984)
4. Austria	RBS-56 (1990)
5. Bahrain	TOW (1983)
6. Belgium	Milan (1977)
7. Botswana	TOW (1989)
8. Cameroon	Milan (1982); HOT (1983)
9. Canada	TOW (1975); Eryx (1994)
10. Chad	Milan (1984)
11. Chile	Milan (1978); Mapats (1994)
12. China	HOT (1980), HJ-8 (????); AT-11 (1996?)
13. Colombia	TOW (1987)
14. Cyprus	Milan (1986); HOT (1989); AT-10 (1996); AT-11 (1996)
15. Czechoslovakia	AT-4 (1981); AT-5 (1986)
16. Denmark	TOW (1975)
17. East Germany	AT-4 (1981); AT-5 (1987)
18. Egypt	HOT (1977); Milan (1977); TOW (1981); AT-5 (????)
19. Finland	AT-4 (1984); TOW (1985); AT-5 (1989)
20. France	Harpon (1971?); Milan (1974); HOT (1975); Eryx (1993)
21. Gabon	Milan (1990)
22. Greece	TOW (1975); Milan (1976); AT-4 (1997)
23. Hungary	AT-4 (1983); AT-5 (1989); AT-7 (1997)
24. India	Milan (1983); AT-4 (1989); AT-5 (1992)
25. Iran	TOW (1972); Dragon (1976)
26. Iraq	Milan (1979); HOT (1981); AT-4 (1987)
27. Ireland	Milan (1980)
28. Israel	TOW (1974); Dragon (1977); Mapats (1989); Hellfire (????)
29. Italy	TOW (1975); Milan (1981)
30. Japan	KAM-9 (1977); TOW (1982)
31. Jordan	TOW (1975); Dragon (1977)
32. Kenya	Milan (1980); TOW (1982)
33. Kuwait	TOW (1975); Harpon (1976); HOT (1976)
34. Lebanon	TOW (1976); Milan (1979)
35. Libya	Milan (1980); AT-4 (1990)
36. Mauritania	Milan (1988)
37. Mexico	Milan (1986)
38. Morocco	Dragon (1978); TOW (1978); Milan (1982); HOT (1983)
39. Netherlands	TOW (1975); Dragon (1982)
40. North Korea	AT-4 (1994); AT-5 (1994)
41. North Yemen	TOW (1980); Dragon (1982)
42. Norway	TOW (1975)
43. Oman	TOW (1976); Milan (1984)
44. Pakistan	TOW (1984); HJ-8 (1991)
45. Poland	AT-4 (1981); AT-5 (1989); AT-7 (1989); AT-6 (1991)

46. Portugal	TOW (1978); Milan (1986)
47. Qatar	Milan (1987); HOT (1988)
48. Saudi Arabia	TOW (1977); Dragon (1977); Harpon (1978); HOT (1982?)
49. Senegal	Milan (1980)
50. Singapore	Milan (1989)
51. Somalia	Milan (1980); TOW (1983)
52. South Africa	Milan (1975); ZT-3 (1991)
53. South Korea	TOW (1977)
54. South Yemen	AT-6 (1988)
55. Spain	Milan (1976); Dragon (1979); HOT (1982); TOW (1983)
56. Sweden	TOW (1984); RBS-56 (1991); Hellfire (????)
57. Switzerland	Dragon (1981); TOW (1984)
58. Syria	Milan (1979); HOT (1981); AT-4 (1982); AT-5 (1985)
59. Taiwan	Kun Wu (1980); TOW (1982); Hellfire (????)
60. Thailand	Dragon (1980); TOW (1980)
61. Tunisia	Milan (1982)
62. Turkey	TOW (1976); Milan (1984)
63. Uruguay	Milan (1987)
64. UAE	Harpon (1976); TOW (1985) HOT (1988); Milan (1989); Hellfire (????)
65. U.K.	Milan (1978); TOW (1982)
66. U.S.	Shillelagh (1967); TOW (1971); Dragon (1971); Hellfire (1986)
67. USSR	AT-4 (1979), AT-5 (1979), AT-6 (1979), AT-7 (1988), AT-8 (????), AT-9 (1992), AT-10 (1992), AT-11 (????)
68. Venezuela	Mapats (1992)
69. Vietnam (S)	TOW (1972)
70. West Germany	Harpon (????); Milan (1974); TOW (1974); HOT (1976)
71. Yugoslavia	AT-4 (1990); AT-5 (1990)

DIFFUSION OF GENERATION 1 ANTI-TANK GUIDED MISSILES

Total of 32 adoptions by 1970 (exact dates for 19 of these uncertain; listed are all 32): Afghanistan, Belgium, Bulgaria, Canada, Cuba, Czechoslovakia, Denmark, East Germany, Egypt, Finland, France, Greece, Hungary, Indonesia, Israel, Italy, Japan, Kuwait, Netherlands, Nigeria, Pakistan, Poland, Romania, Saudi Arabia, Sweden, Switzerland, Syria, Turkey, U.K., U.S., USSR, and West Germany.

1970	Argentina, India	34
1971	Iran, Iraq	36
1972	Vietnam (N)	37
1973	Libya, Mongolia, UAE	40
1974	Uganda, Yugoslavia	42
1975	Algeria, Australia, Brazil, Lebanon, Norway, South Africa	48
1976	Angola, Chile, Colombia, Peru, Somalia, Spain	54
1977	North Korea, Portugal, Venezuela, Zaire	58
1978	Ethiopia, Mozambique, North Yemen	61

1979	Kenya, Morocco	63
1980	Malaysia	64
1981	China	65
1982	South Yemen, Zambia	67
1983	Sudan	68
1984		68
1985	Nicaragua	69
1986		69
1987	Bahrain	70
1988		70

column on right = cumulative number of adopters

DIFFUSION OF GENERATION 2 ANTI-TANK GUIDED MISSILES

1967	U.S.	1
1968		1
1969		1
1970		1
1971	France	2
1972	Iran, Vietnam (S)	4
1973		4
1974	Israel, West Germany	6
1975	Canada, Denmark, Greece, Italy, Jordan, Kuwait, Netherlands, Norway, South Africa	15
1976	Lebanon, Oman, Spain, Turkey, UAE	20
1977	Belgium, Egypt, Japan, Saudi Arabia, South Korea	25
1978	Chile, Morocco, Portugal, U.K.	29
1979	Iraq, Syria, USSR	32
1980	China, Ireland, Kenya, Libya, North Yemen, Senegal, Somalia, Taiwan, Thailand	41
1981	Czechoslovakia, East Germany, Poland, Switzerland	45
1982	Algeria, Cameroon, Tunisia	48
1983	Bahrain, Hungary, India	51
1984	Australia, Chad, Finland, Pakistan, Sweden	56
1985		56
1986	Cyprus, Mexico	58
1987	Colombia, Qatar, Uruguay	61
1988	Mauritania, South Yemen	63
1989	Botswana, Singapore	65
1990	Angola, Austria, Gabon, Yugoslavia	69
1991		69
1992	Venezuela	70
1993		70
1994	North Korea	71
1995		71
1996		71

column on right = cumulative number of adopters

NOTE

[1] See "Poles Hover Over" (1998). One source (Methehan and Morrocco 1998) specifically describes these missiles as third-generation.

Appendix I
State Diffusion Scores By Region

THIS APPENDIX LISTS THE DIFFUSION SCORES OF ALL 138 NATIONS IN THE data set, as calculated in Chapter 5 by Equation 5.3. States are listed by region, with the states in each region ranked according to their score.

REGION 1: NATO/WESTERN EUROPE

U.S.	11.650
West Germany	7.875
U.K.	7.675
Greece	6.700
Netherlands	6.450
France	6.375
Sweden	6.300
Italy	5.700
Switzerland	5.600
Spain	5.375
Belgium	4.575
Turkey	4.575
Finland	4.425
Denmark	4.325
Norway	3.450
Canada	3.425
Cyprus	2.875
Portugal	2.775
Austria	1.825
Ireland	1.600

REGION 2: MIDDLE EAST

Israel	9.575
Saudi Arabia	7.800
Iran	7.375
Egypt	7.275
UAE	6.250
Iraq	6.175
Kuwait	6.100
Jordan	5.650
Syria	5.375
Libya	5.200
Algeria	5.000
Oman	4.425
Qatar	3.575
Bahrain	3.500
South Yemen	3.375
Tunisia	3.050
Morocco	2.900
North Yemen	2.400
Lebanon	1.550

REGION 3: WARSAW PACT/EASTERN EUROPE

USSR	10.475
East Germany	6.075
Bulgaria	5.425
Czechoslovak.	5.325
Poland	5.275
Hungary	5.175
Yugoslavia	4.000
Romania	3.175
Albania	.675

REGION 4: EAST ASIA/PACIFIC

Japan	7.200
South Korea	6.275
Thailand	5.050
China	4.925
Taiwan	4.675
Australia	4.175
North Korea	4.025
Singapore	3.900
North Vietnam	3.850
Indonesia	2.850
South Vietnam	2.200
Malaysia	2.125
Laos	1.400
Mongolia	1.375
Cambodia	.750
Fiji	.000
New Zealand	.000
Papua NG	.000
Philippines	.000

REGION 5: SOUTH ASIA

India	6.225
Pakistan	4.825
Afghanistan	2.675
Bangladesh	.825
Sri Lanka	.450
Myanmar	.425
Bhutan	.000
Nepal	.000

REGION 6: SOUTH AMERICA

Chile	3.550
Peru	3.525
Argentina	2.975
Venezuela	2.925
Brazil	2.500
Colombia	1.775
Ecuador	1.475
Guyana	.550
Uruguay	.500
Bolivia	.000
Paraguay	.000

REGION 7: LATIN AMERICA/CARIBBEAN

Cuba	4.250
Nicaragua	1.750
Mexico	1.500
El Salvador	.300
Honduras	.300
Dom Republic	.000
Guatemala	.000
Haiti	.000
Jamaica	.000
Panama	.000
Trin & Tobago	.000

REGION 8: AFRICA

Angola	3.325
Ethiopia	3.100
South Africa	3.000
Zamiba	2.475
Somalia	2.400
Kenya	2.375
Mozambique	2.325
Sudan	2.175
Nigeria	2.125
Chad	1.800
Guinea	1.800
Tanzania	1.725
Botswana	1.600
Uganda	1.250
Zaire	1.200
Mauritania	1.025
Gabon	.950
Sierra Leone	.875
Zimbabwe	.875
Burkina Faso	.800
Mali	.800
Senegal	.675
Cameroon	.650
Guinea-Bissau	.600
Malawi	.600
Madagascar	.500
Congo Rep.	.275
Burundi	.175
Ghana	.175
Rwanda	.175
Benin	.000
Cent. Af. Rep.	.000
Djibouti	.000
Eq. Guinea	.000
Gambia	.000
Ivory Coast	.000
Lesotho	.000
Liberia	.000
Niger	.000
Swaziland	.000
Togo	.000

Bibliography

Adelman, Kenneth L. and Norman R. Augustine. *The Defense Revolution: Strategy for the Brave New World*. San Francisco, CA: Institute for Contemporary Studies, 1990.

"Affordable Superiority Eurofighter 2000 Receives the Political Go-Ahead," *Asian Defence Journal*, June 1993, 100–2.

Albrecht, Ulrich. "The Changing Structure of the Tank Industry." In *Restructuring the Global Military Sector Volume II: The End of Military Fordism*, edited by Mary Kaldor, Ulrich Albrecht, and Geneviève Schméder. Washington, D.C.: Pinter, 1998.

Allen, Kenneth W., Glenn Krumel, and Jonathan D. Pollack. *China's Air Force Enters the 21st Century*. Santa Monica, CA: Rand Corporation, 1995

Allison, Graham T. *The Essence of Decision: Explaining the Cuban Missile Crisis*. Boston: Little, Brown, and Co., 1971.

Allison, Graham T., Owen R. Coté, Jr., Richard A. Falkenrath, and Steven E. Miller. *Avoiding Nuclear Anarchy: Containing the Threat of Loose Russian Nuclear Weapons and Fissile Material*. Cambridge, Mass: MIT Press, 1996.

"Already in Service: The 2nd Generation of Soviet Anti-Tank Missiles," *International Defence Review Special Series* #10, 1980, 87–89.

Andrews, William F. *Airpower Against an Army: Challenge and Response in CENTAF's Duel With the Republican Guard*. Maxwell AFB, AL: Air University Press, 1998.

Anthony, Ian, ed. *Russia and the Arms Trade*. New York: Oxford University Press, 1998.

Anthony, Ian, "Economic Dimensions of Soviet and Russian Arms Exports." In *Russia and the Arms Trade*, edited by Ian Anthony. New York: Oxford University Press, 1998.

———. "The Conventional Arms Trade." In *Cascade of Arms: Managing Conventional Weapons Proliferation*, edited by Andrew J. Pierre. Washington, D.C.: Brookings Institution Press, 1997.

Armacost, Michael H. *The Politics of Weapons Innovation: The Thor-Jupiter Controversy*. New York: Columbia University Press, 1969.

Arquilla, John, and David Ronfeldt, eds. *In Athena's Camp: Preparing for Conflict in the Information Age*. Santa Monica, CA: Rand Corporation, 1997.

Bahbah, Bishara. *Israel and Latin America: The Military Connection*. New York: St. Martin's Press, 1986.

Bajusz, William D., and David J. Louscher. *Arms Sales and the U.S. Economy: The Impact of Restricting Military Exports*. Boulder, CO: Westview Press, 1988.

Ball, Desmond. "Arms and Affluence: Military Acquisitions in the Asia-Pacific Region," *International Security* 18, no. 3 (1994): 78–112.

Barber, Benjamin R. *Jihad vs. McWorld*. New York: Random House, 1995.

Bassett, Richard, "Kosovo War Spurs Industry Rethink," *Jane's Defence Weekly*, 30 June 1999, 23–27.

Baugh, William H., and Michael J. Squires. "Arms Transfers and the Onset of War, Part II: Wars in Third World States, 1950–1965." *International Interactions* 10 (1983): 129–141.

Baxter, William. *Soviet Airland Battle Tactics*. Novato, CA: Presidio Press, 1986.

Bee, Ronald J. *Nuclear Proliferation: The Post Cold War Challenge*. New York: Foreign Policy Association, 1995.

Beit-Hallahmi, Benjamin. *The Israeli Connection : Who Israel Arms and Why*. New York: Pantheon Books, 1987.

Belyakov, R. A., and J. Marmain. *MiG: Fifty Years of Secret Aircraft Design*. Annapolis, MD: Naval Institute Press, 1994.

Ben-Menashe, Ari. *Profits of War : Inside the Secret U.S.-Israeli Arms Network*. New York: Sheridan Square Press, 1992.

Bender, Bryan. "Poor U.S. Intelligence May Have Led to Sudan Strikes," *Jane's Defence Weekly*, 2 September 1998, 4.

Bennett, Bruce W., Sam Gardiner, and Daniel B. Fox. "Not Merely Planning for the Last War." In *New Challenges for Defense Planning: Rethinking How Much is Enough*, edited by Paul K. Davis. Santa Monica, CA: Rand Corporation, 1994.

Bergquist, Ronald E. *The Role of Airpower in the Iran-Iraq War*. Maxwell Air Force Base, AL: Air University Press, 1988.

Berman, Robert P. *Soviet Air Power in Transition*. Washington, D.C.: Brookings Institution, 1978.

Betts, Richard K. "American Strategic Intelligence: Politics, Priorities, and Direction." In *Intelligence Policy and National Security*, edited by Robert L. Pfaltzgraff, Jr., Uri Ra'anan, and Warren Milberg. London: Macmillan Press, 1981.

Biddle, Stephen, and Robert Zirkle. "Technology, Civil-Military Relations and Warfare in Southern Asia." In *Military Capacity and the Risk of War: China, India, Pakistan, and Iran*, edited by Eric Arnett. New York: Oxford University Press, 1997.

Bitzinger, Richard A. "The Globalization of the Arms Industry: The Next Proliferation Challenge," *International Security* 19, no. 2 (1994): 170–98.

———. *Chinese Arms Production and Sales to the Third World*. Santa Monica, CA: Rand Corporation, 1991.

Blair, David. "How to Defeat the United States: The Operational Military Effects of the Proliferation of Weapons of Precise Destruction." In *Fighting Proliferation: New Concerns for the Nineties*, edited by Henry Sokolski. Maxwell Air Force Base, AL: Air University Press, 1996.

Blanche, Ed, and Duncan Lennox, "Shifting Balance," *Jane's Defence Weekly*, 10 March 1999, 59–69.

Bonds, Ray, ed. *The US War Machine: An Encyclopedia of American Military Equipment and Strategy*. New York: Crown Publishers, Inc., 1983.

———. ed. *Russian Military Power*. New York: Bonanza Books, 1982.

Brzoska, Michael, and Thomas Ohlson. *Arms Transfers to the Third World, 1971–85*. New York: Oxford University Press, 1987.

———. *Arms Production in the Third World*. Philadelphia, PA: Taylor and Francis, 1986.

Buchan, Glenn C. "The Use of Long-Range Bombers in a Changing World: A Classical Exercise in Systems Analysis." In *New Challenges for Defense Planning: Rethinking How Much is Enough*, edited by Paul K. Davis. Santa Monica, CA: Rand Corporation, 1994.

Bugos, Glenn E. *Engineering the F-4 Phantom II: Parts Into Systems*. Annapolis, MD: Naval Institute Press, 1996.

Butowski, Piotr, "Thrust-Vectoring MiG-35 Ready to Fly Next Year," *Jane's Defence Weekly*, 5 June 1996, 3.

Buzan, Barry. *An Introduction to Strategic Studies: Military Technology and International Relations.* New York: St. Martin's Press, 1987.

Campany, Richard C., Jr. *Turkey and the United States: The Arms Embargo Period.* New York: Praeger, 1986.

"The Case for the B-2," *Air Combat*, August 1991, 26–37, 66–74.

Cashman, Greg. *What Causes War? An Introduction to Theories of International Conflict.* New York: Lexington Books, 1993.

Catrina, Christian. *Arms Transfers and Dependence.* New York: Taylor and Francis, 1988.

Chadwick, Frank, and Matt Caffrey. *Gulf War Fact Book.* Bloomington, IN: GDW, Inc., 1991.

Clark, Asa A. IV. "The Role of Technology in U.S. National Security: An Introduction." In *Defense Technology*, edited by Asa A. Clark IV and John F. Lilley. New York: Praeger, 1989.

Clark, Mark T. "Emerging Security Threats," *Orbis* 42, no. 1 (Winter 1998): 121–130.

Clark, Ronald W. *War Winners.* London: Sidgwick and Jackson, 1979.

Clarke, Duncan. "Israel's Unauthorized Arms Transfers," *Foreign Policy* 99 (1995): 89–109.

Clawson, Robert W., and Lawrence S. Kaplan. *The Warsaw Pact: Political Purpose and Military Means.* Wilmington, DE: Scholarly Resources, Inc., 1982.

Cockburn, Andrew. *The Threat: Inside the Soviet Military Machine.* New York: Random House, 1984.

Cook, Nick, "Russian Air Force Is Down But Not Out," *Jane's Defence Weekly*, 19 March 1997, 21–23.

———. "Air Force in Dilemma as Programmes Soar," *Jane's Defence Weekly*, 4 November 1995, 49–52.

———. "AA-11 is 10 Years Ahead of ASRAAM," *Jane's Defence Weekly*, 20 July 1991, 89.

Cooper, Julian. "Russia." In *Cascade of Arms: Managing Conventional Weapons Proliferation*, edited by Andrew J. Pierre. Washington, D.C.: Brookings Institution Press, 1997.

Cordesman, Anthony H. *Iran's Military Forces in Transition: Conventional Threats and Weapons of Mass Destruction.* Westport, CT: Praeger, 1999.

———. *Saudi Arabia: Guarding the Desert Kingdom.* Boulder, CO: Westview Press, 1997.

———. *Iran and Iraq: The Threat from the Northern Gulf.* Boulder, CO: Westview Press, 1994.

————. *Jordanian Arms and the Middle East Balance: Update.* Washington, D.C.: Middle East Institute, 1985.

————. *The Gulf and the Search for Strategic Stability.* Boulder, CO: Westview Press, 1984.

———— . *Jordanian Arms and the Middle East Military Balance.* Washington, D.C.: Middle East Institute, 1983.

Cordesman, Anthony H., and Abraham Wagner. *The Lessons of Modern War Volume II: The Iran-Iraq War.* Boulder, CO: Westview Press, 1991.

Cordesman, Anthony H., and Ahmed S. Hashim. *Iran: Dilemmas of Dual Containment.* Boulder, CO: Westview Press, 1997.

Cornish, Paul. *The Arms Trade and Europe.* London : The Royal Institute of International Affairs, 1995.

Coulter, Robert M., Laure Despres, and Aaron Karp. "The Political Economy of East- South Military Transfers," *International Studies Quarterly* 31 (1987): 273–299.

Covault, Craig, and Boris Rybak, "Russia Revamping Aerospace Identity," *Aviation Week and Space Technology,* 7 June 1993, 58, 61.

Crabtree, James D. *On Air Defense.* Westport, CT: Praeger, 1994.

Crano, William D., Suellen Ludwig, and Gary W. Selnow. *Annotated Archive of Diffusion References: Empirical and Theoretical Works.* Lansing, MI: Michigan State University,1981.

"Creation of a Missile System—the RBS70," *Asian Defence Journal,* January 1991, 49–52.

Crescenzi, Mark C., and Andrew J. Enterline. "Ripples From the Waves? A Systemic, Time-Series Analysis of Democracy, Democratization, and Interstate War," *Journal of Peace Research* 36 (January 1999): 75–94.

David, Steven R. "Saving America From the Coming Civil Wars," *Foreign Affairs* 78, no. 1 (January/February 1999): 103–106.

Davis, Paul K. "Planning Under Uncertainty Then and Now: Paradigms Lost and Paradigms Emerging." In *New Challenges for Defense Planning: Rethinking How Much is Enough,* edited by Paul K. Davis. Santa Monica, CA: Rand Corporation, 1994.

Davis, Richard G. *Decisive Force: Strategic Bombing in the Gulf War.* Washington, D.C.: Air Force History and Museums Program/U.S. Government Printing Office, 1996.

Davis, Zachary S., and Benjamin Frankel. *The Proliferation Puzzle: Why Nuclear Weapons Spread and What Results.* Portland, OR: Frank Cass, 1993.

Day, Samuel H., Jr., "Vanunu: Israel's Embarrassment," *The Bulletin of the Atomic Scientists*, November 1992, 12–13.

Demin, Methehan, and John D. Morrocco, "Turkey Sets Framework for Attack Helo Buy," *Aviation Week and Space Technology*, 18 May 1998, 34–35.

Dickson, Paul. *The Electronic Battlefield*. Bloomington, IN: Indiana University Press, 1976.

Donald, David, "F-15E Strike Eagle," *World Air Power Journal*, Summer 1995, 38–75.

Donnelly, Christopher, Bill Gunston, and James E. Dornan. *Soviet Ground and Rocket Forces*. Hickesville, NY: Paradise Press, 1997.

Douglas, Susan J. "Technological Innovation and Organizational Change: The Navy's Adoption of Radio, 1899–1919." In *Military Enterprise and Technological Change: Perspectives on the American Experience*, edited by Merritt Roe Smith. Cambridge, Mass.: MIT Press, 1985.

Doyle, Michael W. "Liberalism and World Politics," *American Political Science Review* 80 (1986): 1151–69.

Drifte, Reinhard. *Arms Production in Japan: the Military Applications of Civilian Technology*. Boulder, CO: Westview Press, 1986.

Dunn, Lewis A. *Controlling the Bomb: Nuclear Proliferation in the 1980s*. New Haven, CT: Yale University Press, 1982.

Dunnigan, James F. *Digital Soldiers: The Evolution of High-Tech Weaponry and Tomorrow's Brave New Battlefield*. New York: St. Martin's Press, 1996.

———. *How to Make War: A Comprehensive Guide to Modern Warfare for the Post Cold War Era*, 3rd ed. New York: William Morrow and Company, Inc., 1993.

Ebata, Kensuke, "Japan Joins the World Arms Control Lobby," *Jane's Defence Weekly*, 23 January 1993, 5.

El-Shazly, Nadia El-Sayed. *The Gulf Tanker War: Iran and Iraq's Maritime Swordplay*. New York: St. Martin's Press, 1998.

Epstein, Joshua M. *Measuring Military Power: The Soviet Air Threat to Europe*. Princeton, NJ: Princeton University Press, 1984.

Erlanger, Stephen, "Moscow Insists It Must Sell the Instruments of War to Pay the Costs of Peace,"*New York Times*, 3 February 1993, A6.

Etcheson, Craig. *Arms Race Theory: Strategy and Structure of Behavior*. New York: Greenwood Press, 1989.

Evangelista, Matthew. *Innovation and the Arms Race: How the United States and the Soviet Union Develop New Military Technologies*. Ithaca, NY: Cornell University Press, 1988.

Eyestone, Robert. "Confusion, Diffusion, and Innovation," *American Political Science Review* 71 (1977): 441–47.

Farrell, Theo. *Weapons Without A Cause: The Politics of Weapons Acquisition in the United States*. New York: St. Martin's Press, 1997.

Forsberg, Randall. *The Arms Production Dilemma: Contraction and Restraint in the World Combat Aircraft Industry*. Cambridge, Mass: MIT Press, 1994.

Forty, George. *United States Tanks of World War II*. New York: Blandford Press, 1983.

Foss, Christopher S. "Raising the Low-Level Air Defense Umbrella." *Jane's Defence Weekly*. 11 December 1996; pp. 19–23.

———. "Revolutionary Russian MBT Prototype Built," *Jane's Defence Weekly*, 28 January 1995, 2.

———. ed. *Jane's Armour and Artillery, 1992–1993*. Alexandria, VA: Jane's Information Group, 1992a.

———. "Manportable SAMs and Target Acquisition," *Jane's Defence Weekly*, 25 April 1992b, 712–18.

———. "Stinger-Style SAM Detailed," *Jane's Defence Weekly*, 20 July 1991, 88.

Francillon, René J. *Naval Institute Guide to World Military Aviation, 1997–1998*. Annapolis, MD: Naval Institute Press, 1997.

Franko-Jones, Patrice. *The Brazilian Defence Industry*. Boulder, CO: Westview Press, 1992.

Friedman, Alan. *Spider's Web: The Secret History of How the White House Illegally Armed Iraq*. New York: Bantam Books, 1993.

Friedman, Norman. *The Naval Institute Guide to World Naval Weapons Systems 1997– 1998*. Annapolis, MD: Naval Institute Press, 1997.

———. "'It's Dangerous Out There...'" *Proceedings of the U.S. Naval Institute*, October 1992a, 122.

———. "Russia Stages A Fire Sale," *Proceedings of the U.S. Naval Institute*, April 1992b, 123.

Friedman, Richard S., David Miller, Doug Richardson, Bill Gunston, David Hobbs, and Max Walmer. *Advanced Technology Warfare: A Detailed Study of the Latest Weapons and Techniques for Warfare Today and into the 21st Century*. New York: Crescent, 1985.

Fukuyama, Francis. "The End of History?" *The National Interest* 16 (Summer 1989): 3–18.

Fulghum, David A, "Improved Air Defenses Prompt Pentagon Fears," *Aviation Week and Space Technology*, 6 July 1998, 22–24.

————. "Expanding Roles May Shield F-22," *Aviation Week and Space Technology*, 6 January 1997, 42–43.

————. "Defense Dept. Confirms Patriot Technology Diverted," *Aviation Week and Space Technology*, 1 February 1993, 26–27.

————. "Advanced Arms Spread Defies Remote Detection,"*Aviation Week and Space Technology*, 9 November 1992, 20–22.

Gabriel, Richard A. *Military Incompetence: Why the American Military Doesn't Win.* New York: Hill and Wang, 1985.

Galeotti, Mark, "Soviet Weapon Stockpile is a Volatile Inheritance," *Jane's Defence Weekly*, 15 February 1992, 231.

Garrett, James M. *The Tenuous Balance: Conventional Forces in Central Europe.* Boulder, CO: Westview Press, 1989.

Garrity, Patrick J. "Implications of the Persian Gulf War for Regional Powers." In *Weapons Proliferation in the 1990s*, edited by Brad Roberts. Cambridge, Mass.: MIT Press, 1995.

Gates, Scott, Torbjørn L. Knutsen, and Jonathon W. Moses. "Democracy and Peace: A More Skeptical View," *Journal of Peace Research* 33 (January 1996): 1–10.

Gati, Charles. "From Sarajevo to Sarajevo," *Foreign Affairs*. 71, no. 4 (Fall 1992): 64–78.

Gelbart, Marsh. *Tanks: Main Battle Tanks and Light Tanks.* London: Brassey's (UK) Ltd., 1996.

Gill, Bates, and Taeho Kim. *China's Arms Acquisitions from Abroad: A Quest for 'Superb and Secret Weapons.'* New York: Oxford University Press, 1995.Gill, R. Bates. *Chinese Arms Transfers: Purposes, Patterns, and Prospects in the New World Order.* Westport, CT.: Praeger, 1992.

Gilpin, Robert. "Hegemonic War and International Change." In *Conflict After the Cold War: Arguments on Causes of War and Peace*, edited by Richard K. Betts. New York: Macmillan Publishing Co., 1994.

Glassman, Jon D. *Arms for the Arabs: The Soviet Union and War in the Middle East.* Baltimore, MD: Johns Hopkins University Press, 1975.

Gleditsch, Nils Petter. "Research on Arms Races." In *Arms Races: Technological and Political Dynamics*, edited by Nils Petter Gleditsch and Olav Njølstad. London: Sage Publications, 1990.

Gleditsch, Nils Petter, and Hvard Hegre. "Peace and Democracy: Three Levels of Analysis," *Journal of Conflict Resolution* 41 (1997): 283–310.

Goetz, Gary, and Paul F. Diehl. "Measuring Military Allocations: A Comparison of Different Approaches." In *Measuring the Correlates of*

War, edited by J. David Singer and Paul F. Diehl. Ann Arbor, MI: University of Michigan Press, 1990.

Goertz, Gary, and Paul F. Diehl. "Measuring Military Allocations: A Comparison of Different Approaches," *Journal of Conflict Resolution* 30, no. 3 (September 1986): 553–81.

Goldanskii, Vitalii I., "Russia's 'Red-Brown' Hawks," *The Bulletin of the Atomic Scientists*, June 1993, 24–27.

Gray, Virginia. "Innovation in the States: A Diffusion Study," *American Political Science Review* 67 (1973): 1174–1185.

Greenhouse, Stephen, "Post Soviet Arms Industry Is Collapsing," *New York Times*, 9 June 1992, A3.

Gujarati, Damodar N. *Basic Econometrics*, 3rd ed. New York: McGraw-Hill, Inc., 1995.

Gunston, Bill, ed. *The Encyclopedia of World Aircraft*. New York: Crescent Books, 1986a.

Gunston, Bill. *MiG-23/27 Flogger*. London: Osprey Publishing, 1986b.

———. *AH-64 Apache*. London: Osprey Publishing, 1986c.

———. *Modern Combat Aircraft*. London: Treasure Press, 1985.

Gunston, Bill, and Mick Spick. *Modern Fighting Helicopters*. New York: Crescent Books, 1986.

Hamilton, Lee H. "A Democrat Looks at Foreign Policy," *Foreign Affairs* 71, no. 3 (Summer 1992): 32–51.

Hammond, Paul Y., David J. Louscher, Michael D. Salomone, and Norman A. Graham. *The Reluctant Supplier: U.S. Decisionmaking for Arms Sales*. Cambridge, Mass: Oelgeschlager, Gunn, and Hain Publishers, Inc., 1983.

Hampson, Fen Osler. *Unguided Missiles: How America Buys Its Weapons*. New York: W.W. Norton and Company, 1989.

Harkavy, Robert. "Images of the Coming International System," *Orbis* 41, no. 4 (Fall 1997): 569–90.

———. *The Arms Trade and International Systems*. Cambridge, MA: Ballinger Publishing Company, 1975.

Hartcup, Guy. *The Silent Revolution: The Development of Conventional Weapons, 1945–85*. New York: Brassey's, 1993.

Hartung, William D. *And Weapons for All*. New York: Harper Collins Publishers, 1994.

Haselkorn, Avigdor. *The Continuing Storm: Iraq, Poisonous Weapons, and Deterrence*. New Haven, CT: Yale University Press, 1999.

Heikal, Mohamed. *The Sphinx and the Commisar: The Rise and Fall of Soviet Influence in the Middle East*. New York: Harper and Row Publishers, 1978.

Hewish, Mark, and Joris Janssen Lok, "Air Forces Face Up to NBC Reality," *Jane's International Defense Review*, May 1998, 47–52.

Higgott, Richard. "International Political Economy." In *Contemporary International Relations: A Guide to Theory*, edited by A.J.R. Groom and Margot Light, New York: Pinter Publishers, 1994.

Holland, Lauren. *Weapons Under Fire*. New York: Garland Publishing, 1997.

Homer-Dixon, Thomas F. "On the Threshold: Environmental Changes as Causes of Acute Conflict," *International Security* 16, no. 2 (1991): 76–116.

Howe, Russell Warren. *Weapons: The International Game of Arms, Money, and Diplomacy*. Garden City, NY: Doubleday and Company, 1980.

Huntington, Samuel P. 1993. "Why International Primacy Matters," *International Security* 17, no. 4 (1993): 68–83.

Hussein, Mushahid, "Pakistan in Missile Share Offer with Turkey," *Jane's Defence Weekly*, 25 February 1989, 298.

Ibrahim, Y. M, "Iran Said to Commit to $7 Billion Secret Arms Plan," *New York Times*, 8 August 1992, A3.

[IWD] *International Weapon Developments: A Survey of Current Developments in Weapons Systems*, 4th ed. New York: Brassey's Publishers Ltd., 1980. in text notes]

"Iran Eyes Purchase of Two More Russian Subs," *Aviation Week and Space Technology*, 9 November 1992, 20.

Issacson, Jeffrey A., Christopher Layne, and John Arquilla. *Predicting Military Innovation*. Santa Monica, CA: Rand Corporation, 1999.

Jaggers, Keith and Ted R. Gurr. "Tracking Democracy's Third Wave with the Polity III Data," *Journal of Peace Research* 32, no. 4 (1995): 469–82.

[JLBAD] *Jane's Land-Based Air Defence 1997–1998*. Alexandria, VA: Jane's Information Group, 1997.

Jervis, Robert. *Perception and Misperception in International Politics*. Princeton, NJ: Princeton University Press, 1976.

Johnson, David E. *Fast Tanks and Heavy Bombers: Innovation in the U.S. Army, 1917–1945*. Ithaca, NY: Cornell University Press, 1998.

Jones, Daniel M., Stuart A. Bremer, and J. David Singer. "Militarized Interstate Disputes, 1816–1992: Rationale, Coding Rules, and

Empirical Patterns," *Conflict Management and Peace Science* 15, no. 2 (1996): 163–213.

Joshua, Wynfred and Stephen P. Gilbert. *Arms for the Third World: Soviet Military Aid Diplomacy.* Baltimore: Johns Hopkins Press, 1969.

Kaldor, Mary. *The Baroque Arsenal.* New York: Hill and Wang, 1981.

Kaplan, Robert D. *The Ends of the Earth: A Journey at the Dawn of the 21st Century.* New York: Random House, 1996.

Karinol, Robert, "MANPADS May Help to Revive Sino-Thai Trade," *Jane's Defence Weekly*, 22 January 1997a, 13.

———. "SAM Sale Marks Russia's Debut Deal in Singapore," *Jane's Defence Weekly.* 22 October 1997b, 3.

Karp, Aaron, "The New Politics of Missile Proliferation," *Arms Control Today*, October 1996, 10–14.

———. "The Arms Trade Revolution: The Major Impact of Small Arms." In *Weapons Proliferation in the 1990s*, edited by Brad Roberts, Cambridge, Mass.: MIT Press, 1995.

Karsh, Efraim, Martin S. Navias, and Philip Sabin. *Non-Conventional Weapons Proliferation in the Middle East: Tackling the Spread of Nuclear, Chemical, and Biological Capabilities.* New York: Oxford University Press, 1993.

Katz, James Everett, ed. *Arms Production in Developing Countries: An Analysis of Decision Making.* Lexington, Mass: Lexington Books, 1984.

Kearns, Graham. *Arms for the Poor: President Carter's Policies on Arms Transfers to the Third World.* Canberra: Australian National University Press, 1980.

Keller, William W. *Arm in Arm: The Political Economy of the Global Arms Trade.* New York: HarperCollins Publishers, 1995.

Keller, William W., and Janne E. Nolan. "The Arms Trade: Business as Usual," *Foreign Policy* 109 (Winter 1997–1998), 113–125.

Kelly, Orr. *King of the Killing Zone.* New York: W. W. Norton, 1989.

Kendall, Maurice, and J. Keith Ord. *Time Series*, 3rd ed. New York: Oxford UniversityPress, 1990.

Keohane, Robert O. *After Hegemony: Cooperation and Discord in the World Political System.* Princeton: Princeton University Press, 1984.

King, Gary. *Unifying Political Methodology: The Likelihood Theory of Statistical Inference.* New York: Cambridge University Press, 1989.

Kinsella, David. "Conflict in Context: Arms Transfers and Third World Rivalries During the Cold War," *American Journal of Political Science* 38 (1994): 557–81.

Kiplinger, Knight A. *World Boom Ahead: Why Business and Consumers Will Prosper*. Washington, D.C.: Kiplinger, 1998.

Kissinger, Henry A. "Domestic Structure and Foreign Policy." In *Comparative Foreign Policy: Theoretical Essays*, edited by Wolfram F. Hanrieder. New York: David McKay Company.

Klare, Michael T. *Rogue States and Nuclear Outlaws*. New York: Hill and Wang, 1995.

———. "Adding Fuel to the Fires: The Conventional Trade in Arms in the 1990s." In *World Security: Challenges for a New Century*, 2nd ed., edited by Michael T. Klare and Daniel C. Thomas. New York: St. Martin's Press, 1994.

———. "The Next Great Arms Race," *Foreign Affairs* 72, no. 3 (Summer 1993): 136–52.

———. *American Arms Supermarket*. Austin: University of Texas Press, 1984.

Klieman, Aaron S. *Israel's Global Reach : Arms Sales as Diplomacy*. Washington, D.C.: Pergamon-Brassey's International Defense Publishers, 1985.

Kolodziej, Edward A. *Making and Marketing Arms: The French Experience and Its Implications for the International System*. Princeton, NJ: Princeton University Press, 1987.

Kolodziej, Ed, and Roger E. Kanet, eds. *The Limits of Soviet Power in the Developing World*. Baltimore, MD: Johns Hopkins University Press, 1989.

Kortunov, Sergei. "Non-Proliferation and Counter Proliferation: Russian Perspective." Paper presented at the 1994 National Defense University Topical Symposium "Counterproliferation: Security Dimensions of WMD Proliferation," 1994a

———. "Russian Aerospace Exports." In *The Arms Production Dilemma: Contraction and Constraint in the World Combat Aircraft Industry*, edited by Randall Forsberg. Cambridge, Mass: MIT Press, 1994b.

Kotz, Nick. *Wild Blue Yonder: Money, Politics, and the B-1 Bomber*. New York: Pantheon Books, 1988.Krause, Keith. *Arms and the State: Patterns of Military Production and Trade*. New York: Cambridge University Press, 1992.

Lambeth, Benjamin S. *Russia's Air Power at the Crossroads*. Santa Monica, CA: Rand Corporation, 1996.

———. *The Evolving Soviet Strategic Threat*. Santa Monica, CA: Rand Corporation, 1975.

Laurance, Edward J. "The UN Register of Conventional Arms: Rationales and Prospects for Compliance and Effectiveness." In *Weapons*

Proliferation in the 1990s, edited by Brad Roberts. Cambridge, Mass.: MIT Press, 1995.

———. *The International Arms Trade*. New York: Lexington Books, 1992.

Laurance, Edward J., and Ronald G. Sherwin. "Understanding Arms Transfers Through Data Analysis." In *Arms Transfers to the Third World: The Military Build-Up in Less Industrial Countries*, edited by Uri Ra'anan, Robert L. Pfaltzgraff, Jr., and Geoffrey Kemp, eds. Boulder, CO: Westview Press, 1978.

Lefebvre, Jeffrey Alan. *Arms for the Horn: U.S. Security Policy in Ethiopia and Somalia, 1953–1991*. Pittsburgh: University of Pittsburgh Press, 1991.

Leitner, Peter M. *Decontrolling Strategic Technology, 1990–1992: Creating the Military Threats of the 21st Century*. New York: University Press of America, 1995.

Lesser, Ian O. and Ashley J. Tellis. *Strategic Exposure: Proliferation Around the Mediterranean*. Santa Monica: Rand Corporation, 1996.

Levy, Marc A. "Is the Environment a Security Issue?" *International Security* 20, no. 2 (1995): 35–62.

Lockwood, Dunbar, "Pentagon Begins Policy Review of Post-Cold War Nuclear Strategy," *Arms Control Today*, December 1993, 22, 27.

Lorell, Mark, Daniel P. Raymer, Michael Kennedy, and Hugh Levaux, "The Gray Threat," *Air Force Magazine*, February 1996, 64–68.

———. *The Gray Threat: Assessing the Next Generation European Fighters*. Santa Monica: Rand Corporation, 1995.

Luttwak, Edward N. "Where Are the Great Powers?" *Foreign Affairs* 73, no. 4 (1993): 23–8.

MacKenzie, Donald. *Inventing Accuracy: A Historical Sociology of Nuclear Missile Guidance*. Cambridge, Mass: MIT Press, 1990.

Maddison, Angus. *Monitoring the World Economy 1820–1992*, Paris: Development Centre of the Organization for Economic Cooperation and Development, 1995.

Mahajan, Vijay, and Robert A. Peterson. *Models for Innovation Diffusion*. Beverly Hills: Sage Publications, 1985.

Mandeles, Mark D. "Command and Control in the Gulf War: A Military Revolution in Airpower?" In *The Eagle in the Desert: Looking Back on U.S. Involvement in the Persian Gulf War*, edited by William Head and Earl H. Tilford, Jr., eds. Westport, CT: Praeger, 1996.

"Manportable SAMS and Target Acquisition," *Jane's Defence Weekly*, 25 April 1992, 712–18.

Mansfield, Edwin. "Technical Change and the Rate of Imitation," *Econometrica* 29 (1961): 741–66.

Maoz, Zeev, and Bruce Russett. "Normative and Structural Causes of Democratic Peace, 1946–1986," *American Political Science Review* 87, no. 3 (1993): 624–638.

McIntosh, Malcolm. *Arms Across the Pacific: Security and Trade Issues Across the Pacific.* New York: St. Martin's Press, 1987.

———. *Japan Re-Armed.* New York: St. Martin's Press, 1986.

McKinlay, Robert D. *Third World Military Expenditure: Determinants and Implications.* New York: Pinter Publishers, 1989.

Mearsheimer, John J. "Back to the Future: Instability in Europe After the Cold War," *International Security* 15, no. 1 (1990): 5–56.

Mellinger, George M., ed. *Soviet Armed Forces Review Annual.* Volume 13, 1989. Gulf Breeze, FL: Academic International Press, 1995.

Menaul, Stewart, ed. *Russian Military Power.* New York: Bonanza Books, 1982.

Messinger, Charles. *Anti-Armour Warfare.* London: Ian Allan Ltd., 1985.

Meyer, Stephen M. *The Dynamics of Nuclear Proliferation*, Chicago, IL: University of Chicago Press, 1984.

Miller, Davina. *Export or Die: Britain's Defence Trade With Iran and Iraq.* New York: Cassell, 1996.

Molander, Roger C. and Peter A. Wilson. "On Dealing with the Prospect of Nuclear Chaos." In *Weapons Proliferation in the 1990s*, edited by Brad Roberts. Cambridge, Mass: MIT Press, 1995.

Moodie, Michael. "Beyond Proliferation: The Challenge of Technology Diffusion." In *Weapons Proliferation in the 1990s*, edited by Brad Roberts. Cambridge, Mass: MIT Press.

Mullins, A. F., Jr. *Born Arming: Development and Military Power in New States.* Stanford, CA: Stanford University Press, 1987.

Murray, Williamson. "Armored Warfare: The British, French, and German Experiences." In *Military Innovation in the Interwar Period*, edited by Williamson Murray and Allan R. Millet. New York: Cambridge University Press, 1996.

Myers, Steven Lee, "The Latin Arms Explosion That Fizzled," *New York Times*, 3 December 1998, A3.

Nasbeth, L., and G. F. Ray, eds. *The Diffusion of New Industrial Processes.* New York: Cambridge University Press. 1974.

Nash, T., "Dossier: Manportable Air Defense Systems," *Jane's International Defence Review*, September 1995, 78–93.

Navias, Martin S. *Going Ballistic: The Build-Up of Missiles in the Middle East.* New York: Brassey's, 1993.

Navias, Martin, and Susan Willet. *The European Arms Trade.* Commack, NY: Nova Science Publishers, 1996.

Nelson, Daniel N., "Ancient Enmities, Modern Guns," *The Bulletin of the Atomic Scientists,* December 1993, 21–27.

Neuman, Stephanie G. "International Stratification and Third World Military Industries," *International Organization* 37 (1984): 167–97.

Nicholson, Michael. *Formal Theories in International Relations.* New York: Cambridge University Press, 1989.

Nolan, Janne E. *Trappings of Power: Ballistic Missiles in the Third World.* Washington, D.C.: The Brookings Institution. 1991.

Nordeen, Lon O., and David Nicole. *Phoenix Over the Nile: A History of Egyptian Air Power, 1932–1994.* Washington, D.C.: Smithsonian Institution Press, 1996.

Novichkov, Nicolay, "Sukhoi Set to Exploit Thrust-Vector Control," *Jane's Defence Weekly,* 26 August 1996, 50–5.

Nye, Joseph S. *Bound to Lead: The Changing Nature of American Power.* New York: Basic Books, 1990.

Ogorkiewicz, R. M. "Trends in the Development of Armoured Vehicles." In *Jane's Defence '96: The World in Conflict.* Surrey, UK: Jane's Information Group, 1996.

Ohlson, Thomas. *Arms Transfer Limitations and Third World Security.* New York: Oxford University Press, 1988.

Olson, Mancur. *The Logic of Collective Action: Public Goods and the Theory of Groups.* Cambridge, Mass: Harvard University Press, 1965.

Onuf, Nicholas G., and Thomas J. Johnson. "Peace in the Liberal World: Does Democracy Matter?" In *Controversies in International Relations Theory: Realism and the Neo-liberal Challenge,* edited by Charles W. Kegley, Jr. New York: St. Martin's Press, 1995.

Pearson, Frederic S. *The Global Spread of Arms: Political Economy of International Security.* Boulder, CO: Westview Press, 1994.

Pedatzur, Reuven. "Conventional Arms Transfers to the Middle East." In *The Middle East Military Balance, 1996,* edited by Mark Heller. New York: Columbia University Press, 1998.

Peebles, Curtis. *Dark Eagles: A History of Top Secret U.S. Aircraft Programs.* Novato, CA: Presidio Press, 1995.

Pierre, Andrew J., ed. *Cascade of Arms: Managing Conventional Weapons Proliferation.* Washington, D.C.: Brookings Institution Press. 1997.

――――. ed. *Arms Transfers and American Foreign Policy*. New York: New York University Press, 1979.

"Poles Hover Over Israel Anti-Tank Missile Order," *Jane's International Defence Review*, January 1998, 14.

Porter, Bruce D. *The USSR in Third World Conflicts: Soviet Arms and Diplomacy in Local Wars, 1945–1980*. New York: Cambridge University Press, 1984.

Posen, Barry R. *The Sources of Military Doctrine: France, Britain, and Germany Between the World Wars*. Ithaca, NY: Cornell University Press, 1984.

Postol, Theodore A. "Lessons of the Gulf War Experience With Patriot," *International Security* 16, no. 4 (Spring 1992): 119–71.

Ra'anan, Uri. "Soviet Arms Transfers and the Problem of Political Leverage." In *Arms Transfers to the Third World: The Military Build-up in Less Industrial Countries*, edited by Uri Ra'anan, Robert L. Pfaltzgraff, Jr., and Geoffrey Kemp. Boulder, CO: Westview Press, 1978.

――――. *The USSR Arms the Third World: Case Studies in Soviet Foreign Policy*. Cambridge, Mass: MIT Press, 1969.

Ra'anan, Uri, Robert L. Pfaltzgraff, Jr., and Geoffrey Kemp. *Arms Transfers to the Third World: The Military Build-up in Less Industrial Countries*. Boulder, CO: Westview Press, 1978.

Rapp, Johann, "World Conflicts Reduced to 30, Says SIPRI Report," *Jane's Defence Weekly*, 19 June 1996, 3.

Record, Jeffrey. *Hollow Victory: A Contrary View of the Gulf War*. New York: Brassey's (US), 1993.

Reiser, Stewart. *The Israeli Arms Industry: Foreign Policy, Arms Transfers, and Military Doctrine of a Small State*. New York: Holmes and Meier, 1989.

Risse-Kappen, Thomas. "Collective Identity in a Democratic Community: The Case of NATO." In *The Culture of National Security: Norms and Identity in World Politics*, edited by Peter J. Katzenstein. New York: Columbia University Press, 1996.Roberts, Brad. "Arms Control and the End of the Cold War." In *Weapons Proliferation in the 1990s*, edited by Brad Roberts. Cambridge, Mass: MIT Press, 1995.

――――. "From Nonproliferation to Antiproliferation," *International Security* 18, no. 1 (1993): 139–173.

Rogers, Everett M. *Diffusion of Innovations*, 4th ed. New York: Free Press, 1995.

Rogers, Everett M., and F. Floyd Shoemaker. *Communication of Innovations: A Cross- Cultural Approach*, 2nd ed. New York: Free Press, 1971.

Rosen, Stephen Peter. *Winning the Next War: Innovation and the Modern Military*. Ithaca, NY: Cornell University Press, 1991.

Rosenau, James N. "Armed Force and Armed Forces in a Turbulent World." In *The Adaptive Military: Armed Forces in a Turbulent World*, 2nd ed., edited by James Burk. New Brunswick, NJ: Transaction Publishers, 1998.

———. ed. *Linkage Politics: Essays on the Convergence of National and International Systems*. New York: Free Press, 1969.

———. *Domestic Sources of Foreign Policy*. New York: Free Press, 1967.

Rosenber, Nathan. *Perspectives on Technology*. New York: Cambridge University Press, 1976.

"Russia's Swords and Plowshares," *U.S. News and World Report*, 18 January 1993, 54–55.

Russett, Bruce. *Grasping the Democratic Peace: Principles for a Post Cold War World*. Princeton, NJ: Princeton University Press, 1993.

———. "The Mysterious Case of Vanishing Hegemony; or, is Mark Twain Really Dead?" *International Organization* 39 (1985): 207–31.

Ryan, Stephen L., "Shallow Threats: Has the Shallow Water Submarine Threat to Blue Water Navies Been Overrated?" *Asian Defence Journal*, July 1995, 14–18.

Ryan, Steve, "The Attack Helicopters for ASEAN," *Asian Defence Journal*, June 1995, 28–34.

Safran, Nadav. *Saudi Arabia: The Ceaseless Quest for Security*. Cambridge, Mass: Harvard University Press, 1985.

Sampson, Anthony. *The Arms Bazaar: From Lockheed to Lebanon*. New York: Viking Press, 1977.Sanjian, Gregory S. "Cold War Imperatives and Quarrelsome Clients: Modeling U.S. and USSR Arms Transfers to India and Pakistan," *Journal of Conflict Resolution* 42, no. 1 (1998): 97–127.

———. *Arms Transfers to the Third World: Probability Models of Superpower Decisionmaking*. Boulder, CO: Lynne Rienner Publishers, 1988.

Sapir, Jacques. *The Soviet Military System*. Cambridge, England: Polity Press, 1991.

Sayigh, Yezid. "Arms Production in Pakistan and Iran: The Limits of Self-Reliance." In *Military Capacity and the Risk of War: China, India,*

Pakistan, and Iran, edited by Eric Arnett. New York: Oxford University Press, 1997.

Schmitt, Eric, "Shrewd Tactics Downed Stealth Jet, U.S. Inquiry Shows," *New York Times*, 11 April 1999, A1, A10.

Schneider, Wolfgang, "Gunnery with the Soviet T-72M/M1 Tanks," *Jane's International Defense Review*, May 1991, 491–94.

Schrodt, Philip A. "Arms Transfers and International Behavior in the Arabian Sea Area." *International Interactions* 10 (1983): 101–27.

Segal, Gerald. *Defending China*. New York: Oxford University Press, 1985.

Sherwin, Ronald G., and Edward J. Laurance. "Arms Transfers and Military Capability: Measuring and Evaluating Conventional Arms Transfers," *International Studies Quarterly* 23 (1979): 360–89.

Shishlevskiy, Valentin, "The T-80 Main Battle Tank: Power and Mobility in One Mass," *Asian Defence Journal*, July 1995, 20–27.

Shukman, David. *Tomorrow's War: The Threat of High-Technology Weapons*. New York: Harcourt Brace and Company, 1996.

Simpkin, Richard. *Red Armour: An Examination of the Soviet Mobile Force Concept*. New York: Brassey's Defence Publications, 1984.

Singer, J. David. "The Level-of-Analysis Problem in International Relations." In *The International System: Theoretical Essays*, edited by Kalus Knorr and Sidney Verba. Princeton, NJ: Princeton University Press, 1961.

Singer, J. David, Stuart A. Bremer, and John Stuckey. "Capability Distribution, Uncertainty, and Major Power War, 1820–1965." In *Peace, War, and Numbers*, edited by Bruce M. Russett. New York: Free Press, 1972.

Singer, J. David, and Melvin Small. *Correlates of War Project: International and Civil War Data, 1816–1992*. Ann Arbor, MI: Inter-university Consortium for Political and Social Research, 1994.

Singer, Max, and Aaron Wildavsky. *The Real World Order: Zones of Peace, Zones of Turmoil*. Chathan, NJ: Chatham House Publishers, Inc., 1993.

Slomovic, Anna. *MiG-21 Fishbed: A Case Study in Soviet Weapons Acquisition*. Santa Monica, CA: Rand Corporation, 1987.

Smart, Christopher. "Amid the Ruins, Arms Makers Raise New Threats," *Orbis* 36, no. 3 (1992): 349–364.

Smith, Chris. *India's Ad Hoc Arsenal: Direction or Drift in Defence Policy*. New York: Oxford University Press, 1994.

Smith, Joseph Wayne, Graham Lyons, and Evonne Moore. *Global Meltdown: Immigration, Multiculturalism, and National Breakdown in the New World Disorder.* Westport, CT: Praeger, 1998.

Smith, Merritt Roe, ed. *Military Enterprise and Technological Change: Perspectives on the American Experience.* Cambridge, Mass.: MIT Press, 1985.

Snidal, Duncan. "The Limits of Hegemonic Stability Theory," *International Organization.* 39: 579–614.

Sorenson, David S. *The Politics of Strategic Aircraft Modernization.* Westport, CT: Praeger, 1995.

Spector, Leonard S. *Going Nuclear.* Cambridge, MA: Ballinger Publishers Co., 1987.

Spence, W. R. *Innovation: The Communication of Change in Ideas, Practices, and Products.* New York: Chapman and Hall, 1994.

Spick, Mike. *Mil Mi-24 Hind.* London: Osprey Publishing, 1988.

Stapfer, Hans-Heiri. *MiG-23/27 Flogger in Action (Aircraft Number 101).* Carrollton, TX: Squadron/Signal Publications, 1990.

Starr, Barbara, "New Contracts, But U.S. Arms Trade Ban Stays," *Jane's Defence Weekly.* 31 January 1996, 60.

———. "USA to Pitch PRD-8 Against the Threat of Proliferation," *Jane's Defence Weekly*, 4 September 1993a, 24.

———. "Russians Voice Their Proliferation Fears," *Jane's Defence Weekly*, 6 March 1993b, 10.

Stephens, Alan. "'You'll Remember the Quality Long After You've Forgotten the Cost': Structuring Air Power for the Small Air Force." In *Air Power Confronts an Unstable World*, edited by Richard P. Hallion. Washington, D.C.: Brassey's, 1997.

Stevenson, James P. *The Pentagon Paradox: The Development of the F-18 Hornet.* Annapolis, MD: Naval Institute Press, 1993.

Sweetman, Bill, "'Backfire' Bomber for Export Soon," *Jane's Defence Weekly*, 17 October 1992, 19.

———. "Warsaw Pact Air Power: Present and Next Generations." In *The Warsaw Pact: Political Purpose and Military Means*, edited by Robert W. Clawson and Lawrence S. Kaplan. Wilmington, DE: Scholarly Resources, Inc., 1982.

Taylor, Bill, "Bloodhound Force," *Air Forces Monthly*, January 1990, 10–13.

Taylor, John W. R., "Gallery of Russian Aerospace Weapons," *Air Force Magazine*, March 1993, 67–83.

Taylor, Michael J. H. *Jet Warplanes: The Twenty-First Century.* New York: Exeter Books, 1986.

Taylor, Michael J. H., and John W. R. Taylor. *Missiles of the World.* New York: Charles Scribner's Sons, 1972.

Timmerman, Kenneth. *The Death Lobby: How the West Armed Iraq.* New York: Houghton Mifflin Company, 1991.

Tirman, John. *Spoils of War: The Human Cost of America's Arms Trade.* New York: Free Press, 1997.

Tornatzky, Louis G., and Mitchell Fleischer. *The Process of Technological Innovation.* Lexington, Mass.: Lexington Books, 1990.

Towle, Philip. *Pundits and Patriots: Lessons from the Gulf War.* London: Alliance Publishers Ltd., 1991.

Url, Thomas, and Andreas Wörgötter, eds. *Econometrics of Short and Unreliable Time Series.* Heidelburg, Germany: Physica-Verlag, 1995.

"USA Rejects Saudi Request for AMRAAMs," *Jane's Defence Weekly*, 20 November 1993, 11.

"USN Gets Thai Request for F/A-18s, AMRAAM," *Jane's Defence Weekly*, 4 November 1995, 6.

Valladão, Alfredo G. A. *The Twenty-First Century Will Be American.* New York: Verso, 1996.

Valente, Thomas W. *Network Models of the Diffusion of Innovations.* Cresskill, NJ: Hampton Press, Inc., 1995.

Van Crevald, Martin. *Technology and War: From 2000 B.C. to the Present.* New York: Free Press, 1989.

Vanhanen, Tatu. *Military Rule and Defense Expenditures: A Study of 119 States, 1850–1975.* Hong Kong: Asian Research Service.

Vargas, Augusto. *Militarization and the International Arms Race in Latin America.* Boulder, CO: Westview Press, 1985.

Vasquez, John A. "The Realist Paradigm and Degenerative Versus Progressive Research Programs: An Appraisal of Neotraditional Research on Waltz's Balancing Proposition," *American Political Science Review* 91 (1997): 899–912.

Venter, Al J., "Keeping the Lid on Germ Warfare," *Jane's International Defense Review*, May 1998, 26–29.

Walker, Jack L. "The Diffusion of Innovation Among the American States," *American Political Science Review* 63 (1969): 880–899.

Wallerstein, Peter, and Margareta Sollenberg. "Armed Conflict and Regional Conflict Complexes," *Journal of Peace Research* 35 (1998): 621–634.

Walters, Stewart, "Guns and Missiles for Combat Aircraft," *Asian Defence Journal*, December 1995a, 100–06.

———. "Land-Based Air Defence: Vital But Costly," *Asian Defence Journal*, September 1995b, 50–3.

Waltz, Edward. *Information Warfare Principles and Operations*. Boston: Artech House, 1998.

Waltz, Kenneth N. "Evaluating Theories," *American Political Science Review* 91 (1997): 913–17.

———. *Theory of International Politics*. Reading, MA: Addison-Wesley Publications, 1979.

Watson, Bruce P., and Peter M. Dunn. *Military Lessons of the Falkland Islands War: Views from the United States*. Boulder, CO: Westview Press, 1984.

Wayman, Frank W., and Paul F. Diehl. "Realism Reconsidered: The Realpolitik Framework and Its Basic Propositions." In *Reconstructing Realpolitik*, edited by Frank W. Wayman and Paul F. Diehl. Ann Arbor, MI: University of Michigan Press, 1994.

Weiner, Tim, "Mass Weapons Are Spreading, Pentagon Warns," *New York Times*, 12 April 1996, A5.

Weissman, Steve. *The Islamic Bomb: The Nuclear Threat to Israel and the Middle East*. New York: New York Times Books, 1981.

Williamson, Murray, and Allan R. Millet, eds. *Military Innovation in the Interwar Period*. New York: Cambridge University Press, 1996.

Wulf, Herbert. "The Soviet Union and the Successor Republics: Arms Exports and the Struggle with the Heritage of the Military-Industrial Complex." In *Arms Industry Limited*, edited by Herbert Wulf. New York: Oxford University Press, 1993.

Zakheim, Dov S. *Flight of the Lavi: Inside a U.S.-Israeli Crisis*. Washington, D.C.: Brassey's, 1996.

Zaloga, Steven, "Russia Exporting Top-of-the-Line Weapons," *Armed Forces Journal International*, December 1992, 45–46.

———. *Red Thrust: Attack on the Central Front, Soviet Tactics and Capabilities in the 1990s*. Novato, CA: Presidio, 1989.

Zaloga, Steven J., and George J. Balin. *Anti-Tank Helicopters*. London: Osprey Publishing, 1986.Zarzecki, Thomas W. "Are Arms Transfers from the Former Soviet Union a Security Threat? The Case of Combat Aircraft," *Journal of Slavic Military Studies* 12, no. 1 (1999a): 124–48.

———. "Arming China or Arming India: Future Russian Dilemmas," *Comparative Strategy* 18, no. 3 (1999b): 261–81.

Index